MW00626011

Praise for *The Wordhord*

'A wonderful book heaving with linguistic treasure, a joyfully
clever exploration of early medieval life'
Edward Brooke-Hitching, author of *The Madman's Library*

'Splendid . . . It is the perfect way to be introduced to Old English.
There is insight on every page, in a beautifully clear and down-to-earth
style, with lovely humorous asides'
David Crystal, author of *The Story of English in 100 Words*

'A marvellous book'
Neil Gaiman, author of *Norse Mythology*

'A wonderful book that blends linguistics with a survey of
everyday life in early medieval England'
Tom Holland, *BBC History Magazine*

'Thorough, entertaining and absolutely fascinating. If you're
interested in Old English (and for that matter, even if you're not!)
it's an absolute treat'
Paul Anthony Jones, author of *The Cabinet of Linguistic Curiosities*

'A treasure trove of forgotten words, their meanings and origins,
written with insight and humour'
Marshall Julius, author of *Vintage Geek*

'Engaging, conversational, humorous, and full of surprising
revelations'
Library Journal

'A lovely, lovely read . . . written with such love and care and accessibility to the lay person that you can feel it just doing you good – feeding your soul and your brain at the same time'
Lucy Mangan, author of *Bookworm*

'Eminently giftable . . . A book to be dipped in and out of for the riddles and enjoyable factoids'
James Marriott, *The Times* (London)

'Delightful . . . [Videen's] etymological journeys [are] full of satisfying twists . . . a classy gift to the commonly word-drunk'
Steven Poole, *Guardian*

'Videen is both a passionate medievalist and a relaxed, lucid writer; the pleasure she takes in her subject is infectious. . . . There are enough literary snippets here to suggest why Old English has enchanted so many authors'
Henry Hitchings, *Wall Street Journal*

THE
DEORHORD

THE
DEORHORD
An Old English Bestiary

Hana Videen

Princeton University Press

Princeton and Oxford

Copyright © 2024 by Hana Videen

Published in the United States and Canada in 2024 by
Princeton University Press
41 William Street, Princeton, New Jersey 08540
press.princeton.edu

First published in Great Britain in 2023 by Profile Books Ltd

ISBN 978-0-691-26000-6
Ebook ISBN 978-0-691-26099-0
Library of Congress Control Number 2023943252

Illustrations by Joanna Lisowiec
Text design by Crow Books

All rights reserved. Princeton University Press is committed to the
protection of copyright and the intellectual property our authors entrust
to us. Copyright promotes the progress and integrity of knowledge.
Thank you for supporting free speech and the global exchange of ideas by
purchasing an authorized edition of this book. If you wish to reproduce or
distribute any part of it in any form, please obtain permission.

Requests for permission to reproduce material from this work should be
sent to permissions@press.princeton.edu

Printed in the United States of America

1 3 5 7 9 10 8 6 4 2

For my *sunu* Kai and my *nefene* Charlotte,
who came into the world alongside this book

Contents

The Bad

The Baffling

Prologue
An Old English Bestiary

IN 2018 THE CITY OF Toronto wheeled out a solution to its infamous trash panda dilemma. 'Trash panda' is the half-affectionate, half-resentful epithet for the raccoon, a chubby creature with a bandit's mask of black fur around its eyes and an exceptional ability to survive on scraps from the green plastic food waste bins that residents use throughout the city. While municipal politicians claimed the new design for these bins was 'raccoon-proof', engineered with special handles to prevent the critters from breaking in, Toronto's raccoons seem to have missed the memo. Instead of keeping the raccoons out, the new design merely challenged them to become more innovative in their methods for extracting people's trash. Before long, stories were popping up on social media and news networks about 'genius' and 'superhuman muscular' creatures. The raccoon seemed to have outwitted humans once again with its determination and ingenuity. One article jokingly suggested that the cleverest thieves must be 'armed with diagrams and spreadsheets', spreading their knowledge throughout the raccoon community. Of course, the raccoons were just being raccoons, looking for food in their urban habitat, but the people

who live alongside them can't help but grant them 'human' characteristics and motivations.

Toronto isn't the only city whose streets are shared with creatures
that the human inhabitants begin (begrudgingly) to see as neighbours:
partly beloved, partly vilified, entirely personified. Toronto has its raccoons, New York its rats and London its foxes. There are an estimated
10,000 foxes living within the sprawling reaches of London, and they
can be spotted everywhere from the steps of Downing Street to the
suburbs. Although London foxes receive even more vitriol as a wildlife
menace than Toronto's raccoons, and though they might not have a
cute moniker like 'trash panda', there is no shortage of media reports
that describe their activities like any other person getting on with life
in the big city. An article in *Metro* describes them enjoying recreational
activities like 'bouncing on a makeshift trampoline or sunbathing on
a roof'. A Bloomsbury resident refers to a pair who were 'such polite
neighbours that they used our dog toilet area for its intended purpose', and the Internet delights in tales of foxes living 'rent-free' in
skyscrapers, mugging walkers for their snacks and stealing entire
collections of shoes. Some city-dwellers wish these daring denizens
were quieter – too much loud sex at night – but such a complaint could
apply equally to human neighbours as to those of a furrier nature.

Sometimes loved, sometimes hated, animals are often assigned
human attributes, whether it's disregard for one's neighbours or
innovation in urban exploration. Perhaps it is an attempt to understand another way of being, to imagine a city or the world or ourselves through the eyes of other creatures. Whatever its motivation,
this habit has a long history, one that began centuries before the
invention of TikTok or memes of trash pandas eating pizza. Humans
love to tell stories about animals, and across cultures we imbue them
with the same qualities we admire or abhor in ourselves. I grew up
hearing stories about the loyal dog, the eager beaver, the wise owl,

the wily fox and the busy bee. Perhaps you are more familiar with the antics of Anansi, the trickster spider, or tales of the jolly but mischievous *tanuki* (Japanese raccoon dog). Some animals are inextricably tied to certain stories and legends, like the tortoise who wins the race against the hare at its slow and steady pace, the wolf who consumes grandmothers and foolish pigs, or the serpent who deceives unsuspecting humans. The fables and fairy tales we grow up with, as much as any nature documentary, influence our perspectives on the animal world.

Even the multitude of stories about 'real' animals is not enough to satisfy our imaginations. Our personal libraries include numerous fantastic, mythical creatures, drawn from the stories we are told as children and the media we consume as adults: legends about the phoenix who burns and rises from its ashes, fire-breathing dragons who guard treasure hoards, monsters who lurk in the deepest and darkest of places, and many more. These mythical creatures, too, take on human traits in stories about love, hate, greed and desire.

But where do these associations come from? Humans' obsession with real and mythical creatures is nothing new: it stretches to antiquity and beyond. In ancient Greece Homer wrote about the fire-breathing chimera, in Persian mythology we had the simurgh, a giant bird, and during the medieval period, books of animal lore were bestsellers. These illustrated books, known as bestiaries, contained descriptions and allegorical tales of the various creatures to be found across the medieval world. Some ideas from medieval bestiaries have stayed with us: the lion is still the king of beasts and a white dove still symbolises peace. But other animal associations may be less familiar. In the medieval period, for instance, one might see Jesus in a panther or Satan in a whale. Medieval bestiaries often highlighted lessons in morality through analogies that have gradually become obscure. Be long-sighted like the industrious ant. Take shelter in God's shadow like the dove in the peridexion tree. Remember that through penitence even a sinner can shed past deeds as a snake can shed its skin.

Ancient origins: the *Physiologus*

Although bestiaries were popular texts in medieval Europe, many of their tales derive from a far older text from northern Africa known as the *Physiologus*. The *Physiologus* (meaning *Natural Philosopher*) was originally written in Greek by an unknown author, probably someone living in Alexandria during the third century CE. This text in turn is made up of stories whose influences can be traced even further back in time to texts on natural philosophy and religion by ancient Greek and Roman writers. As the *Physiologus* further developed over the centuries, its age-old tales were often shaped by contemporary authorities like the third-century geographer and grammarian Solinus, or Ambrose, a fourth-century bishop and theologian. So while the bones of a story might stay the same, the interpretation and moral might shift according to the ideas that pleased the contemporary scribe. Perhaps the most significant influence on later versions of the *Physiologus* text came from Isidore of Seville's *Etymologies*. In this text, Isidore, a seventh-century Spanish cleric, explains the supposed stories behind animal names: their 'etymologies'. Foxes, for instance, which are *vulpes* in Latin, are so called because they are 'shifty on their feet' (*volubilis* + *pes*), choosing a twisting path over a straight one. The vulture (Latin *vultur*) is supposedly named for its 'slow flight' (*volatus tardus*). A bird is an *avis* because it has no set 'path' (*via*) but travels by means of 'pathless' (*avia*) ways. Isidore would eventually become canonised after the medieval period, and due to his insatiable desire for the world's knowledge – and compelling need to record it – he is sometimes called the patron saint of the Internet. (And like 'facts' on the Internet, some of Isidore's etymologies are legit, but you shouldn't believe everything you read.)

The original forty or so animals in the Greek *Physiologus* grew to number over a hundred, and the versions of the text itself proliferated, with translations in many languages, especially Latin, the language of learning and the Christian Church. By the ninth or tenth century, these collections of stories – *Physiologi* – were popular across western Europe. No matter the language or country, era or religion, it seemed that people were hungry for tales of animals and their exploits.

Beastly bestsellers

And so the *Physiologus* remained highly influential for more than a millennium, gathering new material over the centuries. By the time these more extensive, often illustrated compendiums of animal lore reached the medieval period, they had become the books known as bestiaries.

In Europe, the heyday for bestiaries was from around 1000 to 1300. But their tremendous popularity was by no means limited to medieval Europe. Just as European bestiary compilers drew upon animal descriptions from the *Physiologus* and other ancient Greek texts, so did Muslim writers from Persia. The scholar Ibn Bakhtishu' wrote the *Manafi' al-hayawan* (*Usefulness of Animals*), an illuminated bestiary, in Arabic during the tenth century, and Zakariya al-Qazwini, a physician, astronomer and geographer, composed his own *'Aja'ib al-makhluqat* (*Book of the Wonders of Creation*) during the thirteenth century. Like those of Christian tradition, Islamic bestiaries contained moralised tales about real and mythical animals, often accompanied by lavish illustrations.

During the twelfth and thirteenth centuries, most of the development of the bestiary tradition was happening in England. During this period, monastic orders involved in preaching, like the Cistercians, often possessed the most bestiaries. Itinerant preachers needed stories for their sermon-making that would be vivid and memorable, and so they turned to animals and illustrations. Monastic scribes produced bestiaries to teach proper living and thinking, following the idea that the world's creatures were created by God for the purpose of instructing humankind. As well as on the road, bestiaries served as teaching tools in schools and monasteries. You can tell they were used in classrooms because of their glosses (translations from a less familiar tongue – usually Latin – into the vernacular), rubrics and other teaching aids.

But some of the lessons in these bestiaries have a dark side. Throughout, there are textual and visual references that were intended to encourage anti-Semitic and misogynist beliefs. They are not always obvious to us today, but their meaning would have been clear to people in medieval England. A story about a siren may seem like a harmless myth, but it was a tale used to demonise women who feel and express sexual desire: the lesson here is that such feelings turn women not only into threats to men but unwomanly 'beasts'. Today, owls are often seen as 'wise' because they are associated with Athena, the Greek goddess of wisdom. Yet medieval bestiaries compare the owl's daytime blindness to the spiritual 'blindness' of the Jews, who refuse to accept the 'light' of Christianity. One bestiary depicts an owl surrounded by other birds. While we might assume this is meant to portray people flocking to the wisest bird in the room, the medieval illustrator would have intended something much more troubling: many virtuous birds pecking at a blind owl, a tacit endorsement of anti-Semitic violence. Is it a mere coincidence that the popularity of bestiaries with anti-Semitic messaging became significantly less popular (and perhaps less relevant) after the expulsion of the Jews from England in 1290? Historians think not.

The owl is just one example of how our perceptions of animals – real or imagined – change over time. Were foxes still wily and bees busy a thousand years ago? No matter what message the scribe hoped to communicate, their words reveal something about the world they lived in and their place within it.

The oldest of Englishes

The earliest European bestiaries are written in Latin, the language of learning and the Christian Church. These were then translated into a variety of vernacular languages, including Middle English, Icelandic, German, French, Italian, Occitan and Catalan. The earliest bestiary made in England that still survives today dates from the early twelfth century.

But what about prior to that? Given the wide distribution of the *Physiologus* in earlier times, it would be surprising if there wasn't also an interest in animal lore in the early medieval period. There is even written evidence for a bestiary from this time in England: a list of gifts made to Peterborough Abbey in 970 includes a *Liber Bestiarum* (*Book of Beasts*), a Latin bestiary now lost to time. But no bestiaries from early medieval England survive today, and none are known to have existed at all in England's vernacular. To read the *Liber Bestiarum* would have required knowledge of Latin, a language limited to the well educated. In early medieval England (*c.*550–1150), the language that most people spoke and could understand was **englisc**, or 'Old English'. And no bestiaries exist in that language.

Old English is the language we think we know until we see or read it. It is quite different from the English used by Wordsworth (modern), Shakespeare (Early Modern) or even Chaucer (Middle), though these are all, of course, 'old' relatively speaking. Old English, though, is the oldest of them all: it was written and spoken over a thousand years ago, as the main language of early medieval England. The vocabulary of Old English is primarily Germanic, with only a small percentage of words borrowed from Latin: it was not until the Norman invasion that the language was forever shaped by a major influx of words from Latin and French. Some words in Old English can look quite familiar to modern English speakers (like **word** itself), but much of the time it is as foreign as any new language, incomprehensible without immersion or study.

One challenge to immersing yourself in Old English, though, compared to even Latin (never mind a language like French or Spanish), is that only a relatively small number of texts survive; the content of all unique works written in Old English could be contained in the space of about thirty novels. This is far less than the records we have in Latin, a language written for millennia, spanning ancient and medieval periods. The best-known work in Old English today is *Beowulf* (which contains 3,182 lines of verse), a poem that may have started out as an oral tale, something to be spoken or sung at feasts. It survived in only one manuscript that made it to modern times, a manuscript that was nearly destroyed in a library fire.

The Old English words that have survived represent the experience of a relatively small portion of the population – those people who could read and write and had the time and resources to do so. When we look at daily life during this period through the words that remain, we understand that we must be seeing the world based on this fairly limited perspective. Another limitation to our view is that some of the words appear only once in the entire body of Old English literature. Such a word may have been commonly used in everyday conversations, may have appeared in many other manuscripts that were lost over time, or may have been the isolated coinage of one lone scribe who couldn't get it to catch on. We will never know. Regardless, like peering through a keyhole, we can still get a sense of the richness of the vast world beyond: these words give us glimpses into lives lived long ago.

Cats and sea-cargo

Although many bestiaries have survived from medieval England, these date mainly from the time when Middle English was the vernacular, from around 1150 to the end of the medieval period (*c*.1450). And even those are in a different language: Latin, not the vernacular. A Middle English translation of the *Physiologus* does survive from the thirteenth century, but it lacks the extensive additional material and illustrations of a proper bestiary. An Old English version of this text is even more limited. The so-called Old English *Physiologus* has only two complete poems and one poetic fragment, which appear together in the tenth-century Exeter Book.

But despite there being no Old English bestiary, there is no shortage of stories about animals. They play a vibrant role in Old English tales, poems and medical texts, riddles and travel logs, sermons and saints' lives: there are many creatures and lessons for the *englisc* speaker to find.

In the world of Old English there is no 'creature' and no 'nature'; instead we have **sceaft** (creation). *Sceaft* includes everything in the world made by God – humans, animals, plants, rocks and the sun, even dragons, phoenixes and other fantastical creatures. People saw themselves as part of *sceaft*, and they looked to other aspects of it to gain a deeper understanding of themselves. There were lessons to be learned from serpents and spiders, eagles and elephants. When we read about animals in Old English, what we get is a human perspective on animal life. Even when animals have the power to speak in words, these words belong to a human scribe and reflect that scribe's own experience. Animal stories reveal far more about the people who wrote them, how these humans interpreted their world, than they do about the animals. If God created animal life to teach humans about themselves, medieval scribes created their books of animal lore for the same purpose. The words and stories that are associated with certain animals reveal something of the beliefs of the people who made them and their cultural background; and maybe they can reveal something about us too, those who weave words into stories in modern English, continuing to tell tales about the animals of our daily lives and imaginations.

What roles did animals play in early medieval life and legend? What Old English words were used to describe them? Would these animal descriptions be as recognisable to us today as a word like **cat** (cat) or as foreign as **brim-hlæst** (sea-cargo, a poetic word meaning 'fish')? And what might they tell us about ourselves? These are some of the questions we will explore in the pages of *The Deorhord* – the Old English bestiary that never existed . . .

A new Old English bestiary

The Old English word for 'animal' is **dēor**. It resembles the modern English word 'deer' but is pronounced DAY-or, and in early medieval England every animal was a *dēor*, not just those with antlers. *Dēor* derives from the Proto-Germanic root *dhus* (to breathe), and in this way it is etymologically similar to our modern word 'animal', which comes from Latin *anima* (breath, life).

This book's title is a compound I invented from real Old English words: *dēor* + **hord** (hoard). *Deorhord* (pronounced DAY-or-HORD) is not a word that actually appears in Old English but is inspired by the real compound **wordhord** (word-hoard). A *wordhord* is a poet's mental stockpile of words to be used in their stories and songs. Tales in the early medieval period were often transmitted orally, with some of the composition done on the spot, so it would have been handy to have a *hord* of poetic words and phrases at the ready. Like a poet's *hord* of words, this is a *hord* of *dēor*, a collection to be kept near and cherished; and as we read stories of creatures big and small, we'll be stocking our own word-hoards too.

Because bestiaries derive from a shared tradition, they all tend to follow the same ordering of creatures, beginning with land animals and continuing with birds, snakes and water-dwellers. *The Deorhord* isn't a traditional bestiary – it's a *hord* of *dēor* – and so I've gone with a different kind of order, collecting creatures into the ordinary and the extraordinary, the good, the bad and the baffling. When humans attempt to generalise and categorise a thing, it quickly becomes clear that that thing is far too complex, and my categories of Old English animals are no different. Something as seemingly ordinary as an ant is in fact extraordinary, and the much-maligned serpent may in fact be 'good' (at least in some ways). Some creatures are baffling due to their limited descriptions, while others are described in great detail – but with utterly bizarre characteristics. Perhaps a *dēor* that baffles modern scholars would have been familiar and easily recognisable in the early medieval period; we'll never know, and must continue to rack our brains. I hope you'll join me in the puzzle.

This Old English bestiary brings together a *hord* of animal words from the farms, forests, rivers and seas of the early medieval landscape. Many of these *dēor* descriptions echo ideas that appeared in the earlier northern African *Physiologus* text, as well as offering a glimpse of the tales yet to be told in later European bestiary lore. Within each chapter we'll often see both, alongside the Old English.

Some of *The Deorhord*'s creatures are real and others legendary, some mythical and others mundane. They pad softly through collections of Old English poetry and soar through saints' lives and homilies. They might necessitate a leechbook remedy, or in fact be a vital ingredient. They creep through the riddles and crawl through the Psalms. They slither into accounts of the world's greatest marvels, even lurking in the letter of an emperor and conqueror to his tutor. Wherever they appear, these *dēor* reveal more about the word-hoarders who underestimate, fear or admire them.

The Prologue's Wordhord

At the end of each chapter I include a *wordhord*, a stockpile of its Old English words. Any time a word appears for the first time in this book I put it in boldface, and you can turn to the chapter's *wordhord* to remind yourself of its meaning or learn its pronunciation. A complete list of all the words is at the end of the book.

Old English spans several centuries, and there are variations to its pronunciation across this period, not to mention differences in dialect. My pronunciations thus reflect only one version of Old English. The pronunciations of each word are given in two styles: a simpler but slightly less precise one, and one that uses the International Phonetic Alphabet.

The macron (the horizontal bar above some vowels) is not used in Old English texts, which is why you'll never see it in a quotation. It is a common editorial device in modern-day Old English dictionaries, indicating that a vowel sound is long rather than short. (A short 'u' sounds like the 'u' in 'pull', for instance, while a long 'ū' is pronounced like the 'oo' in 'cool'.)

brim-hlæst, noun (BRIM-H'LAST / ˈbrɪm-ˌhlæst): Fish (sea-cargo).

cat, noun (KAHT / ˈkat): Cat (plural: *catas*).

dēor, noun (DAY-or / ˈdeːɔr): Animal (plural: *dēor*).

englisc, noun (ENG-glish / ˈɛŋ-glɪʃ): English, the English language.

hord, noun (HORD / 'hɔrd): Hoard.

sceaft, noun (SHEH-oft / 'ʃɛaft): Creation.

word, noun (WORD / 'wɔrd): Word.

wordhord, noun (WORD-HORD / 'wɔrd-ˌhɔrd): Word-hoard, a store of
   words.

The Ordinary

'ORDINARY' IS A RELATIVE TERM. When I lived in London, foxes were quite ordinary sights in the city, although the first time I saw one I was completely taken aback. I had never seen a fox outside of a zoo before. Similarly, when I saw my first Canadian raccoon, I excitedly took a photo and showed it to my friends. The Canadians were about as impressed by it as I would have been by a photo of a mourning dove or a squirrel, prominent denizens of my own home town in the American Midwest.

The animals I label 'ordinary' in this book are creatures that would not be surprising to see in early medieval England. 'Ordinary' changes over time. The animals you'll most likely come across while walking along the city streets are dogs and pigeons, and inside houses you might find cats and spiders. Today it is unlikely you'll see an ox, cow or sheep in central London, but that wasn't always the case. Most people in the early medieval period were farmers, so horses and oxen would be a familiar sight. If you lived in a high-status, urban area you may have come across more cattle, while in a small village the sheep might have outnumbered the human residents. Most cats and dogs you'd see would not be sheltered, household pets but working animals, dogs used for hunting, herding and guarding and cats for controlling the mice population. In a time when acres of land remained wild and unsettled, it was unlikely that the sight of a soaring eagle or a wild boar would be a cause for surprise.

Sometimes 'ordinary' creatures are granted extraordinary abilities – like the urban exploration and clever sabotage technique of a trash panda. The 'ordinary' animals in this book generally have abilities that are not far beyond the realm of reality. Eagles do indeed fly high, even if they don't reach the sun. Doves are gentle creatures and spiders weave webs to catch their prey. These details may not be surprising to us, even if we aren't familiar with the stories that were told about them a thousand years ago.

I

Eagle (*earn*)

P EOPLE HAVE BEEN EAGLE-EYED since the fifteenth century, when the English monk and poet John Lydgate described someone as 'egle-eyed, bryght and cler'. But sharp sight had been associated with the eagle for even longer. The Latin for 'eagle', *aquila*, supposedly comes from the creature's keen sense of sight (*acumen oculorum*: sharpness of the eyes), at least according to Isidore's seventh-century *Etymologies*. Isidore explains that eagles soar high above the ocean, too distant for human eyes to see, and yet the sharp-eyed birds can still spot small fish swimming far below. (The *Oxford English Dictionary* suggests a less appealing but more probable etymology, that *aquila* comes from Latin *aquilus*, or 'dark brown'.)

Our modern English word 'eagle' comes from the Anglo-Norman *aigle*, but before the influence of French this bird was called an **earn**. 'Erne' is in fact still used today, usually referring to the golden eagle or sea-eagle (though 'erne-eyed' doesn't have quite the same ring to it . . .). Old English *earn* has Germanic roots, with cognates in Old Norse (*ǫrn*), Middle Low German (*arn*) and modern Dutch (*arend*). (Incidentally, Old English is closest in structure to Frisian, a language from the coastal Netherlands and north-west Germany, so it is sometimes more easily understood by speakers of modern Dutch or German.) *Earn* even has cognates in non-Germanic languages, like the Greek *órnis* (bird), a word from which we get 'ornithology', the study of birds. Only two species of eagle feature among Britain's native birds, so the word *earn* would probably have been used to talk about either the golden eagle or the white-tailed eagle – and often we can tell which one the writer had in mind by the way they describe it. The golden eagle, known in Scotland as the black eagle, may be the bird referred to in the Old English poem *Judith*, which has an *earn* that is **saluwig-pād** (dark-cloaked). And it is undoubtedly the white-tailed eagle that the poet is thinking about in *The Battle of Brunanburh*, where the *earn* is a **hasu-pāda** (grey-cloaked one) with a **hwīt** (white) tail.

Seeker of the sun

Whether dark-cloaked or grey-cloaked, an eagle is easiest to spot when it is soaring high in the sky. On a sunny day you might have to squint to see it up above the treetops. Bestiaries of the later medieval period seem to be particularly interested in the eagle's flying ability, which – ordinary though it may be – contributed to the bird's role in myth and allegory. These bestiaries explain why the eagle flies so high: it must burn off its old feathers and the mist in its eyes by flying close to the sun, renewing itself in the blazing heat. The eagle is thus made young again. This story of renewal doesn't appear in ancient literature and may have derived from Psalm 102, which says, 'thy youth shall be renewed like the eagle's' (in Old English *bið geedneowod swa swa earnes geogoð ðin*).[*]

---

[*] Throughout this book psalms are numbered according to the Latin Vulgate Bible.

The religious eagle comparisons don't stop there. Flying towards the sun is not just an extreme rejuvenation: when the eagle looks to the sun it is like Christians looking to God, not allowing their spiritual vision to become clouded over time. The way the eagle gazes fearlessly upon the sun is also compared to the way the saints turn their faces towards Christ with unflinching eyes. The notion that eagles can stare directly at the sun without pain or injury goes back at least as far as ancient Rome. Lucan, a Roman poet of the first century CE, refers to the eagle as the 'bird of Jove', who makes his fledglings look upon 'Phoebus' rays', the rising sun, with an unwavering gaze. In the seventh century, Isidore writes that only fledglings who successfully pass the sun-staring challenge are considered worthy enough to belong to the eagle family. A fledgling that draws back from the sun is cast out by its own parents. A thirteenth-century Latin bestiary explains that the parent eagle carries out this harsh sentence 'without any bitterness in its nature, but as an impartial judge'. To the parent, the flinching fledgling is nothing but a stranger. While this image of the cruel eagle parent is present in Latin bestiaries, it doesn't appear in Old English texts or the Middle English *Physiologus*, which focuses on the individual eagle's renewal, not mentioning fledglings at all. And in Old English we only have references to the eagle as a protective parent, like in the Old English translation of Deuteronomy: the baby eagles, *briddas*, are encouraged to fly, but the parent flutters over them to make sure they are safe. **Bridd** is specifically a young bird or chick in Old English but has grown up to become 'bird' today – while **fugel**, far more commonly used to mean a bird generally in Old English, is an etymon of our more specific 'fowl'.

The *earn*'s habit of staring directly at the sun does appear in Old English, though not in the context of testing one's offspring or even of self-renewal. In a homily of the tenth-century English abbot and writer Ælfric of Eynsham, the *earn*'s ability to look unflinchingly at the sun is compared to a saint's ability to behold the full extent of God's glory. The keen eyes of an eagle see God clearly.

Ælfric explains that each of the four evangelists (Matthew, Mark, Luke and John) is represented by a different living creature. He says in an Old English saint's life that the prophet Ezekiel had a vision of the four evangelists as four **nȳtenu** (beasts): a **mann** (human), a **lēo** (lion), an *earn* and a **stirc** (calf). The *mann* represents St Matthew because his gospel explicates Christ's human lineage. St Mark has a *lēo* because his gospel begins with a reference to St John the Baptist, whose voice is compared to a lion's roar. The Gospel of St Luke emphasises Christ's sacrifice, so Luke is accompanied by a *stirc*, an animal traditionally used for sacrifices. The *earn* is a symbol of St John the Evangelist, as Ælfric clarifies:

> The eagle's likeness belongs to John because the <u>eagle</u> (*earn*) flies the highest of all birds and can stare the most fixedly upon the light of the sun. So did John, the divine writer. He flew far up, as with an <u>eagle's wings</u> (*earnes fyðerum*), and wisely beheld how he could write <u>most gloriously</u> (*mærlicost*) of God.

Here we find all the familiar qualities of our *earn* – high-flying, fearless, keen-sighted and able to look directly at the light. **Feþer** (pronounced FEH-ther) in the singular form means 'feather', the same as in modern English, but in the plural *feþra* (or *fyðerum* as it is written here) means 'wings'. St John flies like an *earn* into the heavens, leaving behind earthly concerns to contemplate the divine. Christian allegory has transformed an ordinary bird into a symbol of new life and renewal. The adjective **mǣr-līc** can mean 'great', 'magnificent', 'glorious', 'splendid' or 'illustrious'. John's perspective from his great height, face to face with God, makes his gospel the most *mǣr-līc* of the four.

St John the Evangelist and his eagle in the Lindisfarne Gospels
(England, *c.*700)

In later medieval bestiaries, the eagle's flight to the sun is followed
by a quick descent into a spring below, the water of which further
renews it. Only its beak remains crooked; the eagle must sharpen it on
a rock until it's the right size, the way a Christian is meant to 'sharpen'

their soul on Christ, improving their faith through close contact with the Word of God. The eagle also dives into the spring to catch fish, which bestiaries liken to Christ's descent into hell to rescue deserving souls. This episode, the Harrowing of Hell, was a popular subject of art and literature throughout the Middle Ages (the analogy is not perfect, of course, since during the Harrowing of Hell the souls do not become Christ's dinner). The eagle's renewal through immersion in water can also symbolise the Christian sacrament of baptism, and for this reason the bird sometimes appears on medieval baptismal fonts. Christians who turn their eyes to the Lord, the way the eagle turns its eyes to the sun, will find their spiritual vision refreshed.

A bird of contradictions

As we've seen with the eagle's parenting styles, interpretations of the bird's behaviour sometimes seem to contradict each other. The eagle's rapid fall from on high for the sake of food can also be read as an allegory of Adam's metaphorical fall, when he disobeyed God and ate the forbidden fruit in the Garden of Eden. The eagle can thus signify human frailty, falling for fish the way man falls for forbidden fruit. Like the human soul, the eagle can soar, but it can also fall. Medieval bestiaries also compare the eagle to persecutors who lie in ambush for one's spirit, as well as to secular rulers who fail to focus on spiritual concerns.

So, on the one hand the eagle seems to represent Christ rescuing sinners from hell; on the other it represents Adam, falling again and again. These contrasting attitudes towards the *earn* are not only the preserve of religious texts and poems. Although they too would have been written down by monks and nuns, Old English prognostics are not religious in nature. They are reference texts that make predictions about the future based on everything from the human body to the stars to the days of the week. Seeing an *earn* in your dreams can be either good or bad. Two prognostic texts claim that if you dream about an *earn* above your head, you will have **weorþ-mynd** (honour, glory, favour, fame). Today the eagle is still used as a symbol of leadership and authority, which perhaps align with *weorþ-mynd*. But these texts also warn that if you dream about many eagles together it indicates **nīþ** (hatred), the snares and deceits of men. When eagles gather, it is usually around dead bodies. An Old English translation of the Gospel of Matthew says, 'Wherever the <u>body</u> (*hold*) shall be, <u>eagles</u> (*earnas*) shall be gathered there.' A **hold** is a corpse or carcass, cognate with Old Norse *hold*, which means 'flesh'.

Sometimes, contradictions can be found between predictions that seem otherwise almost identical. Take these two different copies of the same prognostic text, for instance:

Gif him þince, þæt hine earn swyþe ete, þæt byþ deaþ.
(If it appears to him that the eagle fiercely devours him, that means death.)

Þonne him þynce, þæt his earn ehte, þæt bið eað.
(When it seems to him that an eagle pursues him, that means happiness.)

It is odd that these predictions should differ so drastically in texts that otherwise seem like duplicate copies. But if you look carefully, you'll notice some crucial differences – ones that belong to the hand of the scribe rather than the **swefen-reccere** (dream interpreter). *Ete* is a form of the verb **etan** (to eat), while *ehte* is a form of **ēhtan** (to pursue or chase). Did the scribe leave out an 'h', turning the *earn's* pursuit into a feast? *Eað*, which is read as an alternate spelling of **ēad** (happiness or well-being), easily becomes *deað*/**dēaþ** (death) if you add a 'd'. Are these scribal errors, or are the dreambooks portraying two different scenarios? If there is an error, which prognostic is the original and the 'correct', and which is the badly copied? Certainly, if one is being devoured by an eagle, that probably means death. It's less clear why an eagle pursuing you would mean happiness, but this concept is echoed in another prognostic text, which says:

> *Gif him þince, þæt his earn swyþe eahte, þæt byþ mycel gefea.*
> (If it seems to him that an eagle fiercely pursues him, that means great joy.)

It's essentially the same as the other prediction but uses **ge-fēa** (joy) instead of *ēad* (happiness). But repetition of the idea doesn't mean that the joyful interpretation is the correct one: yet another text claims that if you dream about an *earn* flying, it means *dēaþ* for your wife. There are no prognostics, however, that claim that dreaming about an eagle is simply a sign of a mildly upset stomach. It seems that dreams about eagles lead either to joy and prosperity or to malice and death – there's really no in-between.

Beasts of battle

The ordinary sight of an eagle soaring high in the sky might be inspiring, as we imagine the *ge-fēa* (joy) we'd experience with such freedom, but maybe you associate this behaviour with impending *dēaþ* – and this isn't simply due to dream prognostics. If an eagle is circling high above, it is very likely looking for prey, ready to kill for its supper. Or, if it's feeling lazy, it might feed on a pre-killed *hold* (corpse). Eagles hunt for their own food, but they also feed upon the remains of other animals' kills, scavenging like a vulture or raven. For this reason, the *earn* is one of the 'beasts of battle', a trope that appears throughout Old English poetry: three fearsome creatures whose presence accompanies war and destruction.

The Old English poem *The Battle of Brunanburh* describes one such scene of bloody destruction: the battle of English forces (King Athelstan and his brother Edmund) against an alliance of enemies (the kings of Scotland, Dublin and Strathclyde). In the aftermath of the conflict, three beasts of battle come into view: the *earn*, the black and horny-beaked **hræfn** (H'RAV-un) and the grey **wulf** of the woods. If you read these words out loud, it's easy to see how these latter two creatures have become the modern raven and wolf – even if the spelling and pronunciation have morphed along the way. Most noticeably, Old English *hræfn* contains a letter that no longer appears in English words: æ (æsc, pronounced ASH), a ligature that sounds like the 'a' in 'cat'. This is just one of the letters that have disappeared as Old English became new. In this book you'll come across two others: þ (thorn) and ð (eth), which are used interchangeably for a voiced or voiceless 'th' sound (as in 'this' or 'path').

But what is our sharp-eyed *earn* doing among these beasts of battle? The trio of *earn*, *hræfn* and *wulf* loiters near battlefields, waiting to have their fill of carrion: battles mean corpses, and corpses mean dinner. The creatures are depicted as heartless scavengers following their natural instincts, which the medieval literature scholar Heidi Estes compares to the way Old English texts portray pagans plundering the bodies of Christians. In *The Battle of Brunanburh* the poet chooses language that emphasises these negative traits. The *earn* is described as **grǣdig** (greedy), a **gūþ-hafoc** (GOOTH-HA-vock) or 'war-hawk', and elsewhere it is a **gūþ-fugel** (war-bird). Its feathered companion doesn't get off any lighter: other poems describe the *hræfn* as a **wæl-cēasiga** (chooser of the slain) and a **lyft-sceapa** (robber of the air). *The Battle of Brunanburh* is a political text, written for the purpose of celebrating the heroism and victory of the West Saxon dynasty. But Christian heroes can't be seen heartlessly plundering the bodies of the slain, so the poem has the beasts of battle collect the spoils of war rather than the victorious warriors.

In *The Battle of Brunanburh* it is only the excitement of the victorious humans that gets transferred to the beasts of battle, but in *Beowulf* we find a raven with the ability to speak. Having defeated a fierce dragon fighting at King Beowulf's side, the warrior Wiglaf returns to the men who refused to join him, who cowered beyond a nearby cliff. The dragon is dead, Wiglaf says, but so is their leader. He looks towards the imminent future, when their enemies learn that they no longer have a powerful king to protect them. He paints a grim vision of the aftermath of the unavoidable battle:

> Many a morning-cold spear shall be clasped in fists, held in hands. The warriors will not be awakened by the sound of the harp. Instead, the dark raven (*hrefn*), eager for the fated, speaks (*reordian*) at length, telling (*secgan*) the eagle (*earne*) how he was successful at his meal, while plundering the slaughtered with the wolf (*wulf*).

This scene is devastating, utterly devoid of human life. It is less about the specific enemy who will bring down Wiglaf's people than the inevitability of their demise. The warriors cannot be awakened by music because they lie dead, and it is the beasts of battle who speak up in the absence of humans. The *hræfn* boasts like any warrior after battle, going into detail (we imagine – since he does talk 'at length'), describing the exploits that led to his sumptuous feast. There is something here that might remind us of the dinner-party bore, and the poet uses words like **reordian** (to speak) and **secgan** (to tell) to emphasise the raven's human qualities. The eagle, noticeably, stays silent.

The eagle is more vocal in *Judith*, a retelling of the story of the Old Testament heroine who beheads an enemy general and saves her people. It is just before Judith's people, the Hebrews, launch their successful attack on the Assyrian camp. The warriors march confidently, newly inspired by Judith's bravery – they are **hæleþas** (heroes). Meanwhile, both the lean *wulf* and the black *hræfn* rejoice at the thought of impending slaughter, knowing the *hæleþas* will provide them with a feast. The *earn* eagerly follows along behind the marching men, singing a **hilde-lēoþ** (battle-song) as if to inspire them further. This is no normal birdsong: a **lēoþ** usually refers to a poem, ode or song with verses. **Lēoþ-cræft** is the art of poetry, a musical medium that uses words. Just as the beasts of battle take on the traits of human blood-thirstiness, here the *earn* takes on the role of a **scop** (poet) . . .

Isolation or inspiration?

While the song of the *earn* in *Judith* inspires warriors to victory, to the ears of the traveller in the poem *The Seafarer* the eagle's cries are only desolate screeches. In the midst of stormy weather, this lonely soul hears the dewy-feathered eagle *bigeal* (pronounced bih-YEH-all). This verb, **be-gyllan** (beh-YUEL-lahn), is a hapax legomenon, or a word that appears only once in extant Old English texts. If the pronunciation 'YEH-all' makes you think of 'yell', you wouldn't be far off: the Toronto *Dictionary of Old English* defines *be-gyllan* as 'to cry out against or in answer to', which seems quite specific to this scenario: a man alone at sea, speaking about his hardships, with no one to respond to his stories but the birds. The slightly more common verb **gyllan** has been defined in a variety of ways:

1.   (of birds) to make a loud cry, to screech
2.   (of a wolf/dog) to bay, howl
3.   (of an inanimate object) to make a strident, grating or crashing noise

Regardless of who or what makes the sound, it seems that it is never pleasant.

In *The Seafarer* a lonely man is isolated by storms and unable to see a better future. He cannot see, only hear the eagle who soars with a freedom far removed from the man's own state. But what if instead he had the perspective of the eagle soaring above the clouds? In an Old English translation of Boethius' *Consolation of Philosophy*, Wīsdōm tells Mōd that when he ascends he will look down upon the tempestuous world below, *swa se earn ðonne he up gewit bufan ða wolcnu styrmendum wedrum* (like the eagle when he goes above the clouds in stormy weather). Boethius, a Roman statesman and philosopher, wrote his *Consolation of Philosophy* while in prison before his execution in 524 CE, so it is no wonder that he is fantasising about an eagle's freedom and fearless flight. Boethius' text is written in the form of a conversation between Philosophy personified and his own suffering soul. In the Old English translation, Boethius' soul is Mōd and Philosophy Wīsdōm. The meaning of **wīsdōm** was the same as it is today, referring to knowledge, learning or philosophy. **Mōd** can be translated in many ways: 'the inner person or spiritual element of a person', 'soul', 'heart', 'spirit' or 'mind'. It eventually became modern English 'mood'. Not every Latin text was translated into Old English, but Boethius' *Consolation of Philosophy* was popular throughout the Middle Ages. Its translation into different languages tells us that it spoke to many people, some of whom may have felt 'trapped' by their situation, even if they weren't actually imprisoned. Could the idea that one's *mōd* eventually rises above all earthly ills have been a comfort? Whether we are a lonely seafarer or not, the ability to imagine our spirits ascending like the high-flying *earn* soars above the clouds – where no troublesome storm can harm it or hinder its flight – is an inspiring vision. As long as you don't also think about the eagle's grim, haunting screech.

Sometimes *earnas* can actively show us inspiration by guiding our souls to wondrous visions. In the Old English poem *Andreas*, some young seafarers say that while they were sleeping, *earnas* allowed them to glimpse the wonders of heaven. They describe their dream or vision to St Andrew:

> Eagles (*earnas*) came over the surge of the waves, flying, exultant in their wings (*feðerum*). They carried away our souls as we slept, conveying them joyfully, flying through the air with happy (*bliðe*), clear (*beorhte*) and gentle (*liðe*) sounds. They jubilantly showed us affection, dwelling in love. There was unending singing and heaven's circuit, many beautiful troops and a host of glory.

The *earnas* guide the sleeping souls to heaven, allowing them – even while still alive – to glimpse the eternal, heaven and a host of angels singing. They contrast significantly with the screeching, dewy-feathered *earn* of *The Seafarer* and the chattering scavenger of *Beowulf*. Instead of eliciting a sense of loneliness or doom, the song of the eagle is **blīþe**, **beorht** and **līþe** (happy, bright and gentle), a line which is itself musical in its use of alliteration and rhyme (BLEE-thuh, BEH-orh't and LEE-thuh).

The eagle's behaviour in Old English texts is fairly ordinary but heavy in meaning, whether inspiring hope or reminding us of our isolation. *Earnas* fly over desolate waters, screeching at lonely seafarers, making us realise we are ultimately alone on the journey to our salvation. Alongside the *hræfn* and the *wulf*, the *earn* haunts the battlefield, eager to plunder the corpses, reminding us that death comes to us all. But there is also something joyful in the *earn*'s flight as it soars through the air. *Earnas* can escape storm clouds, finding security in the rays of the sun. And, of course, their eagle eyes see all.

Eagle's Wordhord

be-gyllan, verb (beh-YUEL-lahn / bɛ-ˈjyl-lan): To cry out against or in answer to.

beorht, adjective (BEH-orh't / ˈbɛɔrxt): Bright, clear, lucid.

blīþe, adjective (BLEE-thuh / ˈbliː-θə): Happy, joyful; gentle, kind, gracious.

bridd, noun (BRID / ˈbrɪd): Young bird, chick.

dēaþ, noun (DAY-ath / ˈdeːaθ): Death.

ēad, noun (AY-ahd / ˈeːad): Happiness, well-being.

earn, noun (EH-arn / ˈɛarn): Eagle (plural: *earnas*).

ēhtan, noun (AY-h'tahn / ˈeːx-tan): To pursue or chase.

etan, noun (EH-tahn / ˈɛ-tan): To eat.

feþer, noun (FEH-ther / ˈfɛ-θɛr): Feather; (in plural) wings (plural: *feþra*).

fugel, noun (FUH-yell / ˈfʌ-jɛl): Bird (plural: *fuglas*).

ge-fēa, noun (yeh-VAY-ah / jɛ-ˈveːa): Joy, gladness.

grǣdig, adjective (GRADD-ih / ˈgræː-dɪj): Greedy, covetous.

gūþ-fugel, noun (GOOTH-FUH-yell / ˈguːθ-ˌfʌ-jɛl): War-bird (an epithet for the eagle).

gūþ-hafoc, noun (GOOTH-HA-vock / ˈguːθ-ˌha-vɔk): War-hawk (an epithet for the eagle).

gyllan, verb (YUEL-lahn / ˈjyl-lan): To make a loud cry, to screech; to bay, howl; to make a strident, grating or crashing noise.

hasu-pāda, noun (HA-zuh-PAH-da / ˈha-zʌ-ˌpaː-da): Grey-cloaked one (an epithet for the eagle).

hæleþ, noun (HAL-eth / ˈhæ-lɛθ): Hero, (noble) man (plural: *hæleþas*).

hilde-lēoþ, noun (HILL-duh-LAY-oth / ˈhɪl-də-ˌleːɔθ): Battle-song.

hold, noun (HOLD / ˈhɔld): Corpse, carcass.

hræfn, noun (H'RAV-un / ˈhræ-vən): Raven.

hwīt, adjective (H'WEET / ˈhwiːt): White.

lēo, noun (LAY-oh / 'leːɔ): Lion (plural: *lēon*).

lēoþ, noun (LAY-oth / 'leːɔθ): Song, poem, ode.

lēoþ-cræft, noun (LAY-oth-KRAFT / 'leːɔθ-ˌkræft): The art of poetry.

līþe, adjective (LEE-thuh / 'liː-θə): Soft, gentle, mild, serene.

lyft-sceaþa, noun (LUEFT-SHEH-ah-tha / 'lyft-ˌʃea-θa): Robber of the air (an epithet for the raven).

mann, noun (MAHN / 'man): Man, human being (plural: *menn*).

mǣr-līc, adjective (MAER-leech / 'mæːr-liːtʃ): Great, magnificent, glorious, splendid, illustrious.

mōd, noun (MOAD / 'moːd): Inner person, soul, mind, heart, spirit.

nīþ, noun (NEETH / 'niːθ): Hatred, enmity, rancor, spite, malice.

nȳten, noun (NUE-ten / 'nyː-tɛn): Animal, beast (plural: *nȳtenu*).

reordian, verb (REH-or-di-ahn / 'rɛɔr-di-an): To speak, say.

saluwig-pād, adjective (SA-luh-wi-PAWD / 'sa-lʌ-wɪj-ˌpaːd): Dark-cloaked, having dark plumage.

scop, noun (SHOP / 'ʃɔp): Poet.

secgan, verb (SEDG-ahn / 'sɛdʒ-an): To say words, tell.

stirc, noun (STIRK / 'stɪrk): Calf.

swefen-reccere, noun (SWEH-ven-REH-cheh-ruh / 'swɛ-vɛn-ˌrɛ-tʃɛ-rə): Interpreter of dreams, soothsayer.

wæl-cēasiga, noun (WAEL-CHAY-ah-zi-ga / 'wæl-ˌtʃeːa-zɪ-ga): Chooser of the slain (an epithet for the raven).

weorþ-mynd, noun (WEH-orth-muend / 'wɛɔrθ-mynd): Honour, glory, favour, fame.

wīsdōm, noun (WEEZ-doam / 'wiːz-doːm): Wisdom, knowledge, learning, philosophy.

wulf, noun (WULF / 'wʌlf): Wolf.

2

Spider (*gange-wæfre*)

THE OLD ENGLISH **wyrm** is far grander than its humble descendant is today. Today a 'worm' is usually a small, slender, segmented creature that lives in gardens and occasionally one's intestines. In Old English, a *wyrm* is essentially any 'creepy-crawly' – an insect, a worm, a snake, a reptile or even a dragon. Isidore of Seville explains that worms come into the world mainly 'from flesh or wood or some earthy substance, without any sexual congress', although sometimes they hatch from eggs, like the scorpion. Isidore puts his 'worms' into categories based on the source from which he believed them to be generated: earth, water, air, flesh, leaves, wood and clothing. An example of an 'air worm' is the spider, with its Latin name *aranea* deriving from *aer* (air).

Words for 'spider' in Old English sound like poetry – **gange-wæfre** (walker-weaver) and **wæfer-gange** (weaver-walker). These are kennings, or riddle-like compounds of two ordinary nouns that when combined mean something else. 'Walker' and 'weaver' on their own do not mean 'spider', but when they are joined together in a kenning they do. Not many animal kennings survive from Old English, and although we do still have the **gærs-hoppa** (grasshopper), its poetic cousins the **gærs-stapa** (literally 'grass-stepper' – a locust), walker-weaver and others have long faded from our language. Another word for 'spider' that has disappeared is **attor-coppa**, which literally means 'poison-top' or 'poison-vessel', depending on how you translate *coppa*: **cop** (top) or **copp** (vessel). At some point in linguistic history, 'coppa' or 'cop' on its own came to mean 'spider'. In the fourteenth century a 'coppe' spun a 'cop-web', and this spidery word has survived in today's 'cobweb'.

Leechbooks and spider bites

Kennings are usually found only in poetry, but we find both *attor-coppa* and *gange-wæfre* in the practical prose of medical texts. In Old English spiders are typically found in one of two types of texts: leechbooks and psalters. In neither place are they particularly desirable or admirable, just decidedly ordinary. A **lǣce-bōc** (leechbook) is a book of medical remedies, and the spiders in these texts have usually been up to no good: Old English *lǣce-bēc* (the plural) specify various methods of treating spider bites. As well as the kennings used for these creatures, the prosaic leechbooks also use the word **hunta** (hunter), which the Toronto *Dictionary of Old English* hypothesises is a word for a venomous spider, possibly arising from confusion of Latin *venator* (hunter) with *venenatus* (filled with poison). Although it may be that *hunta* means 'hunting spider', a spider that hunts its prey rather than lying in wait for it, the earliest usage of 'hunting spider' isn't until 1665, when the scientist Robert Hooke names them in his *Micrographia*. So we can fairly say that it's unlikely to be a hunting spider (although, happily, venomous spiders are just as unlikely on the British Isles).

Bald's Leechbook, a tenth-century Old English text, provides six different remedies for a *hunta* or *gange-wæfre* bite:

1. Cut three scarifications near the bite, directed away from it, letting the blood flow on to a green stick of hazel wood. Toss away the stick across a road.

2. Cut a scarification on the wound and place pounded **lǣce-wyrt** upon it. (*Lǣce-wyrt* is thought to be ribwort plantain, a herb widespread in the British Isles; its name literally means 'doctor-plant'.)

3. Take **æferþe** (a plant that has not been identified) and lichen from a blackthorn. Make these into a powder. Moisten with honey and apply to the wound.

4. Fry black snails in a hot pan, then grind them into powder with pepper and betony. This concoction may be eaten, drunk or applied to the wound.

5. Place the lower part of a mallow plant upon the wound.

6. Cut five scarifications, one on the bite and four around it. Put blood from the scarifications on to a stick, and silently throw the stick across a wagon road.

The first and the last of these remedies are particularly intriguing, since nothing is done to the wound itself aside from some very light bloodletting, and, more importantly, the blood must be transferred to a piece of wood that is physically cast away from the patient. Perhaps it was thought that the poison could be transferred to another object in this way, outside the patient's body. Another curious detail is the modification of 'silently' in the final suggestion: no yelling, please, when tossing your poison stick!

Another *lǣce-bōc* recommends a different concoction to treat a *gange-wæfre* bite, a combination of a raw hen's egg, ale and a fresh sheep's **tord** (turd). Significantly, the leechbook recommends preparing this *swa he nyte* (so he doesn't know) before giving him a good cupful to drink. *He*, in this case, is the person with the spider bite – not the spider. The verb **nytan** is a combination of **ne** (not) + **witan** (to know), so it seems you're meant to hide the fact that you are presenting the patient with a cupful of sheep *tord*. The Old English scholar Thijs Porck playfully suggests that, as ineffective as this remedy seems, perhaps it would prevent the patient from complaining about spider bites again. And it's true – even if you were not *told* about the sheep's *tord*, the taste would probably give it away, no matter how much ale you added.

A rather less repugnant tonic appears in the Old English *Herbarium*, a book of herbal remedies from the early eleventh century. Instead of a sheep's *tord*, this remedy uses **æsc-þrote** (verbena), an herbaceous flowering plant. Boil the *æsc-þrote* leaves in wine, pound them, and place them on the swollen *attor-coppa* bite. The wound will then open up. Once this has occurred, pound the *æsc-þrote* (it's not clear if this is more leaves or another part of the plant) with honey and apply it to the wound – you'll be better in no time.

One thing that casts doubt upon the effectiveness of the *Herbarium*'s remedy is the accompanying illustration of the so-called *attor-coppan*, which are not particularly convincing drawings of spiders. If we disregard the horse's heads, the horns and the wings, we might commend the illustrator of these 'spiders' on at least getting the number of legs right. Spiders are not a common subject of illustration in medieval texts, and they often have the wrong number of legs – six or ten, for instance.

Spiders in the Old English *Herbarium* (England, eleventh century)

Looking again at the *Herbarium* spiders, we might infer artistic licence rather than error: it's possible to see that they resemble dragons (another kind of *wyrm*). These fierce *attor-coppan* are not to be trifled with, resembling the spider of the later Middle English *Physiologus*, who is always ready to seize any unfortunate flies caught in her net: 'She bites them cruelly, becoming their slayer. She kills them and drinks their blood.'

Years and souls like spiders

As well as leechbooks, the other place that spiders are most commonly found in Old English is in psalters. Here, medical prose gives way to more dreamy, metaphorical language. For all their apparent ferocity and harmful poisons in the leechbooks, spiders are quite weak and vulnerable in the Psalms. The Latin Vulgate Bible, a late-fourth-century Latin translation by Jerome, was the Bible version most familiar to Christians living in early medieval England, and the Douay-Rheims version is its modern English translation. In the Douay-Rheims translation, Psalm 38 says:

> The strength of thy hand hath made me faint in rebukes: Thou hast corrected man for iniquity. And thou hast made his <u>soul</u> (*anima*) to waste away like a <u>spider</u> (*aranea*).

As the Old English scholar Megan Cavell points out, this psalm's meaning is clear – 'sin eats away at the soul, which withers like a fragile spider' – and its translations into Old English are pretty straightforward. The Vespasian, Regius and Lambeth Psalters – Latin psalters containing Old English glosses or translations – all describe the soul as languishing, dwindling, wasting away and becoming useless like a spider. The Paris Psalter, an Old English translation of the Psalms from the late ninth century, has a slight variation: a sinner's *mōd* (mind/heart/spirit), it says, becomes as **tīdre** (fragile) as a *gange-wæfre*'s **nett**. It is the spider's web, rather than the spider, that is fragile. This is not unlike the way in which many people think of spiders today: although it's easy to sweep their frail webs away, although they are 'more scared of you than you are of them', the sight of a spider is often enough to strike fear into the hearts of even the bravest among us.

The image of the spider has developed gradually over the centuries. Classical literature (by Roman writers like Ovid and Pliny the Elder in the first century CE) and late antique literature (Symphosius in the fourth or fifth century) portray spiders as artists and master craftspeople. This 'diligent artist' concept eventually gave way to a competing biblical tradition which associated spiders with weakness and fragility. The *tīdre* spider is the one that appears in early medieval England. Spiders' webs were easily broken and caught only the smallest flies; their work was not seen as artistic like it was in earlier periods but instead symbolic of what the medieval literature scholar

E. Ruth Harvey describes as 'useless ingenuity'. By the fourth century, Ambrose was using the spider as an example of what Katarzyna and Sergiusz Michalski call 'mindless industriousness', explaining that 'he works on his web day and night without achieving anything usable in the form of clothing'. In the sixth century, the Roman writer Cassiodorus links the fragile spider to sin. Because the spider is 'weak and feeble', it must catch its dinner using cunning and deceitful traps. By the time we get to Old English texts, it seems that the spider has become if anything feebler, and by the time Middle English is in use the emphasis is on the creature's cruel violence. So much for the artistic crafts-spider of ancient Rome.

If the symbolic nature of the spider has changed over time, so has the creature featured in the psalm's comparison. The original Hebrew version of the psalm does not say anything about a spider at all. Instead, it uses a moth attacking clothing as a metaphor for life fleeing the body. In their natural and cultural history of the spider, the Michalskis explain that the Greek translator of the psalm replaced the moth with a spider, comparing the drying up of a sinner's soul to the dryness of a spider's web. It's for this reason that some modern editions of the Bible refer to moths, others to spiders: it depends on whether they are based on the Hebrew psalm or the Greek. The King James Version published in 1611 leaves out the spider entirely, perhaps to avoid the complicated metaphor. The Catholic Public Domain Version (2009) has a spider, but several other editions, like the New International Version (2011), have moths – 'you consume their wealth like a moth'. Whether a hungry moth or a fragile spider, the point is that the soul is vulnerable in the presence of sin.

While Psalm 38 likens the fragile spider to a sinner's soul, Psalm 89 compares time to a spider. The Latin Vulgate says, 'For all our days are spent; and in thy wrath we have fainted away. Our years shall be considered as a spider (*aranea*).' The meaning here is far from obvious, and scribes clearly struggled a bit more translating this Latin verse into Old English. The Lambeth Psalter uses 'spider' for the comparison (in fact two different words for spider, **lobbe** and **renge**), as does the Cambridge Psalter (which uses *wæfer-gange*). However, the Regius Psalter compares 'our years' to a *renge* or **frocga** (frog), while the Vespasian Psalter makes the comparison to a *gange-wæfre* or **grytt** (dust). *Grytt* makes sense; if you're trying to emphasise the transitory, ephemeral nature of the years of one's life, 'dust' is a more obvious metaphor than 'spider'. But there is nothing particularly fragile or fleeting about a frog. Perhaps the Lambeth Psalter scribe got confused when writing their translation, misreading the Latin text as *rana* (frog) instead of *aranea* (spider). (They didn't have the benefit of a copy-editor back then.) Meanwhile, the Paris Psalter reveals some of the spider's desire for bloodshed that appears in the Middle English *Physiologus*: 'Our winters [or years] were most like a spider (*geongewifran*), when it is most eager to frighten flies into its web (*nette*).'

Yet as fragile and fleeting as a walker-weaver and its web can be, an Old English homily about Judgement Day refers to their longevity despite the passing of time:

> God's Law will be destroyed, and then there will be great people-troubles (*folcgedrefnesse*) before Doomsday. And God's house will be laid to waste and the altars very neglected, so that spiders (*attorcoppan*) will have woven inside.

The *Dictionary of Old English* defines **folc-gedrēfnes** (literally 'people-trouble') as 'disturbance of the people' or 'confusion of mankind'. When human-made churches are destroyed and their altars forgotten, still the *attor-coppa*'s webs will remain.

Whether they're like a frog, dust or a spider, 'our years', the Psalms warn, are fragile and fleeting, fading away. Even a bloodthirsty hunter, like the spiders in the Paris Psalter and Middle English *Physiologus*, is ultimately a vulnerable, *tīdre* creature who weaves a fragile *nett*. But that *nett* will outlast human ambition and confusion, the 'people-trouble' of the world. Such an ordinary thing as a cobweb holds eternity in its silky threads.

Spider's Wordhord

attor-coppa, noun (AHT-tor-KOP-pa / ˈat-tɔr-ˌkɔp-pa): Spider (plural: *attor-coppan*).

æferþe, noun (AE-ver-thuh / ˈæ-vɛr-θə): Unidentified medicinal herb.

æsc-þrote, noun (ASH-THROT-uh / ˈæʃ-ˌθrɔ-tə): Verbena, vervain.

cop, noun (KOP / ˈkɔp): Top, summit.

copp, noun (KOP / ˈkɔp): Cup, vessel.

folc-gedrēfnes, noun (FOLK-yeh-DRAVE-ness / ˈfɔlk-jɛ-ˌdreːv-nɛs): Disturbance of the people, confusion of mankind (people-trouble).

frocga, noun (FRAW-ja / ˈfrɔ-dʒa): Frog.

gange-wæfre, noun (GONG-guh-WAV-ruh / ˈgaŋ-gə-ˌwæv-rə): Spider (walker-weaver).

gærs-hoppa, noun (GARZ-HOP-pa / ˈgærz-ˌhɔp-pa): Grasshopper.

gærs-stapa, noun (GARZ-STAH-pa / ˈgærz-ˌsta-pa): Locust (grass-stepper).

grytt, noun (GRUET / ˈgryt): Dust.

hunta, noun (HUN-ta / ˈhʌn-ta): Possibly a venomous spider or a hunting spider.

lǣce-bōc, noun (LATCH-uh-BOAK / ˈlæː-tʃə-ˌboːk): Leechbook, book of medical remedies (plural: *lǣce-bēc*, pronounced LATCH-uh-BAYCH).

læce-wyrt, noun (LATCH-uh-WUERT / 'læː-tʃə-ˌwyrt): Ribwort
plantain, a medicinal herb.

lobbe, noun (LOB-buh / 'lɔb-bə): Spider.

ne, adverb (neh / nɛ): Not.

nett, noun (NET / 'nɛt): Web, net.

nytan, verb (NUE-tahn / 'ny-tan): To not know.

renge, noun (RENG-guh / 'rɛŋ-gə): Spider.

tīdre, adjective (TEE-druh / 'tiː-drə): Fragile, weak, easily broken.

tord, noun (TORD / 'tɔrd): Turd, dung.

wæfer-gange, noun (WAV-er-GONG-guh / 'wæ-vɛr-ˌgaŋ-gə): Spider
(weaver-walker).

witan, verb (WIT-ahn / 'wɪ-tan): To know, be aware.

wyrm, noun (WUERM / 'wyrm): Worm, insect, snake, dragon, reptile
(plural: *wyrmas*).

3

Field Creature (*feoh*)

PERHAPS THE MOST ORDINARY of the ordinary animals is the *feoh*. A *feoh* is a creature of the field, or livestock, typically of the four-legged variety. The word can refer specifically to cattle, but the crucial characteristic of a *feoh* was the fact it was domesticated, not wild. If an *earn* is happiest beside a battlefield and a *gange-wæfre* weaving webs on church altars, the *feoh*'s place is on a farm.

On the farm

Most people in early medieval England would have been farmers, people who worked the land, growing whatever food they needed to survive. A **gebūr** (yeh-BOOR) was a free but economically dependent peasant, someone who held land that belonged to a lord. (Not all farming was done by free peasants, and enslaved labourers would have undertaken a great deal of the work.) A *gebūr* needed to pay compensation to the lord of the land, in the form of either goods or labour. Whether you were paying rent or compensation or acquiring goods and services, trade and transactions mainly took the form of foodstuffs. People of means in early medieval England did trade with the world beyond, enjoying exotic items like silks and spices, but all the essentials of life came from local farms – food from crops and animals, clothing from sheep's wool and building materials from the trees and fields.

Other Old English words for 'farmer' are **eorþ-tilia** (EH-orth-TIH-li-ah, tiller of the earth), **æcer-mann** (ACK-er-MAHN, literally 'acre-person') and **irþling** (IRTH-ling, someone who does **irþ**, or ploughing). Modern English 'farmer' derives from **feormere**, a noun that seems to have been uncommon – a hapax, appearing only once in extant Old English. The Toronto *Dictionary of Old English* defines *feormere* as 'purveyor', a supplier or provider in goods. **Feorm** is 'food' or 'provisions', but it could also refer to 'hospitality' or 'entertainment' or simply 'a benefit'. The verb **feormian** has varied meanings: 'to foster or maintain', 'to entertain or welcome a guest', 'to harbour a fugitive or criminal', 'to maintain someone with basic necessities', 'to supply food as an obligation or rent' or 'to provide a feast for someone'. *Feormian* could also mean 'to feed on', 'to consume' or even 'to cleanse'. After all, an important aspect of farming is emptying or clearing out a ditch or latrine, or removing dung and soiled straw from a stable. In an Old English translation of the Gospel of Luke (*c.*1000), St John the Baptist says Christ will come with a winnowing fan to clean out his **bern** (barn):

He will <u>cleanse</u> (*feormað*) the <u>barn's floor</u> (*bernes flore*) and gather the wheat into his <u>barn</u> (*berne*); the chaff he will burn in an unquenchable fire.

John is referring to Christ's separation of the wheat from the chaff, a metaphor for separating the worthy people destined for heaven from the worthless sinners. It wasn't until the sixteenth century that 'farm' took on an agricultural definition – 'to use (land) for growing crops or rearing animals; to cultivate (land)'.

A farm in early medieval England typically consisted of a house, an outbuilding and an enclosure. A *gebūr* would probably have kept their harvested crops in ricks or stacks, since owning a *bern* (like the metaphorical one in the Gospel of Luke) or **corn-hūs** (granary, literally 'grain-house') was less common. Farmers would thresh and use grain as needed; it was not a large commercial operation. Without a *bern*, a *gebūr* may have kept their *feoh* living outside all year round. England's weather was a bit more clement during this period, so that might have helped. The 'Medieval Warm Period' had average temperatures similar to those of the early twenty-first century, while the earlier Roman period is thought to have been a bit chillier.

So what *dēor* would a *gebūr* have kept on their farm? The **cū** (cow) was mainly used for farm labour (especially ploughing), its meat and milk being of secondary importance. Instead, a **scēap** (sheep, pronounced SHAY-op) was more likely to have been kept for its meat, manure and wool. Sheep skins were also most likely to be turned into parchment (while sheep, calf and goat skins were all used to make the parchment, sheep were the most readily available). A **swīn** (pig) was a useful source of meat and fat. The **hors** was a more prestigious animal, a luxury gift or a warrior's form of transport. But horses could still be found on a humble farm, used for riding as well as carrying burdens. Perhaps there would also be a **hund** (dog) or a *cat* (cat) or some **cicenu** (chickens), but these are not really *feoh*, creatures of the field.

Many *feoh* appear in an eleventh-century calendar, where each month's labours or activities are illustrated with a number of domesticated critters, the most ordinary of animals in early medieval life. The page for January has a plough pulled by a team of four **oxan** (oxen – the reason we say 'oxen' instead of 'oxes'!). On the page for May, a shepherd tends his flock of *scēap*. June shows a pair of cattle wearing a yoke, perhaps waiting to pull a cart that's being filled with timber nearby. September depicts five hairy *swīn* rooting around in a forest, feeding on fallen acorns, chestnuts or other nuts. On October's page a falconer sits astride a *hors*, ready to hunt wild *fuglas* (birds) with his **heoru-swealwe** (hawk or falcon, literally 'fierce swallow'). Unlike the spiders of the previous chapter, these animals look fairly realistic (although whether this is due to artistic choices or skills is unknown).

A shepherd tending sheep on a calendar page for May (England, eleventh century)

The Old English name for May is **þrimilce-mōnaþ** (three-milkings-month), supposedly because the *feoh* had plenty to eat and produced a great quantity of milk, enough for three milkings a day. You might wonder, then, why the May calendar page features sheep instead of cows. Of the various lactating *feoh*, in the early Middle Ages the *cū* was not used as much for dairy products as the *scēap* and **gāt** (goat), *scēap* being the most common. It requires a lot less food to feed a *scēap* than a *cū*; cattle, more expensive to keep in large numbers, were used where they were most needed, ploughing and working the fields. **Meolc** (milk) was not only for drinking or churning into butter and cheese: **cū-meoluc** (cow's milk), **ēowo-meoluc** (ewe's milk) and **gāte meoluc** (goat's milk) all appear in leechbook remedies. It seems that these three varieties of *meolc* were thought to heal gastrointestinal ailments, ranging from stomach pain to dysentery.

And, as we already know, milk wasn't the only animal by-product to feature in leechbooks. As well as sheep dung, there are two remaining leechbook remedies that call for *hors* manure. While sheep *tord* (dung) might be used to treat a spider bite, the *tord* of a *hors* can be used in two ways, each related to blood flow. If a wound made for bloodletting won't stop bleeding, *Bald's Leechbook* says, 'Take a <u>fresh horse's turd</u> (*horses tord niwe*); dry it in the sun or by a fire. Rub it into a powder and lay this powder very thickly on a linen cloth. Bind the bloodletting wound with this for a night.' Another leechbook describes a remedy for when one's **mōnaþ-gecynd** (period, literally 'month-condition') is too heavy: 'If a woman's <u>period</u> (*monaðgecynd*) is heavy of flow, take a <u>fresh horse's turd</u> (*niwe horses tord*), lay it on hot burning coals, and make it smoke strongly between the thighs up under the clothes so that the woman sweats a lot.' (This sounds like a good way to make one's *mōnaþ-gecynd* even less bearable, but I suppose it's preferable to a sheep *tord* in your drink.)

Clearly, *feoh* were valuable in many ways to those who kept them. Domesticated animals by their nature belong to someone, and *feoh* can sometimes mean 'property', as well as 'wealth' or 'money'. It is from this word that we get modern English 'fee'. *Feoh* is inherently valuable, regardless of whether it's a cow or a tax payment, treasure or household possessions. **Feoh-spilling** is the wasting of money, and if you are **feoh-strang** (wealth-strong) you are rich. **Here-feoh** (battle-wealth) is the spoils of war, which may or may not include farm animals. A **feoh-hord** is not a hoard of cattle but of riches – a treasury.

The runic alphabet of early medieval England begins with *feoh*, the Old

English F-rune: ᚠ. Today this alphabet is known as 'fuþorc' or 'futhark', named by modern scholars for its first six letters. Unlike the letters of our modern English alphabet, Old English runes represent words as well as sounds, so ᚠ can represent the letter F as well as a cow or wealth.

Feoh is not the only word that means both 'livestock' and 'money'. The Old English words *yrfe* (cattle) and *irfe* (inheritance, property) are also quite similar. This coincidence is not unique to the English language: 'cattle', 'chattel' (property) and 'capital' (wealth) all derive from Latin *capitalis* and thus from *caput* (head). Latin *pecu* means 'cattle' or 'livestock' as well as 'wealth' or 'property'; today we use 'pecuniary' to refer to financial matters.

The importance of cows to the early medieval economy is clear from the overlapping meanings of *feoh* – cattle, property, wealth – but it's also evident because of the sheer number of words Old English has for this animal. In addition to *feoh*, *yrfe* and *cū*, a cow might be called a **hrȳþer**, *oxa*, *stirc*, **cealf** or **nēat**. A *hrȳþer* (pronounced H'RUE-ther) is an ox or cow, which became 'rother' in later periods, a term for cattle that was still used in certain parts of England, particularly the Midlands, long after Old English was a distant memory. (Next time you accuse someone of talking bullshit, why not use the alternative historical term 'rother-soil'?) *Hrȳþer* has survived in place names like Rotherhithe in London (**hȳð**: landing place for boats or port) and Rotherfield in East Sussex (**feld**: field or pasture). *Oxa* is, of course, Old English for 'ox', and the place name **Oxna-ford** (Oxford) refers to a **ford** for oxen, a shallow place in the river where the animals can cross.

Holy cows and the value of *feoh*

Feoh – cows or otherwise – were clearly the most 'ordinary' of creatures in early medieval England, the ones you see most often in daily life and think of when considering the standard labours from month to month. But *feoh* also appear in literary and artistic representations of the holiest and most extraordinary of people – the saints.

In medieval literature and art, a *stirc* or *cealf* (two words meaning 'calf') often represents a saint. If you recall Ælfric of Eynsham's explanation for the four animals of the evangelists in Chapter 1, the *stirc* represents St Luke:

> The <u>calf's likeness</u> (*celfes gelicnyss*) belonged to Luke because he began his gospel, as God ordered him, from the priest that was called Zacharias, because people offered, in the old custom, a <u>calf</u> (*cealf*) for the priest and slew it at the altar.

There isn't any slaying of *cealfru* (calves) in the first chapter of Luke's Gospel; only incense and prayers are offered to God. But the Gospel

St Luke and his calf in the Lindisfarne Gospels (England, *c.*700)

of Luke generally emphasises Christ's sacrifice, and a *cealf* or *stirc* is traditionally a sacrificial beast.

If a *cealf* is meant for sacrifice, a *nēat* is for service. A *nēat* could be non-specific livestock (even as general as 'animal' or 'beast'), although it's most often bovine. The word may be related to Old English **nēotan**, which means 'to enjoy', 'to have the benefit of' or 'to make use of'. One 'makes use of' a *nēat*, a domesticated animal; the animal doesn't exist for its own sake. In the poem *Beowulf*, someone who serves their leader is called a **heorþ-genēat** (hearth-companion), **genēat** being a word for 'companion' or 'vassal', a person who both benefits from and serves another. 'Neat' has survived into modern English, although its pronunciation changed from NAY-aht (as in Old English *nēat*) to NEET; the English poet and novelist Thomas Hardy uses it in 'Growth in May', saying that a meadow is 'possessed of the neats', which rhymes nicely when that meadow's grass 'brushes their teats'. The modern English cattle 'neat' is archaic and used only regionally, unlike the adjective 'neat' that means 'elegant', 'smart' or 'free from additional embellishments'. Unrelated to the cattle 'neat', the elegant 'neat' first appears in the fifteenth century, referring to a 'nete broch of gold', and derives from French *net* (clean, clear).

Whether or not the *nēat* is 'neat' like a brooch, it is ultimately an object of value, *feoh* for one's *hord*. Like Hardy's neats, *feoh* are possessions, whether of a meadow or farmer. The *feoh* exists for the *gebūr's* pleasure. The *cealf* does have the honour of representing one of the evangelists, but it does so as a symbol of sacrifice; it is a creature to be used for the good of others. Yet this does not lessen its religious significance, for Christ too sacrificed himself for the good of others.

But no matter whether the *feoh* is a traditional *cū* or *oxa*, or if it is a 'field creature' more generally like a *hors*, *scēap* or *gāt*, its importance in early medieval life cannot be emphasised enough. *Feoh* are the most common *dēor* of the medieval agricultural landscape, and indeed it would be impossible to imagine it without them. People relied on *scēap*, *gǣt* (goats) and *swīn* for food, *oxan* for labour, *hors* for transportation of people and goods, *scēap* for wool and manure. Other farm (but not field) animals included *hund* for guarding, herding and hunting, *catas* for catching **mȳs** (mice), *cicenu* for meat and eggs and **gēs** (geese) for grease and down. The villages of early medieval England had not yet reached the fullest extent of their territories, and the *feldas* between them were open rather than enclosed. Every generation or so might add to the cultivated areas by clearing more woodland. This would have looked very different to the enclosed pastures and self-contained farms of today.

Would the omnipresence of these *dēor* have made them less appealing for symbolism in literature? The *hors* might appear as a status symbol, the *scēap* as representing one who follows a leader, the *stirc* as a sacrifice for the good of others. The cats and dogs, chickens and geese, pigs and mice mostly turn up in more literal contexts. Sometimes they appear in glosses – lists of words in Latin with Old English definitions – and nowhere else. As such, they are useful words to know but apparently not as intriguing to write about, which is why they don't have their own chapters in this book. But every once in a while an ordinary *dēor* is granted more significance, accumulating symbolism through Bible verses, homilies and poetry – like the next creature we are about to meet.

Field Creature's Wordhord

ǣcer-mann, noun (ACK-er-MAHN / ˈæ-kɛr-ˌman): Farmer.
bern, noun (BERN / ˈbɛrn): Barn.
cealf, noun (CHEH-alf / ˈtʃɛalf): Calf (plural: *cealfru*).
cicen, noun (CHIH-chen / ˈtʃɪ-tʃɛn): Chicken (plural: *cicenu*).

corn-hūs, noun (KORN-hoos / ˈkɔrn-huːs): Granary.

cū, noun (KOO / ˈkuː): Cow.

cū-meoluc, noun (KOO-MEH-o-luk / ˈkuː-ˌmɛɔ-lʌk): Cow's milk.

eorþ-tilia, noun (EH-orth-TIH-li-ah / ˈɛɔrθ-ˌtɪ-lɪ-a): Farmer, tiller of the earth.

ēowo-meoluc, noun (AY-o-wo-MEH-o-luk / ˈeːɔ-wɔ-ˌmɛɔ-lʌk): Ewe's milk.

feld, noun (FELD / ˈfɛld): Field, pasture (plural: *feldas*).

feoh, noun (FEH-oh / ˈfɛɔx): Cattle, livestock; property, wealth, money; value, price, fee; name of the F-rune ᚠ.

feoh-hord, noun (FEH-oh-HORD / ˈfɛɔx-ˌhɔrd): Hoard of money or wealth.

feoh-spilling, noun (FEH-oh-SPIL-ling / ˈfɛɔx-ˌspɪl-lɪŋ): Wasting of money.

feoh-strang, adjective (FEH-oh-STRONG / ˈfɛɔx-ˌstraŋ): Rich (money-strong).

feorm, noun (FEH-orm / ˈfɛɔrm): Food, provisions; entertainment, feast; benefit, profit.

feormere, noun (FEH-or-meh-ruh / ˈfɛɔr-mɛ-rə): One who supplies with food, purveyor.

feormian, verb (FEH-or-mi-ahn / ˈfɛɔr-mɪ-an): To foster or maintain; to entertain or welcome a guest; to harbour a fugitive or criminal; to maintain someone with basic necessities; to supply food as an obligation or rent; to provide a feast for someone.

ford, noun (FORD / ˈfɔrd): Ford; a shallow place, natural or artificial, across a stream, river or other water, by which a crossing can be made.

gāt, noun (GAHT / ˈgaːt): Goat (plural: *gǣt*).

gāte meoluc, noun (GAH-tuh MEH-o-luck / ˈgaː-tə ˈmɛɔ-lʌk): Goat's milk.

gebūr, noun (yeh-BOOR / jɛ-ˈbuːr): Farmer, a free but economically dependent peasant.

genēat, noun (yeh-NAY-aht / jɛ-'neːat): Companion, associate, vassal.

gōs, noun (GOHS / 'goːs): Goose (plural: *gēs*).

heorþ-genēat, noun (HEH-orth-yeh-NAY-aht / 'hɛɔrθ-jɛ-ˌneːat): Hearth-companion.

heoru-swealwe, noun (HEH-oh-ruh-SWEH-all-wuh / 'hɛɔ-rʌ-ˌswɛal-wə): Falcon, hawk.

here-feoh, noun (HEH-reh-FEH-oh / 'hɛ-rɛ-ˌfɛɔx): Booty, spoils of war.

hors, noun (HORS / 'hɔrs): Horse (plural: *hors*).

hrȳþer, noun (H'RUE-ther / 'hryː-θɛr): Ox, cow.

hund, noun (HUND / 'hʌnd): Dog, hound (plural: *hund*).

hȳð, noun (HUETH / 'hyːθ): Landing place for boats, low shore, port.

irfe, noun (IR-vuh / 'ɪr-və): Inherited property, property that passes to an heir.

irþ, noun (IRTH / 'ɪrθ): Ploughing, tilling; ploughed land.

irþling, noun (IRTH-ling / 'ɪrθ-lɪŋ): Ploughman, farmer.

meolc, noun (MEH-olk / 'mɛɔlk): Milk.

mōnaþ-gecynd, noun (MO-nath-yeh-KUEND / 'moː-naθ-jɛ-ˌkynd): Period, menstruation.

mūs, noun (MOOS / 'muːs): Mouse (plural: *mȳs*).

nēat, noun (NAY-aht / 'neːat): Ox or cow; beast, animal.

nēotan, verb (NAY-o-tahn / 'neːɔ-tan): To enjoy, have the benefit of, make use of.

oxa, noun (AWK-sa / 'ɔk-sa): Ox (plural: *oxan*).

Oxna-ford, noun (AWK-sna-vord / 'ɔk-sna-vɔrd): Oxford.

scēap, noun (SHAY-op / 'ʃeːap): Sheep (plural: *scēap*).

swīn, noun (SWEEN / 'swiːn): Pig, swine (plural: *swīn*).

þrimilce-mōnaþ, noun (THRI-mill-chuh-MO-nath / 'θrɪ-mɪl-tʃə-ˌmoː-naθ): May (three-milkings-month).

yrfe, noun (UER-vuh / 'yr-və): Cattle.

4

Dove (*culfre*)

THE DOVE IS A UBIQUITOUS symbol in England today – in fact, its symbolism reaches across religions, cultures and centuries. Today doves live on every continent aside from Antarctica, so perhaps it isn't surprising that they are symbolic to so many different people. White doves are released at weddings, representative of love, purity and innocence, and they appear on the logos and banners of organisations for the promotion of peace and non-violence. Originally representing peace of the soul and later symbolising peace between peoples, the white dove's symbolism has remained fairly consistent over the millennia. But not all doves are white. In London and other big cities, the main 'dove' you see might be the pigeon. There is no scientific difference between 'doves' and 'pigeons', which all belong to the *Columbidae* family, and in the English language their differentiation is inconsistent. (A common pigeon might be called a 'rock dove' or a 'rock pigeon'.) The widespread rock pigeon is mostly grey. Depending on where in the world you live, you might be very familiar with mourning doves (light grey and brown), spotted doves (brown with a rosy breast) or turtle doves (brown and pinkish-grey).

In the bestiaries of the later Middle Ages, doves congregate in multi-coloured flocks. It is unlikely that people actually saw doves in all the different colours that appear in bestiaries, but that didn't stop the artists and theologians from playing around with colour symbolism. The colours of these doves represented different people or concepts. A blood-red dove represented Jesus, who redeemed humankind with his blood. Naturally, this red dove is the flock's leader – and it can persuade even wild pigeons (non-believers) to leave behind their forests and follow it into the dovecote (Church). Speckled doves signified the diversity of the twelve prophets. Ash-coloured doves were associated with Jonah, who preached in a hair shirt and ashes, and gold doves represented the three boys who refused to worship the golden idol. The prophet Elisha, who was snatched up in a whirlwind, was represented by a dove that is 'air-coloured'. While thematically appropriate for airborne Elisha, it is not so easy to imagine an 'air-coloured' dove, air being largely invisible. Rather than see-through, the dove might be a shade of blue, a celestial colour often used to symbolise heaven. If you are wondering what shade of blue, don't go too pale. After all, the colour of the sky on a clear day is like sapphires, according to Bede, a monk, scholar and historian of early-eighth-century Northumbria. A less positive symbol, perhaps, was the black dove, who was associated with obscure sermons (obscure to whom or in what way remains unclear).

A dove's love and fear

While later medieval bestiaries feature doves in many different colours, the doves in Old English tend to be white, if their colour is mentioned at all.

Culfre is the Old English word for 'dove', and not only is it very distinct from the word we use for this creature today, but cognates of it are not found in other Germanic languages, which makes it rather mysterious – it's still unclear where the word originated. The word 'dove' does derive from Germanic languages, with cognates in Old Saxon (*dūva*) and Old Norse (*dūfa*), but it didn't appear in English until around 1200 (with Middle English's 'douve'). Until then, *culfre* was our only word for a dove, and it even survived the arrival of its rival: 'culver' remains a word in modern English, and though its use is quite rare it is a valid entry in Scrabble. If anyone challenges you, you can tell them it was once a common name specifically for the wood pigeon in the south and east of England.

The most famous of the white *culfran* (doves) is the one sent out by Noah during the Flood, which you can see in the illustration from the Old English *Hexateuch*, a late-eleventh- or early-twelfth-century man-uscript containing the first six books of the Bible. It is often forgotten that the *culfre* was not Noah's first choice as ambassador to land in the Book of Genesis. In order to find out if the waters are receding after the Flood, Noah initially sends a raven – a **hremn** or *hræfn* – from his **þel-fæsten** (plank-fortress – a very grand name for an ark). The *hremn* doesn't return; when he leaves the boat and discovers the feast left by the Flood's destruction, he becomes too busy flying about and feeding on carcasses to think of Noah and his task. The *hremn* is the opposite to the white dove in both colour and character: he cannot be trusted to do anything outside of his own self-interest. Noah is patient: he waits for the *hremn* for seven days before sending out a *culfre*. The *culfre* cannot find any dry land, so she returns to the ark in the eve-ning. After another seven days, Noah sends out the *culfre* again. An Old English poetic translation of Genesis says:

<u>She</u> (*heo*) flew far and wide, rejoicing in the spaciousness, until she found a fair resting place and then stepped with her feet on to a tree.

She rejoiced, cheerful-minded, because she, very weary, could sit on the tree's bright branches. She shook her wings and went flying back with her gift. She brought to the sailor's hands a single twig from the olive tree, a green leaf.

A white dove returning to Noah with an olive branch in the Old English *Hexateuch* (England, late eleventh to early twelfth century)

The *culfre* returns to Noah bearing an olive branch, which tells him that there is dry land ahead. The English clergyman Arthur Collins explains the significance of the dove's return in his *Symbolism of Animals and Birds Represented in Church Architecture* (1913): 'Just as the dove could find no rest for the sole of her foot save in the ark, so the Christian soul can find no safety or peace outside the Church.' Another seven days go by and Noah sends out the *culfre* one last time. This time the *culfre* does not return, and Noah knows this must mean she has reached dry land. As the Old English poem says, 'Not gladly would she ever show herself again under the dark deck in the plank-fortress (*þellfæstenne*) when she had no need.' This statement rather undermines Collins's analogy, though, since the *culfre* does eventually decide she's spent enough time in the ark, that cramped *þel-fæsten*. Presumably Christians are not meant to grow weary of their time within the constricting Church.

Meanwhile, the *hræfn* continues to feast on carcasses until long after the floodwaters have finally dried. We don't need to dig too deep for this significance.

If the dove distinguishes herself from the raven by returning to Noah, it is not simply from a sense of obedience (or because she was tired). The *culfre* is inspired both by her love and by her fear. This pair of inspirations – love and fear – appear in one of Ælfric of Eynsham's sermons, in which he instructs women to present two *culfran briddas* as an offering to God after they have given birth (you might remember from Chapter 1 that a *bridd* is a young bird or chick). Ideally a woman should also bring a yearling **lamb** (lamb) as her post-partum offering, but Ælfric acknowledges that some impoverished women may not be able to afford such a creature. Yet there is no such get-out clause for providing the *culfran briddas*, and even poor women were expected to supply not one but two of them. If two baby doves were attainable by even a poor woman, they must have been fairly common.

The pair of doves represent the two things that inspire humankind: **ege** (fear, pronounced EH-yuh) and **lufu** (love). Although *ege* means 'terror', it can also be a respectful kind of fear, like 'reverence' or 'awe'. In fact, modern English 'awe' comes from Old English *ege*. The word increasingly takes on the 'reverence' meaning over the course of the Middle Ages, and by the eighteenth century reverence, not fear, is its primary association. In the context of Ælfric's sermon, however, there is no doubt it means 'fear'; one is inspired by *ege* because one dreads hell's torments. Humans must weep for their sins when they confront this fear, and yet they continue to feel *lufu* towards God.

Holiness in a dove's form

Throughout medieval literature, white doves are not just associated with love and peace but also with the cleansing power of baptism, and because of this St John the Baptist is often depicted with one. During St John's baptism of Jesus, the Holy Spirit appears above Jesus in the form of a dove. In Old English religious texts we often find the **hālga gāst** (Holy Spirit) or **godes gāst** (God's Spirit) in the **hīw** (form) of a *culfre*. The main definition of 'hue' in modern English is 'colour'. But while Old English *hīw* can refer to the colour of something, or indeed to one's complexion, it was more often used to refer to something's general appearance or form. This *hīw* is often a form that, through natural or supernatural intervention, differs from the norm.

Ælfric writes about the *hīw* of the *culfre* in his sermon for the Lord's Epiphany, and here he is quite clearly referring to the Holy Ghost's assumed appearance in the *form* of a dove rather than the Holy Ghost being a dove-like colour:

> Then John consented to baptise <u>Christ</u> (*crist*). When he was baptised, heaven opened above his head and <u>God's Spirit</u> (*godes gast*) came in the <u>appearance of a dove</u> (*culfran hiwe*) and sat above Christ, and the voice of the <u>Father</u> (*fæder*) cried out from the heavens and said, 'This is my beloved son, and he pleases me well.'

All parts of the Holy Trinity, or **þrinness** ('three-ness'), are present here: the **fæder** (Father, a voice from the heavens), **crist** (Christ, the Son, a human being) and *godes gāst* (the Holy Spirit, in the *hīw* of a *culfre*).

Godes gāst, or the *hālga gāst*, might appear in a dove's *hīw* in moments of danger and desperation as well as times of celebration. In the Old English *Martyrology*, a collection of narratives about the lives of over 200 saints, a holy man named Ananias has been imprisoned without food for twelve days by the pagan emperor Diocletian. After the twelve days have passed, a prison guard named Petrus goes to check on the saint. The Old English *Martyrology* says:

> Then [Petrus] saw the <u>Holy Spirit</u> (*halgan gast*) in the <u>form of a dove</u> (*culfran hiwe*), sitting in the window of the prison and speaking to Ananias, the man of God, and afterwards flying to the heavens. Then the prison guard believed in God.

Even though he is pagan, Petrus recognises that the ordinary-looking *culfre* with whom his starving prisoner is having a chat is not just a pigeon sitting on the windowsill of a prison but is in fact the *hālga gāst*. He immediately converts to Christianity.

While St Ananias is visited by a holy dove, St Basil the Great, bishop of Caesarea, makes one. Ælfric explains in his *Lives of Saints* that one night, when Basil is praying at the holy altar, Christ and his apostles suddenly appear. Christ consecrates the **hūsel** (Eucharist) himself and hands it to Basil, who is (quite understandably) astonished. Basil breaks the Eucharistic wafer into three pieces. The first portion he consumes (which is what one usually does with the *hūsel*). The second portion he sets aside to be buried with him upon his death. Basil then orders the likeness of a *culfre* to be fashioned for him from pure gold, and inside this he places the third portion of the *hūsel*. He hangs the gold *culfre* over the altar, and afterwards it always moves three times when he blesses the Eucharist. The story does not specify whether this particular metal dove is moved by the Holy Spirit or by a special form of puppetry, but clearly it is meant to inspire faith among the Christians who gather for Mass.

In his sermon on the Epiphany, Ælfric explains that the *hālga gāst* appears to Christ in the *hīw* of a *culfre* because of the dove's **un-sceþþigness** (innocence). The *hālga gāst*

> . . . came over Christ in the <u>appearance of a dove</u> (*culfran hiwe*) because he wished to signify that Christ in his humanity was very gentle and <u>not eager for harm</u> (*unhearmgeorn*).

The dove is also **un-hearmgeorn** (not 'harm-eager'), as Ælfric explains its pacifistic **ge-cynd** (nature):

> We read in books about the <u>nature of the dove</u> (*culfran gecynde*) that she is a very peaceful bird, innocent and without <u>bile</u> (*geallan*), not fierce with her talons. She lives not on worms but on earthly fruits.

Gealla can refer to black bile and red bile, two of the four humours. According to humoural theory, which goes back to ancient Greece, one's body is composed of four humours – blood, phlegm, red or yellow bile and black bile – and to stay healthy they must be kept in balance. Bede associated a dominance of red bile with boldness and black bile with cunning. But Old English *gealla* could in fact refer to any bitter substance, venom or poison. In the context of the *culfre*, *gealla* means 'bitterness' or 'rancour'.

A short note on gentle doves, irresponsible ravens and the natural gender system

You may have noticed that some of the quotations from Ælfric's sermon use a feminine pronoun for the dove. Meanwhile, the raven is given a masculine pronoun. Ælfric uses **hē** (he) for the *hremn* and **hēo** (she) for the *culfre*. This is not necessarily because the raven's and the dove's characteristics were considered masculine or feminine. In Old English (as in Latin, and many modern languages, including German) nouns are classified as masculine, feminine or neuter. Today, modern English uses a 'natural gender system', where only nouns that refer specifically to males and females take gendered pronouns like 'he' or 'she', and inanimate objects or animals take the neutral pronoun 'it'. A woman might ponder how she can strive for herself and not for God and a man might love his deceit, but a raven would strive for *itself*, and enjoy *its* deceit. The linguistics scholar Anne Curzan points out that calling this the 'natural gender' system is a bit of a misnomer, since our system is not 'natural', and in fact 'stands as the exception, not the rule among the world's languages'. The natural gender system is uncommon among Indo-European languages, in which you are much more likely to find gendered nouns and the common use of he/she for objects and animals.

The grammatical gender categories of Old English are very similar to those of modern German. There is no obvious reason for the nouns to be gendered as they are, but it is not determined by a word's actual meaning. Old English **wīf-mann** (woman), for example, is a masculine noun because its root (*mann*: human) is masculine. Synonyms for the same thing might even be gendered differently, like these three words for 'sword': **ecg** (feminine), **mēce** (masculine) and **sweord** (neuter). It clearly, then, has nothing to do with the nature of the sword. Thus, while it may be tempting to assume that the dove is feminine due to her gentle manner, and the raven is masculine thanks to his dastardly character, the *culfre* is a *hēo* and *hremn* a *hē* because of Old English grammar, not cultural gender stereotypes.

Be like a dove!

The *culfre* represents such positive qualities – it lacks *gealla*, is not eager for harm and embodies pure innocence – that it is no surprise that Christ recommends imitating this *dēor*'s behaviour. In the Old English Gospel of Matthew, Jesus tells his apostles:

> Now I will send you as sheep among wolves. Therefore be wise as serpents and <u>meek as doves</u> (*bylwite swa culfran*).

Bile-wit has a number of positive meanings: 'meek', 'peaceable', 'gentle', 'merciful', 'pure', 'innocent' or 'virtuous'. (The corresponding word in the Latin Vulgate Bible's Gospel of Matthew is *simplices*, which means 'simple' or 'unaffected'.) *Bile-wit* is not used beyond the thirteenth century, and its etymology is unclear. It is tempting to try to link modern English 'bile' (the humour) to the *bile* of *bile-wit*, but remember that the Old English for this is *gealla*. Modern English 'bile' doesn't come into use until the seventeenth century and is wholly unrelated. And indeed, how could the two words be connected, when a dove is *bile-wit* and thus lacks *gealla* (bile)?

Ælfric explains how a *bile-wit* dove's behaviour makes it superior to other birds:

> He who loves deceit, who ponders how he can strive for himself and not for God, does not have the ways of a <u>dove</u> (*culfran*) but those of a black <u>raven</u> (*hremmes*). He who loves plundering is a <u>glede</u> (*glida*) and not a <u>dove</u> (*culfre*).

The *culfre* is gentler than the *hremn* (raven) and the **glida** (glede or kite, a bird of prey) but also smaller birds. Even if a bird is **lytel** (little), it might kill another creature (like a fly) for its dinner. The *culfre*, says Ælfric, does not kill anything, living off of 'earthly fruits': *ne leofað heo be nanum deaðe* (she lives not by death). It's true that pigeons and doves mainly eat seeds and fruit, although certain species are known to take insects, reptiles, snails or moths as prey. I guess those aren't the *culfran* with which Ælfric was familiar. He may also have had trouble fitting the modern-day scavenging habits of urban pigeons into his metaphor, although perhaps it's not so bad to be like those *culfran*. Clean up human trash and food waste like the *bile-wit* pigeon!

Though common and familiar to people both past and present, doves have always been rich in symbolism. In Old English a *culfre* might be the site of a Eucharistic miracle, and the Holy Spirit chooses to take this bird's *hīw*. Of all the animals on Noah's ark, only the *culfre* brings the promise of land to weary travellers. Even real-life habits – like consuming without ever killing – make the *culfre* rather miraculous. The seemingly ordinary dove is actually quite wondrous in many ways . . . but the animals in the next part of this book are unquestionably extraordinary.

Dove's Wordhord

bile-wit, adjective (BILL-uh-wit / ˈbɪ-lə-wɪt): Meek, peaceable, gentle, merciful, pure, innocent, virtuous.

crist, noun (KRIST / ˈkrɪst): Jesus Christ.

culfre, noun (KULL-vruh / ˈkʌl-vrə): Dove (plural: *culfran*).

ecg, noun (EDGE / ˈɛdʒ): Sword.

ege, noun (EH-yuh / ˈɛ-jə): Fear, terror, dread; awe, respectful fear, reverence.

fæder, noun (FADD-er / 'fæ-dɛr): Father (a human father or God the Father).

gealla, noun (YEH-al-la / 'jɛal-la): Gall, bile, or any bitter substance; bitterness.

ge-cynd, noun (yeh-KUEND / jɛ-'kynd): Nature, kind, condition.

glida, noun (GLID-ah / 'glɪ-da): Kite, glede (a bird of prey).

godes gāst, noun (GOD-ess GAHST / 'gɔd-ɛs 'gaːst): God's Spirit (Holy Spirit).

hālga gāst, noun (HALL-ga GAHST / 'haːl-ga 'gaːst): Holy Spirit.

hē, pronoun (hay / heː): He (or a pronoun that refers to a grammatically masculine noun).

hēo, pronoun (hay-oh / heːɔ): She (or a pronoun that refers to a grammatically feminine noun).

hīw, noun (HEE-ew / 'hiːw): Form, figure, appearance, likeness.

hremn, noun (H'REH-mun / 'hrɛ-mən): Raven.

hūsel, noun (HOO-zull / 'huː-zəl): The Eucharist (especially the bread or wafer).

lamb, noun (LAHMB / 'lamb): Lamb.

lufu, noun (LUH-vuh / 'lʌ-vʌ): Love.

lytel, adjective (LUE-tell / 'ly-tɛl): Little.

mēce, noun (MAY-chuh / 'meː-tʃə): Sword.

sweord, noun (SWEH-ord / 'swɛɔrd): Sword.

þel-fæsten, noun (THELL-FAST-en / 'θɛl-ˌfæs-tɛn): Plank-fortress (Noah's ark).

þrinness, noun (THRIN-ness / 'θrɪn-nɛs): Trinity, as in the Holy Trinity (Father, Son and Holy Spirit).

un-hearmgeorn, adjective (UN-HEH-arm-yeh-orn / 'ʌn-ˌhɛarm-jɛɔrn): Not eager for harm.

un-sceþþigness, noun (UN-SHETH-thi-ness / 'ʌn-ˌʃɛθ-θɪ-nɛs): Innocence, harmlessness.

wīf-mann, noun (WEEV-mahn / 'wiːv-man): Woman.

The Extraordinary

ORDINARY *DĒOR* GIVE US ACCESS to the everyday – the creatures that would have occupied the lives and dreams of Old English speakers. But they can also offer a glimpse of the unimaginable. Descriptions of strange animals in Old English texts often refer to characteristics of more common creatures, because if you are asked to imagine the unbelievable, sometimes it's helpful to start with the familiar. An extraordinary creature might have the head of a *hors* or the body of a *cū*. Perhaps it barks like a *hund* or bleats like a *gāt*. It might be feathered like a *gōs* or furry like a *mūs*. The choice of animal for a comparison also gives us an idea of which animals would have been the most familiar and distinctive to people in early medieval England. If you were trying to describe an unknown animal today, for instance, you probably wouldn't describe it as having 'gills like an axolotl' or 'limbs like a tardigrade' unless addressing an audience with specialised knowledge. A *hors*, *hund* or *cū* is easier to picture.

Many of the extraordinary animals that appear in Old English texts like *Alexander's Letter to Aristotle* and *Wonders of the East* don't give a lot of information beyond a physical description. We know that they look strange or have unusual behaviours, but those two texts in particular lack the allegorical explanations that we've seen for animals like the *culfre* and the *earn*. Because of this, I've grouped a number of them together in one chapter. As fascinating as they are, there is very limited information about them. This lack of information might indicate that they'd be just as much a novelty to people living in early medieval England as they are to us today.

The extraordinary animals that do have more stories associated with them also appear in poetry, saints' lives and homilies. They continued to be popular subjects in later medieval bestiaries. Creatures that live in a region as distant as India might as well be mythical, and the stories shared about them in Old English are always a long time ago in a faraway land, giving them a fairy-tale quality. These *dēor* aren't always animals we'd consider 'extraordinary' today, but in Old English texts, at least, they have some surprising habits and characteristics.

5

Animals Unheard Of
(*un-gefrægelican deor*)

A MODERN-DAY READER might imagine that a **henn** (hen), found scratching and pecking in farmyards across the country, would be the most ordinary of creatures. Surely back in early medieval England, in a time when most people were involved in farm work, a *henn* would be an everyday sight. But in Old English texts the strangest creatures aren't always what you think.

The particular *henn* I have in mind appears in the Nowell Codex, a manuscript from around the turn of the first millennium, a text teeming with extraordinary creatures. Most famous for containing the sole surviving copy of *Beowulf* (which itself has some marvellous creatures), the Nowell Codex also contains a prose *Life of St Christopher*, the poem *Judith* and two prose texts that take a special interest in the extraordinary – *Alexander's Letter to Aristotle* and *Wonders of the East*. Although these last two texts are purportedly thrilling first-hand accounts, I'm afraid they are more the adventures of library-bound scholars poring over their old books than those of explorers travelling to the far reaches of the known world. They belong to a tradition of Alexander the Great lore that was extremely popular throughout the Middle Ages. The real-life Alexander the Great lived in the fourth century BCE, but ever since writers had indulged in describing the fantastic events of his life, some of which were more believable than others. Yes, Alexander probably did travel all the way to southern Asia and wrought a lot of destruction through his conquests of various peoples. But did Alexander ever ride in a flying machine powered by griffins? Probably not. Some writers of the so-called 'historical' accounts of Alexander's life are known for having what one scholar describes as 'enthusiasm for rhetorical elaboration'.

Unlike some of the previous descriptions of *dēor* in this book, the accounts of creatures in *Alexander's Letter to Aristotle* and *Wonders of the East* focus on physical characteristics, including little to nothing about their personalities and not attempting to link them to allegorical tales. These texts are written more as travel logs, describing the incredible, horrifying and awe-inspiring sights that the explorer discovers rather than homilies or poetry, which might take more care to draw out a scriptural or moral comparison.

Both texts were translated from Greek to Latin sometime during the early medieval period and were eventually translated from Latin to Old English in the tenth century, for an even wider audience. The Old English translation of *Wonders of the East* appears in two manuscripts, both of which now reside in the British Library: Cotton MS Vitellius A XV (the Nowell Codex) and Cotton MS Tiberius B V/1 (which, for simplicity, I'll call the Tiberius manuscript). The Nowell Codex was produced around the year 1000, while the Tiberius manuscript was created slightly later, in the mid eleventh century. Clearly, the appetite for these tales had not waned in over a hundred years – people had no less interest in outlandish creatures and Alexander fan-fic.

While *Wonders of the East* doesn't specifically refer to Alexander, it has similar content to *Alexander's Letter to Aristotle* and it is likely that they share at least some source material. Whoever wrote *Wonders of the East* says nothing about themselves but presents the material as a scientific treatise or traveller's report on various places in the known world and whom and what you might encounter there. Both Old English translations of *Wonders of the East* include descriptions of strange creatures and peoples, accompanied by rather unhelpful geographical references (like place names that are no longer in use) and illustrations that reflect the content of the text to varying degrees. The Tiberius manuscript's written descriptions are slightly longer and more complete, and its illustrations are not only more numerous but arguably demonstrate greater artistic skill (but you'll get the opportunity to judge this for yourself).

On the way to the Red Sea . . .

Early on in *Wonders of the East*, we are told of a place called Lentibelsinea. Today no one knows where Lentibelsinea was meant to be, other than vaguely 'east' from the perspective of Europeans, possibly the Middle East. It's apparently 'on the way to the Red Sea'. Wherever Lentibelsinea might be, it is home to some truly ***un-gefrægelican*** *dēor* (animals unheard of). Old English ***gefrǣge*** means 'known', 'celebrated' or 'famous', so these *dēor* are not *gefrǣge*, which is to say that they are the opposite: unknown, uncelebrated, unheard of. Of course, the fact that they are described in the text at all makes them animals that have been 'heard of', but perhaps calling them *un-gefrǣgelīcan* makes your literary encounter with them all the more extraordinary. The literal meaning sits like a promise within the word itself: it is the *un-gefrǣgelīcan dēor* that are best suited to be *gefrǣge*, most worthy of celebration and renown.

    According to *Wonders of the East*, Lentibelsinea is home to one particular extraordinary creature: a kind of ***rēad*** (red) bird, which the text simply calls a *henn*. The hen illustrations in both the Nowell Codex and the Tiberius manuscript are fairly ordinary-looking, red-feathered chickens. They are, the scribe writes, 'like the ones we have' (*gelice ðam þe mid us*). This *henn*, however, is unlike any hen encountered in a medieval (or modern) English farmyard in one crucial manner:

> Hens (*henna*) are born like the ones we have that are <u>red in colour</u> (*reades hiwes*). And if anyone wishes to seize or touch one of them, it will immediately burn its entire body. That is <u>unheard-of sorcery</u> (*ungefregelicu lyblac*)!

Self-immolating chickens – certainly a kind of sorcery I'd never heard of before!

Whoever is describing these flaming chickens is probably not marvelling at them as an avid ornithologist, excited to see a new species of bird. They would be more likely to be suspicious, since the chickens are **lyb-lāc**, which *Bosworth-Toller's Anglo-Saxon Dictionary* defines as 'sorcery, witchcraft, the art of using drugs or potions for the purpose of poisoning, or for magical purposes'. In Old English, *lyb-lāc* belongs to the same taboo category as **wicce-cræft** (witchcraft) and **attor-cræft** (literally 'poison-craft'), crafts of deadly evil. (Remember *attor-coppa*, the spider from Chapter 2.) The **lyb** (LUEB) part of *lyb-lāc* can simply mean 'medicine'; for instance, one leechbook refers to a *lyb* to treat 'dimness of the eyes' (*lyb wið eagena dimnesse*). **Lāc** has several different meanings: 'battle, struggle', 'an offering, sacrifice', 'a gift, present, grace, favour', 'a message (offering of words)' and 'medicine'. But even though *lyb* might appear in a *læce-bōc* (leechbook), the **lybbestre** (witch or sorcerer) has quite a different image from the helpful **læce** (doctor or physician). *Lyb* seems to have fallen out of use in the Middle English period, although it continued to be used in Scotland at least as late as 1577. An account of court proceedings from October 1577 tells of the case of Violet Mar, a Perthshire woman convicted of bringing down the ruler of Scotland, Regent Morton (who was ruling on behalf of the

Hens in the Tiberius manuscript's *Wonders of the East* (England,
mid eleventh century)

infant James VI), through her use of 'sorcerie, libbis and charmes',
against 'the lawis of God and manne'. We know Violet was tried and
convicted based on the testimony of primed witnesses under the
direction of a very determined countess, but there is no record of
what ultimately happened to her. As for Regent Morton, he lived for
four more years, at which point he died not by a witch's curse but by
execution following the guilty verdict at his own trial (for his alleged
participation in the murder of a lord). So even though *lyb* could technically be a charm for healing, it has more of a reputation for super-
naturally malicious effects. One wonders, however, which *lybbestre* in

Lentibelsinea decided that creating self-immolating hens was a wise idea.

Perhaps it was the same *lybbestre* who thought to create another strange, self-immolating animal, an unnamed *dēor* that flees upon hearing a human's voice. Just like the *henn*, it sets its own **līc-hama** (body) on fire whenever it feels threatened, and it also makes its home in Lentibelsinea. These *un-gefrægelīcan dēor* have two heads, eight feet, and the eyes of a **wæl-cyrige** (valkyrie), and this is really all we know about them. Perhaps, because they fled upon hearing human voices, it was hard to get close enough to make any other observations, and because they are unnamed, it's hard to say if they appear in texts by other writers.

The *Oxford English Dictionary* says that the word 'valkyrie', from Norse mythology, doesn't enter the English language until the eighteenth century, a borrowing from Old Icelandic *valkyrja*, literally 'chooser of the slain'. (Valkyries were beautiful women, usually wearing helmets and shields, who served the god Odin, choosing who lives and who dies in battle.) But as early as the Old English period we have the word *wæl-cyrige* (WAEL-KUE-ri-yuh), which may be cognate with or formed similarly to the Icelandic. Old English **wæl** means 'the slain' or 'slaughter' in general, while **cyre** means 'choice' or 'free will'. So if the unnamed, two-headed *dēor* has the eyes of a *wæl-cyrige*, what does that actually mean? One ninth-century Norse poem describes valkyries as 'bright-eyed', so perhaps that's how we are meant to imagine these unnamed creatures. Or maybe their eyes just look eager for *wæl*.

The unnamed *un-gefrægelīcan dēor* in both the Tiberius manuscript and the Nowell Codex are depicted as two-headed creatures with eight legs, although there is some variation in the placement of their heads. The Tiberius manuscript shows two heads of equal size facing away from each other, a creature with a head on the back of its head. The Nowell Codex's illustration shows two heads of different sizes

Two-headed beast in the Nowell Codex's *Wonders of the East*
(England, *c.*1000)

facing the same direction, positioned so that the smaller head appears to emerge from the creature's throat. Both are quite hairy; the Nowell Codex animal is orangey-red and the Tiberius one is grey with a long tail and fierce claws. The Nowell Codex beast is partially damaged by fire (oddly apropos given its habit of self-immolation). It's hard to say whether the creatures have the eyes of valkyries. There is nothing exceptional about the eyes of the Tiberius *dēor*, although those of the animal in the Nowell Codex do look rather manic, large with dilated pupils.

Wæl-cyrige eyes are a bit difficult to imagine, but comparisons to more ordinary creatures are useful for describing the extraordinary.

You're more likely to have seen a sheep before than a valkyrie. For this reason, it may be easier to picture a different *dēor* from *Wonders of the East* – *lertices*. *Lertices* have the ears of an **eosol** (donkey), the wool of a *scēap* (sheep) and the feet of a *fugel* (bird). The Tiberius manuscript illustrator renders this description fairly accurately, depicting a woolly, llama-like beast with tall ears and feet that fork out like talons. Each of its physical characteristics is ordinary enough on its own, but taken together they make up an animal that is rather astonishing.

. . . and on through the desert

After discussing the various fiery creatures of Lentibelsinea, the anonymous narrator of our wondrous travel guide takes us to the desert south of Babylon to a city called Persia, from Egypt and the Nile to a river called the Brixontes. East of the Brixontes (perhaps somewhere in eastern Africa) there is a race of cannibalistic giants, but if you manage to avoid them you'll encounter yet another strange animal. Even the name for these animals – *lertices* – is mysterious. While *lertices* (the plural) appears in both the Latin and Old English translations of *Wonders of the East*, neither of these versions provides a singular form. *Lertices* seems to be a Latin word (it's not Old English), but it doesn't appear in Latin dictionaries. A single one of these might be called a *lertex*, a form that doesn't exist in extant manuscripts. This singular form makes sense if *lertices* is Latin, working the same as modern English 'vertex' (the plural of which is 'vertices'). However, the singular form could also be *lertix*, since the Latin plural of *phoenix* is *phoenices*. The dilemma is such that it's tempting to call it a 'ler-whatsit' and leave it at that, for there's no way to know for sure what the creature was called in the Middle Ages. But for simplicity's sake I will call it a *lertex*.

Lertex in the Nowell Codex's *Wonders of the East* (England, *c.*1000)

It's hard to tell how big the *lertex* is, since the text doesn't give any clues. But the Nowell Codex's *lertex* appears with a person beside it. The top of the *lertex*'s head is just about level with the person's chest, making it look about the size of a pony. But, of course, in this world the person might not necessarily be an ordinary human. Before the section on *lertices*, *Wonders of the East* describes the aforementioned cannibals called *Hostes* ('enemies' in Latin). These people have feet and legs that are twelve feet long and flanks and chests that stretch to seven feet. If you add to that the height of neck and head, the *Hostes* must be around twenty feet tall! If one of them is the man pictured petting his *lertex*, the creature would need to be at least twelve feet tall.

But drawing to scale is not a common feature of medieval manuscripts – a saint might hold a tiny church in his hand, an elephant might be the height of a castle, a cat might have a face-off with an equivalently sized bee. The size of people or things is more about their importance or symbolism than their actual height. So the *lertex* of the Nowell Codex could just as likely be the size of a kitten as of a house (that is, of course, if we believe it ever existed in real life).

The southern side of the ocean

From eastern Africa we move on to 'the southern side of the ocean' (wherever that is) to where the *Homodubii* ('maybe-people') live and where precious oil-producing balsam trees grow. There is an island of multilingual, cannibalistic soothsayers somewhere in the Red Sea, and another island where people's eyes shine bright as a lamp on a dark night. We pass through Babylonia and end up in a location where the people are called 'Ethiopians' (although at this point it seems we must be in the Middle East or western Asia). *Wonders of the East* doesn't provide us with maps. But eventually we end up in a region where grapevines grow profusely and where there is a 306-foot-long elephant's bone **rest** (bed or couch). The narrator doesn't bother expanding on the purpose of such a peculiar object and moves swiftly on to a certain **dūn** (mountain) there called Adamant.

While we don't know where this Mount Adamant might be, you will probably recognise the creature that lives there. It appears in children's books and fantasy games, on coats of arms and school emblems. *Wonders of the East* describes a kind of bird called a **griffus**

– the creature we know and love today, the griffin. The *griffus* has four feet, the tail of a *hrȳþer* (ox) and the head of an *earn* (eagle). Although the text does not mention them, the creature presumably has wings as well since it's called a *fugel* (bird). In the Tiberius manuscript an illustration depicts the *griffus* with a pair of feathery wings, in addition to four talon-like feet and an *earn*'s hooked beak.

Griffin in the Tiberius manuscript's *Wonders of the East* (England, mid eleventh century)

Although *Wonders of the East* makes no reference to lion-like traits, the classic description of a griffin in bestiaries has the hindquarters of a lion (the king of beasts) and the head and wings of an eagle (the king of birds). These particular details do appear in a Latin-Old English glossary that describes the griffin as a **fiþer-fōte** *fugel* (a four-footed bird), with a stature like that of a *lēo* and a head and wings like those of an *earn*. Despite being a combination of two respectable, kingly creatures, the griffin does not have a great reputation. The Latin-Old English glossary says, 'It is so great that it seizes horses and men' (*se is swa micel, þæt he gewylt hors and menn*). For some reason the *griffus* is particularly hostile towards the poor *hors* (horse). In the third century, Solinus writes that griffins are 'extremely ferocious' with 'a rage worse than any madness', and they 'mangle anyone they see, as though born to punish the rashness of greed'. Solinus explains that the people who unwisely visit the griffin's lands are greedy for the region's multitude of gold and gems, including the smaragdus, a stone 'greener than water-grass and river herbs' that can restore tired eyes with its gorgeous colour. The medieval bestiaries of later centuries show the griffin carrying various live creatures back to its nest: a horse, a boar, a ram or an ox. However, the Tiberius manuscript *griffus* has no victims or gemstones in its grasp and seems content to stand sedately with one taloned foot in the air, perhaps revelling in its own kingly superiority.

Old English *griffus* derives from Latin *griphus*, meaning 'enigma' or 'riddle', but there's an alternative Old English name for the creature that most likely has Germanic origins: **gīw** (pronounced YEE-ew). *Gīr* means 'vulture' in Old High German, the version of German spoken during the early medieval period (from around 750 to 1050). In modern English a 'gyrfalcon' is a large falcon of the northern regions (especially the white gyrfalcon of Iceland), and even though this word comes from Old French *gerfaucon*, the prevailing view among philologists is that the ultimate source of this 'gyr' is Old High German *gīr*. Could *gīw* have been a vulture before it was a griffin? As far as we can tell from extant texts, the word *gīw* only means 'griffin' in Old English. Today there is a specific kind of vulture known as the 'griffon-vulture', but this term doesn't appear until the nineteenth century.

The words *gīw* and *griffus* appear together in a line from an Old

English poem known as *Solomon and Saturn*. In the poem, the wise King Solomon answers the questions of Saturn, a Chaldean prince. (Chaldea was a small country that existed during the first millennium BCE, located in south-eastern Mesopotamia, in the vicinity of modern-day Iraq.) Solomon represents the knowledge of the Judeo-Christian world, Saturn the knowledge of the ancient (pagan) world. Although the poem follows a straightforward question-answer format, Saturn's questions and Solomon's answers are among the most enigmatic passages in Old English literature. Saturn wants to know things like why weeping and laughter are close companions, how to open the door to heaven, what the four 'ropes' are that are doomed to death and who the 'speechless one' is who sleeps in a certain valley. The answers can be just as confusing as the questions.

The part of *Solomon and Saturn* that refers to griffins is a passage about a strange bird called the *Vasa Mortis* (Latin for 'Vessel of Death'). Solomon describes the *Vasa Mortis*, which is held prisoner by the Philistines (an ancient people who lived in what is now Israel and Egypt, before their territory was subsumed by the Babylonian Empire). Unlike the *lertex*'s description, Solomon's speech about the *Vasa Mortis* gives us some idea of the creature's size:

> The <u>bird</u> (*fugel*) has four heads of an average man's size, and its middle is the size of a whale. It has the <u>wings of a griffin</u> (*geowes fiðeru*) and <u>feet of a griffin</u> (*griffus fet*). It lies secured in fetters, looking about fiercely, beating its wings greatly and ringing its trappings, shrieking mournfully and sighing forth its grief, tormented in its punishment, dwelling without pleasure, singing strangely. Seldom do its limbs ever lie still.

Two hundred men guard this frightening bird, and the Philistines fear that other nations will come and steal it away. What I find particularly puzzling about Solomon's description is the fact it has the *feþra* (wings) and *fēt* (feet) of a *gīw* or *griffus*. The griffin has the wings and feet of an eagle, so why not compare *Vasa Mortis* to an *earn* instead? Are a griffin's wings and feet subtly different from those of an eagle? Or perhaps the poet compared *Vasa Mortis* to a griffin in order to emphasise its monstrosity . . .

The *griffus*, the *lertex* and the various self-immolating creatures of Lentibelsinea are certainly all quite monstrous, but what really stands out about them among the *dēor* in this book is the lack of human characteristics or motivations granted to them. They might be violent, but they are not deliberately antagonistic or vengeful. We don't get more human-centric descriptors like the 'cruel' and 'bloodthirsty' spider, or the 'gentle' dove who is 'free of bile'. They don't speak or sing like the eagle. The ones that set themselves on fire do so as an (albeit questionable) defence mechanism, but there's no deeper reason for it, no moral or allegory. I suppose this makes them more *un-gefrægelīcan*. Throughout the Middle Ages, animals were important in the lessons they taught humanity, but here in the Old English text this critical aspect of their existence remains unspoken, unheard of. There is a fundamental unknown that makes them even more unknowable.

The *un-gefrægelīcan dēor* in this chapter are extraordinary in quite obvious ways, whether in their ability to set themselves on fire or the fact that they are unlikely animal mash-ups. But a *dēor* doesn't need two heads or valkyrie eyes to be extraordinary. As the next chapter reveals, some of the most extraordinary animals in Old English are creatures that we perceive as ordinary today.

Wordhord of Animals Unheard Of

attor-cræft, noun (AHT-tor-KRAFT / ˈat-tɔr-ˌkræft): Art of using poison or poisonous potions, witchcraft, sorcery.

cyre, noun (KUE-ruh / ˈky-rə): Choice, free will.

dūn, noun (DOON / ˈduːn): Mountain, hill.

eosol, noun (EH-oh-zoll / ˈɛɔ-zɔl): Donkey, ass.

fiþer-fōte, adjective (FITH-er-FOAT-uh / ˈfɪ-θɛr-ˌfoː-tə): Four-footed.

fōt, noun (FOAT / ˈfoːt): Foot (plural: *fēt*, pronounced FATE).

gefrǣge, adjective (yeh-FRAE-yuh / jɛ-ˈfræː-jə): Known, celebrated, famous.

gīw, noun (YEE-ew / ˈjiːw): Griffin.

griffus, noun (GRIFF-fuss / ˈɡrɪf-fʌs): Griffin.

henn, noun (HEN / ˈhɛn): Hen.

lāc, noun (LAHK / ˈlaːk): Battle, struggle; a gift, present, grace, favour; a message (offering of words); medicine.

lǣce, noun (LATCH-uh / ˈlæː-tʃə): Doctor, physician.

līc-hama, noun (LEECH-HA-ma / ˈliːtʃ-ˌha-ma): Body.

lyb, noun (LUEB / ˈlyb): Medicine, drug.

lybbestre, noun (LUEB-bes-truh / ˈlyb-bɛs-trə): Witch, sorcerer.

lyb-lāc, noun (LUEB-lahk / ˈlyb-laːk): Sorcery, witchcraft.

rēad, adjective (RAY-ahd / ˈreːad): Red.

rest, noun (REST / ˈrɛst): Bed, couch; a place of rest; (in other contexts) rest, repose, sleep.

un-gefrǣgelīcan, adjective (UN-yeh-FRAE-yuh-lee-kahn / ˈʌn-jɛ-ˌfræː-jə-liː-kan): Unheard of, unusual, extraordinary.

wæl, noun (WAEL / ˈwæl): The slain, the dead; slaughter, carnage.

wæl-cyrige, noun (WAEL-KUE-ri-yuh / ˈwæl-ˌky-rɪ-jə): Valkyrie, chooser of the slain.

wicce-cræft, noun (WITCH-uh-KRAFT / ˈwɪ-tʃə-ˌkræft): Witchcraft, sorcery.

6

Ant (*æmette*)

O F ALL THE ANIMALS in this book, perhaps the humble ant seems least likely to fall into the 'extraordinary' category. They are small but numerous, and they appear single-minded in their quest for food. The simplicity of their daily lives does not make them less admirable. According to the Middle English *Physiologus*, the ant reminds us to gather food in times of plenty, long-lasting provisions to help us survive the winter. We live in the world a short while, and when we depart it, that is our winter. So be like the ant! Find food (or faith) during your life so that you won't worry about winter (or Judgement Day).

The Latin name for the ant is *formica*, which Isidore claims is because it carries (*fert*) bits of grain (*micas farris*), but the Old English word is **æmette**. *Æmette* has cognates in Germanic languages like Old High German *meizan* and Old Icelandic *meita*, which mean 'to cut'. The *Oxford English Dictionary* theorises that this 'cutting' has to do with the creature's 'very visible segmented body structure', although it could also refer to an ant's habit of cutting things with its pincers. *Æmette* becomes 'ant' in modern English, but the forms 'yemmet' and 'nemot' still survive in south-western England and in Scotland respectively. In the 1970s people living in Cornwall began using 'emmet' humorously or deprecatingly for a tourist, a reference to the large crowds of visitors that crawl across that scenic area during the summer. But while the emmets of Cornwall are all on holiday, the ants of medieval texts have a reputation for unrelentingly industrious behaviour.

St Malchus and the anthill

The admirable qualities of the *æmette* are described in the tale of St Malchus in a collection of Old English saints' lives. The *Vitae Patrum* (*Lives of the Fathers*) is an encyclopaedia-like collection of stories about the Desert Fathers and Desert Mothers of early Christianity. Originally composed in Greek, the *Vitae Patrum* was translated into Latin, and from Latin into Old English (and this, of course, is the version to which I refer).

The story tells of a man named Malchus, who lived near Nisibis (in modern-day Turkey) during the fourth century. When his parents pressure him to get married, Malchus says he would rather live the life of a celibate monk. He runs away from home to join a group of monks in the **wēsten** (desert or wilderness), not far from Antioch. Years later, after his father passes away, Malchus decides to return home to claim his inheritance. His abbot objects, since collecting inheritance goes against the ideals of an ascetic Christian life. But Malchus goes anyway without the abbot's blessing, and on his way home he is captured and sold into slavery. (This is why you should never leave home without the approval of your spiritual mentor.)

For a while Malchus endures his unhappy situation, but one day he has something of an existential crisis. While out herding sheep for his master, he observes the behaviour of an ant colony. This passage from the Old English *Vitae Patrum* is narrated in Malchus' own voice:

I saw a large <u>group of ants</u> (*æmettena hēap*) climbing up, carrying burdens greater than their own bodies. Some of them plucked grasses with their mouths, while others flung up the soil, blocking streams of water. They kept their future hunger in mind.

Malchus goes on to explain that the **hēap** (group or 'heap') of *æmettan* takes care not to get the grain wet, since that would make it sprout and ruin the harvest. He observes how the ants show genuine concern for their community, carrying the bodies of their dead upon their heads, almost like a funeral procession. But what Malchus is most impressed by is that despite there being a large *hēap* of *æmettan* walking from the **æmett-hyll** (anthill), not one of them blocks the way of the *æmettan* trying to enter. Malchus adds:

If one of them saw another fall beneath its burden, then it gave assistance to the other at once, setting the burden upon its own shoulders.

The ants' spirit of cooperation is truly admirable, and it forces Malchus to consider the wisdom of life apart from his monastic brothers.

Malchus says he was **ge-myndig** (mindful) of the wise King Solomon that day, who said that 'the slow mind would be right to be like the ants' (*þa latan mod wæron gereht in æmettena onlicnysse*). These words are a reference to Proverbs 6.6–8:

Go to the <u>ant</u> (*formicam*), O sluggard, and consider her ways, and learn wisdom: which, although she hath no guide, nor master, nor captain, provideth her meat for herself in the summer, and gathereth her food in the harvest.

The same sentiment appears in the Old English translation of Gregory the Great's *Pastoral Care*:

> To him who is <u>at leisure</u> (*æmetig*) to do as he pleases, to him say: 'You sluggard, go to an <u>anthill</u> (*æmetthylle*) and observe how they do things. Learn wisdom there.'

Coincidentally, the word *æmette* is quite similar to **_æmtig_** (AM-tih), even though it is those who are *æmtig* who ought to learn from the *æmette*. *Æmtig*'s primary definition is 'empty' or 'devoid of', but it can also mean 'bearing or having nothing', 'not engaged in any activity' or 'at leisure'. It can even mean 'unmarried', although that meaning didn't last beyond the Old English period. The word becomes 'empty' in modern English, the most common definition of which is 'devoid of its usual contents, without anything inside'.

But back to the *ge-myndig* ex-monk. Malchus explains, 'I began to grow discontent because of my captivity, yearning to seek my monastery again.' In a good monastery, he says, 'nothing is separate but it is all in common', the same as it is for a *hēap* of *æmettan*. Such an idea draws upon debates of the late fourth century over the best way to be a monk. This is apparent in the *Life of Malchus* written by Jerome, the theologian who first translated the Bible into Latin. The classicist Christa Gray explains that Jerome's *Life of Malchus* was ideal for representing Jerome's own perspective in the debate, juxtaposing eremitical life with cenobitical monasticism. Eremitical life means living as a hermit, a solitary life in the desert, while cenobitical relates to monastic life in a community like a monastery. Jerome makes clear in his *Life of Malchus* that he favours cenobitical monasticism, living in an organised community of monks or nuns governed by rules. Fellowship is essential to a monastic community: worshipping together multiple times a day, sharing a common meal, performing manual labour with others, etc. The benefits of cenobitical monasticism are demonstrated by Malchus' hard-working, cooperative, supportive *hēap* of *ǣmettan*.

Gold-digging ants

But sometimes the cooperative labour of ants is aimed at collecting things other than grain, and this is where we find some of the more extraordinary ants.

The Old English *Wonders of the East* describes a special sort of *ǣmette* that hunts not for grain but for **gold** (gold). These gold-gathering ants live in a place called Capi or Gorgoneus, which the scribe unhelpfully explains is also known as *Wælcyrginc* – another spelling for *wæl-cyrige*, 'valkyrie' from Chapter 5. (It seems that 'valkyrie' can be a place as well as a creature, although it is not clear if the place is the creature's home.) *Wonders of the East* says:

> Ants (*ǣmættan*) are produced there as big as <u>hounds</u> (*hundas*). They have feet like a <u>grasshopper</u> (*græshoppan*). They are red and black in <u>appearance</u> (*hiwes*).

As we've already observed, the illustrations of the *Wonders of the East* manuscripts do not always match their textual descriptions. Indeed, the creature depicted in the Nowell Codex in no way resembles an ant; instead it is a red and black, chunky creature somewhere between a tailless rat and a dog. The Tiberius manuscript illustrates them in a similar way: reddish, dog-like creatures with four long-toed feet. These ants are a little more elegant than their Nowell Codex cousins – more like long-snouted greyhounds than rodents, and they even get long tails. But in neither manuscript do the *ǣmettan* look anything like ants. The text itself does, I suppose, have some ambiguity about whether the red and black colouring applies only to the grass-hopper-like feet or to the entire ant (though these feet are paws and have claws). Perhaps the illustrators saw the word *hund* (dog) in the description and chose to focus on that, going beyond a size compari-son to a more obvious resemblance.

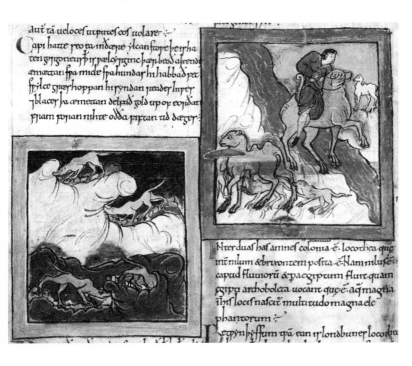

Gold-digging ants in the Tiberius manuscript's *Wonders of the East*
(England, mid eleventh century)

But the most intriguing characteristic of these *æmettan*, even more than their extraordinary size, is their obsession with *gold*. It's not just dragons that guard a **gold-hord** (a hoard of treasure) in medieval lit-erature! The Old English *Wonders of the East* explains that the *æmettan* dig up *gold* from the earth from dusk until the fifth hour of the day (shortly before noon, around eleven in the morning). Presumably this is because the heat is too much for them in the afternoon – this isn't England, after all.

But where *do* these creatures live? Where is Capi/Gorgoneus/Valkyrie? Back in the fifth century BCE, Herodotus, a Greek historian born in the Persian Empire, wrote about gold-digging ants in India. In the first century CE this is corroborated by Pliny the Elder, who says that ants collect gold from caves in a region of northern India. In the third century, however, Solinus claims that giant ants which dig up golden sand live by the River Niger in West Africa, while several medieval sources specify that such activity can be observed in Ethiopia in East Africa. Perhaps this confusion can be forgiven. In the antique and medieval periods, place names like 'India' and 'Ethiopia' were, in the words of the scholar Pamela Gravestock, 'more ideas than actual places'. To us these words correspond to specific regions of the world, but in medieval Europe the phrases 'in India' and 'in Ethiopia' were a bit like saying 'in a faraway land'. 'Ethiopia' might be found in Africa, India or even both at once. Back in the time of Alexander the Great, the emperor's campaign in 'India' included an expanse of land from the eastern regions of present-day Afghanistan and Pakistan to the eastern part of the Indus valley. *Wonders of the East* places the gold-digging *æmettan* in **Indea**, which was a broad geographical term for much of southern Asia.

Wherever the *æmettan* and the place called 'Valkyrie' might be, *Wonders of the East* sensibly assumes that some readers will want to see them for themselves, whether out of curiosity or greed. For this reason, the text describes the best method for stealing *gold* from *æmettan*, should you ever come across one. It requires **olfendas** (camels), and you must also be rather **dyrstig** (daring or rash):

> Those who are <u>daring</u> (*dyrstige*) enough to take that <u>gold</u> (*gold*) should bring <u>female camels</u> (*olfenda-myran*) with them, along with their <u>calves</u> (*folan*) and the <u>males</u> (*stedan*).

An **olfend-mere** is a female *olfend*, or a 'mare'. Today we call a camel baby a 'calf' (like a cow), but it used to be a **fola** (a 'foal', like a horse). Old English *folan* were mainly equine but they could also be the off-spring of camels or elephants. (Today elephant babies are also called calves.) The gold-stealing procedure goes something like this:

1. Begin your gold-gathering quest after the fifth hour of the day (around 11 a.m.), when the *æmettan* have finished digging up *gold* and have taken refuge from the heat.
2. Tie up the *folan* on dry land. (Evidently, the *æmettan* live near an **ēa**, or river.)
3. Cross the *ēa* with your *olfend-meran* and *stēdan*. (**Stēda**, from which we get 'steed', is a male camel.)
4. Load the *gold* on to the *olfend-meran* and lead them back across the *ēa*, leaving your *stēdan* behind.

The logic of this strategy is that when the *æmettan* discover the thievery, the *stēdan* will keep them busy, allowing humans and *olfend-meran* to escape with the *gold*. But while the Old English *Wonders of the East* uses the verb **a-bysgian** (to preoccupy), the Latin translation says that the ants will find the male camels and *comedunt eos* (eat them). Truly, going after ant gold is a *dyrstig* business and a sizeable investment if you must sacrifice several camels in the process. And you definitely want to avoid getting caught if the *æmettan* can consume a full-grown camel! But what use are the baby ones? The text assures its readers that the *olfend-meran* will run so swiftly towards their *folan* that it will feel as though they are **flēogende** (flying). You might wonder if these ants' greedy desire for gold is at odds with the industrious practicality of the *æmettan* that inspired St Malchus. The medievalist Marilina Cesario does point out a more positive interpretation for the gold-digging ants from Clement of

Alexandria, a Christian theologian and philosopher of the second and early third centuries CE. Clement believes the ants to be 'generous and helpful creatures guarding God's gold from greedy people'.

But the *Wonders of the East* is not the only place where these ants appear. The earliest reference to the gold-digging creatures is in the fifth century BCE by Herodotus, who describes them as 'smaller than dogs but larger than foxes'. Scholars have long tried to determine the kind of animal Herodotus meant, although taking too much of a rationalist approach can be problematic. If we always try to explain extraordinary creatures described by ancient and medieval writers as 'mistakes', we risk making the assumption that these writers didn't have imaginations. Perhaps reality isn't always the point. Yet the desire for a rationalist approach is understandable. I myself can't help wanting to understand such creatures beyond their literary and spiritual meanings – particularly when they appear again and again, in contexts that otherwise do not appear to be allegorical.

One theory about the gold-digging ants is that they are honey badgers. Bodley 764, a thirteenth-century Latin bestiary made in England, says the 'ants' live in 'Ethiopia' rather than 'India'. The honey badger is a carnivorous animal that lives in Africa as well as South-west Asia and the Indian subcontinent. It has few natural predators due to its strength and fierce defensive abilities, and the bestiary scholar Richard Barber suggests that the 'gold' could have been 'the honey which it digs out of the ground and on which it feasts'. Honey badgers are known to raid beehives in search of honey and bee larvae.

In 1984 the French ethnologist Michel Peissel published *L'or des fourmis* (*Ant Gold*), a book detailing his theories on the identity of these mysterious 'ants'. Peissel had made expeditions to remote areas of the Himalayas and the Tibetan-speaking world since the 1960s and managed to slip into an area prohibited to foreigners due to its proximity to the tense ceasefire line between Pakistan and India. And what marvellous creature did Peissel behold in this prohibited region? The marmot, an adorable, furry brown rodent that makes its home in mountainous areas and which, weighing as much as 11kg or more, is the largest member of the squirrel family. Peissel claimed that the Dansar plain, a high plateau overlooking the River Indus, was home to marmots that, in the process of digging out burrows, flung gold-bearing sand into the air. Supposedly, long ago, the Brog-pa, the people indigenous to the region, once collected this gold dust.

The theory that Herodotus' gold-digging ants are marmots has been around for quite some time, at least as early as the 1830s when Godfrey Vigne, an English traveller and amateur cricketer, noticed a lot of marmots around gold-digging sites in Baltistan, a mountainous region of Pakistan-administered Kashmir. In 1904 the Scottish explorer Jane Duncan noted that Aziz Khan, her servant from Peshawar, had seen with his own eyes the phenomenon of the gold-tossing marmots on the banks of a stream that flows into the Indus. Khan confirmed that 'the natives collect the gold, make it into ingots, and sell it in the bazaar at Gilgit', where he had purchased some.

Despite the historical acceptance of the marmot theory, a 1988 review of Peissel's book was not particularly favourable. In it, the scholars Janet Rizvi and G. M. Kakpori write:

It is perhaps a pity that Dr. Peissel should have chosen to present his revolutionary thesis to the world in the form of a travelogue. The travel writer is allowed – perhaps even expected – to embroider reality with those little touches that make all the difference between routine and high drama.

The review points out numerous 'inaccuracies and inconsistencies' in Peissel's account, including the fact that the Dansar plain is 'no high mountain-encircled, marmot-infested plateau' but a cultivated area. It was not the Brog-pa but a different group of people in a different location who extracted gold from the earth, and they did so without the assistance of marmots. Rizvi and Kakpori do not, however, conclude that the marmots could not possibly be Herodotus' 'ants' but rather that Peissel misrepresents the evidence and traditions of people in the region, exoticising their way of life for the sake of his theory. It seems that no matter what century – what millennium – we're living in, travel writers can be tempted to weave engaging tales that don't always represent reality.

So what are we meant to think of the humble ant in the end? It is admirable for a human like Malchus to imitate the hard-working *ǣmette*, but should an *ǣmette* dare to act like a human – stealing and hoarding gold – it becomes a threat to be conquered (unless, of course, it is guarding God's wealth against human greed, as Clement suggested). Whether or not it comes across as a good example or some kind of monster, the *ǣmette* is nothing if not busy and industrious, a far cry from the emmets of Cornwall and truly extraordinary in its efficiency.

Ant's Wordhord

a-bysgian, verb (ah-BUEZ-yi-ahn / a-ˈbyz-jɪ-an): To busy, engage, involve, preoccupy.

ǣmette, noun (AM-et-tuh / ˈæː-mɛt-tə): Ant (plural: *ǣmettan*).

ǣmett-hyll, noun (AM-et-HUELL / ˈæː-mɛt-ˌhyl): Anthill.

ǣmtig, adjective (AM-tih / ˈæːm-tij): Empty, devoid of; bearing or having nothing; not engaged in any activity, at leisure; unmarried.

dyrstig, adjective (DUER-stih / ˈdyr-stɪj): Daring, bold, rash.

ēa, noun (AY-ah / ˈeːa): River.

flēogende, verb (FLAY-oh-yen-duh / ˈfleː-ɔ-jɛn-də): Flying.

fola, noun (FOLL-ah / ˈfɔ-la): Young animal (mainly equine but also the young of camels and elephants) (plural: *folan*).

ge-myndig, adjective (yeh-MUEN-dih / jɛ-ˈmyn-dɪj): Mindful, remembering.

gold, noun (GOLD / ˈɡɔld): Gold.

gold-hord, noun (GOLD-HORD / ˈɡɔld-ˌhɔrd): Treasure, a hoard of valuables.

hēap, noun (HAY-op / ˈheːap): Group, company, multitude, crowd.

Indea, noun (IN-deh-ah / ˈɪn-dɛa): 'India', an imprecise term for a broad geographical region in southern Asia.

olfend, noun (OL-vend / ˈɔl-vɛnd): Camel (plural: *olfendas*).

olfend-mere, noun (OL-vend-MEH-ruh / ˈɔl-vɛnd-ˌmɛ-rə): Female camel (plural: *olfend-meran*).

stēda, noun (STAY-da / ˈsteː-da): Stallion (mainly equine but also used for a male camel) (plural: *stēdan*).

wēsten, noun (WAY-sten / ˈweː-stɛn): Desert, wilderness.

7

Elephant (*ylp* or *elpend*)

E VEN TODAY THE ELEPHANT is extraordinary. It uses its trunk for breathing (both on land and underwater), smelling, bathing, gathering food, drinking, digging, trumpeting – not just as a nose but also as a hand or extra foot. Elephant tusks are actually teeth that keep growing throughout their lives. The mother elephant gestates for twenty-two months, producing a baby that can weigh as much as 120kg at birth. These babies are able to stand within twenty minutes of birth and can walk within one hour. Elephants can communicate with each other in a variety of ways, not only through trumpeting but through body language, touch, scent and vibrations in the ground.

To some people this will be strange to hear

The African elephant is the largest living land animal, with an adult male weighing as much as 6,800kg, so it should be no surprise that people in the medieval period also marvelled at its great size. Ælfric of Eynsham describes the **ylp** (elephant) in his *Lives of Saints*:

To some people this will be <u>strange</u> (*syllic*) to hear, for <u>elephants</u> (*ylpas*) have never come to England. An <u>elephant</u> (*ylp*) is an <u>immense beast</u> (*ormæte nyten*), greater than a <u>house</u> (*hus*), all surrounded with bones within the skin except at the navel.

Syllic (strange) indeed!

The elephant has always been known for its size. Isidore writes in his *Etymologies* that the Latin name *elephans* comes from Greek *elephio* (mountain) – an even more exaggerated comparison than Ælfric's **hūs** (house). The salient characteristic of *ylpas* in Ælfric's Old English *Hexameron*, a text about the six days of Creation, is that these *dēor* are **or-mǣte** (immense):

> So, then God created through his wondrous might all <u>kinds of beasts</u> (*nytencynn*) after their kind, and the wild <u>animals</u> (*deor*) that dwell in the woods, and all that is four-footed from the aforesaid earth, and all kinds of worms that creep, and the fierce lions that are not here in this land, and the swift tigers and wonderful leopards, and the terrifying bears and <u>immense elephants</u> (*ormætan ylpas*), which are not born in the <u>country of the English</u> (*Engla ðeode*), and many other kinds, all of which you cannot know.

In this text, Ælfric is in agreement with Isidore in his comparison, claiming that some *ylpas* can grow to be the size of **muntas** (mountains).

In both the *Hexameron* and *Lives of Saints*, Ælfric describes the *ylp* as a kind of *nīten* (or *nȳten*). A variant of *nēat* (ox/cow/beast), **nīten** can mean 'ox' or 'cow' but can also refer to a non-specific animal. Ælfric names a number of **nīten-cynn** (kinds of *nīten*) that would have been unknown to his contemporaries in early medieval England: *lēo* (lion), **tiger** (tiger), **pard** (leopard), **bera** (bear) and *ylp*.

How to draw an elephant

If you've ever seen a medieval illustration of an elephant – and it is a popular subject in bestiaries – you might assume that its strangeness is due to a lack of knowledge about its appearance; but, as we've seen with spiders, an artist's familiarity with a creature does not necessarily mean they'll be able to produce a recognisable drawing on the page. A fourteenth-century encyclopaedia from Flanders portrays generally the correct features, but they are oddly proportioned, with an unrealistically large trunk that resembles a cyclone. Other medieval elephants resemble horses with trunks, or have trunks that protrude from the forehead like a unicorn's horn. Such differences can be attributed to an illuminator's ability and stylistic choices and are not necessarily inaccurate due to a lack of knowledge. The primary characteristics of these early elephant drawings are the long nose and the tusks, but how exactly these fit together was up to one's imagination. Some tusks point up, others down; some elephants even have four tusks, two up and two down. Later illustrations are usually (but not always) more realistic.

Ælfric recognises that in his own time very few people in the **Engla þéod** (country of the English) would know about *ylpas* from a first-hand encounter. The first elephant seen in *Engla þéod* didn't arrive until 1255, long after the Old English period, a royal gift to Henry III of England from Louis IX of France. Matthew Paris, an English monk and chronicler, records this gift of the African elephant in his *Liber Additamentorum* (*Book of Additional Things*) as well as his *Chronica Majora* (*Greater Chronicles*). The art historian Suzanne Lewis suggests that the *Liber Additamentorum* illustration (pictured opposite) may have been Matthew's first attempt to draw the elephant from life, pointing out the inclusion of a second rendering of the trunk in a different position, as well as the convincing detail.

Matthew Paris's drawing of the elephant given to Henry III in the
Liber Additamentorum (England, 1250–59)

This attention to detail from first-hand observation is not typical in
Europe's later medieval bestiaries. By far the most common depiction
of elephants in these bestiaries is the 'elephant and castle'. Medieval
texts describe how Persians and Indians placed archers on the backs
of elephants to fight as though they were atop a castle wall. In reality,
these are probably based on exaggerated tales of travellers who saw
a howdah, a seat usually fitted with railings and a canopy that could
carry a couple of people on an elephant's back. In medieval Europe,
elephants and their 'castles' are associated with enemies in the East,
evoking the Crusades. The elephant and castle image remained so
popular over the centuries that it became the name and symbol of
a medieval cutlery guild, and later a popular name for pubs and
coaching inns. Today Elephant and Castle is still a road junction and
Underground station in London.

Beasts of battle or gentle giants?

Whether or not elephant-and-castle warfare was a reality, it is described in numerous medieval texts. Ælfric writes about teams of 500 men on horseback leading an **elpend** (another Old English word for 'elephant') into battle. The *elpend* bears a **wīg-hūs** (battle-house or tower), and each *wīg-hūs* can hold thirty warriors. Sadly, for those of us who want a clearer vision of an elephant hefting a castle overflowing with soldiers, illustrators of the bestiaries of later centuries tend to under-represent the elephant's great size relative to its 'castle'. The thirteenth-century Rochester Bestiary depicts an elephant that's half the size of a horse (and rather hairy to boot). Perhaps the artist required more space to squeeze in a castle on top of the creature, but this castle can scarcely hold four warriors, much less thirty. Such are the constraints of reality versus imagination.

How might you coax something as big and strong as an *or-mǣte* elephant into battle? Ælfric explains that *ylpas* can be tamed through their love of **mōr-berian** (mulberries). Heathens, Ælfric says, embolden their elephants with *mōr-berian* because these are their most beloved food. Thus, even though the *ylp* is the greatest of all beasts, it can be tamed by man's **ge-scēad** (reason). Because of this, he says, humans 'can train them marvellously for battle'. Alexander the Great seized 400 *elpendas* from one of the kings he conquers to take with him on his expedition, an advantageous addition to his army.

Bestiary elephants might carry soldiers into battle, but when left to their own devices they are shown to be gentle and caring creatures. Elephants travel in herds, always looking out for one another. They cannot swim, so if they must cross a river they make sure the smallest of their herd walks at the front so the water won't get too deep. (The bigger elephants wear away the river bottom with their steps, making the water deeper.) When elephants are surrounded by

Elephant and castle in the Rochester Bestiary (England, *c.*1230)

hunters, they protect their weak, weary or wounded, keeping them at the centre of the group. Pliny the Elder seems to prefer elephants to humankind, claiming they are closest to humans in intelligence but with positive qualities not often seen in humans, such as honesty, wisdom and justice. There is a majesty to the elephant that raises it above other animals, making it truly extraordinary – in reality, not allegory. Cassiodorus says, 'There is a sort of kingly dignity in its appearance, and while it recognises with pleasure all that is honourable, it seems to despise scurrilous jests.' Scandalous humour is clearly detestable to such a superior creature. The thirteenth-century scholar Bartholomaeus Anglicus seems to agree with Pliny's and Cassiodorus' sentiments, noting that of all the animals the elephant is the one 'most of virtue'.

Perhaps this gentler, more virtuous side of the *ylp* is reflected in an entry from an Old English prognostic text based on the dreams of the prophet Daniel. This dreambook explains that if you see an *ylp* that is **lāð** (hostile) or **gram** (angry) in a dream, it indicates that you are being accused of something. If the *ylp* – a naturally kind and gentle creature – is mad at you, you must have done something truly deserving of censure!

Although many writers of the antique and medieval periods sing the elephant's praises, Alexander the Great seems to have seen the *elpend* solely as a threat. *Alexander's Letter to Aristotle* tells how the renowned ruler of Macedon encounters elephants in the Indian subcontinent, following his conquest of Persia. Alexander and his army reach a river called Biswicmon, a name that may mean 'deceive the man' or 'evade the man' in Old English. (The verb **be-swīcan** means 'to deceive, seduce, evade or betray'.) The *Letter* says:

> We came to the forests of 'India' (*Indea*) and the remotest borders of the land, and I commanded my troops to make camp there by the river that is called Biswicmon ... We longed to sit down to our meal. It was the eleventh hour of the day [near evening]. But all of a sudden we were told to gather our weapons, for there was a great need for us to protect ourselves, and we did so, seizing our weapons. Then there came a great multitude of elephants (*elpenda*), an immense host of animals (*diora*). They had come there to attack our camp.

But gathering weapons and running headlong into the fray is perhaps not the best choice that Alexander could have made. After all, Pliny the Elder says that if you are not actively trying to harm an elephant, it will leave you alone. Elephants, he explains, are naturally gentle and kind to anyone weaker than themselves. An even-tempered and peaceful creature, the elephant will even help a harmless human who crosses its path, showing them the way if they are lost. Pliny tells about an elephant that needed to get past a flock of sheep, and so it lifted each sheep very carefully out of its way with its trunk, to avoid treading on one inadvertently. Medieval bestiaries tell similar stories. The Aberdeen Bestiary (*c.*1200), for instance, extends Pliny's sheep story to include a rescued herd of cattle. The gentleness of the elephant in these accounts contrasts with the ferocity of Alexander's *elpendas*. However, the sixth-century scholar Cassiodorus does say that the elephant 'pays to good princes a homage which it refuses to tyrants'. Perhaps Alexander's *elpendas* merely saw him for the tyrant that he was and thus refused to treat him with the respect due to a 'good prince'.

As intimidating as these *elpendas* are in the *Letter*, Alexander manages to defeat them using an ingenious choice of ally: *swīn* (pigs). Despite their superior size, strength and nobility, *elpendas* are frightened by *swīn* – particularly their noisy **rȳung** (grunting). Alexander says:

> I immediately ordered that our <u>horses</u> (*hors*) be made ready and the horsemen leap up. And I ordered a great band of <u>swine</u> (*swina*) to be taken and driven by the <u>horses</u> (*horsum*) towards the <u>elephants</u> (*elpendum*), because I knew that <u>swine</u> (*swin*) were loathsome to those <u>animals</u> (*deorum*) and that their <u>grunting</u> (*rying*) could frighten them. And as soon as the <u>elephants</u> (*elpendas*) saw the <u>swine</u> (*swin*), they were afraid, and they departed immediately into the forest.

This was not just a ruse thought up on the spot by the explorer: the practice of scaring war elephants with pigs is described by various historians across ancient Greece and Rome. Everything, even the fierce *elpend*, has its weakness.

But though they might be afraid of pigs, the main threat to

elephants in the Middle Ages (as is still the case today) is human hunters. When Alexander the Great storms King Porus' palace in the city of Fasiacen, he marvels at its untold luxuries and riches, which include carvings in **elpend-bān** (ivory, literally 'elephant-bone'). Carved *elpend-bān* adorns the palace's exterior, which Alexander describes as 'marvellously white and beautiful'. Such wealth is obtained through cruel butchery. An Old English translation of the history of Paulus Orosius, a Roman historian of the fourth and fifth centuries, describes a brutal method of taking down elephants in battle which emphasises the animals' suffering and pain. But if they keep away from hunters and battlefields, *elpendas* can live quite a long time – 300 years, according to Ælfric. (Today's biologists would give a more conservative estimate; although an elephant has a long lifespan in comparison to many animals, it lives only sixty to seventy years on average.)

The fallen can rise

One way in which hunters take down elephants relies on a peculiar characteristic – their alleged inability to bend their legs. According to Ælfric, the *ylp* never lies down (*næfre ne lið*). This notion may go all the way back to Ctesias, who wrote a fabulous account of India in the fourth century BCE in which he made this claim. Alexander the Great's tutor Aristotle refutes the idea, but it resurfaces in the second century BCE in the account of the Greek historian and geographer Agatharchides. The Roman author Aelian then discounts Agatharchides' claim, but the idea continues to be passed on through late antiquity and the Middle Ages. It even appears in Shakespeare's *Troilus and Cressida* (first printed in 1609): 'The elephant hath joints, but none for courtesy; his legs are legs for necessity, not for flexure.'

The Middle English *Physiologus* explains how this alleged disability is advantageous to elephant hunters. A hunter can use a saw to cut most of the way through a tree, propping it in such a way that it looks normal to an elephant. When an unwary elephant comes wandering by and decides to lean on the tree for a nap, both the tree and the elephant fall down. The elephant, unable to stand, is trapped. Now is the time for the hunter to pounce – and before the immobile elephant can use the only weapon left to it. If it makes enough noise, it can attract its fellow herd members. Its larger companions might be unable to help (since they can't exactly bend down to lift him up), but if a 'ȝungling' ('young-ling' or child) elephant comes, it can place its trunk beneath its elder and begin to lift. With some assistance from the other elephants, the 'ȝungling' can get the fallen elephant back on its feet.

This unlikely scenario is one that seems to have been invented for the sake of a good allegory. The *Physiologus* explains that the fallen elephant (representing God's Law) ultimately fails to keep humankind from committing sin. The other adult elephants (prophets of the Old Testament) try to help their brother without success. Only with the help of the 'ȝungling' (Christ himself) can the fallen rise again. The thirteenth-century bestiary Bodley 764 explains that even though Christ was 'greatest of all', he 'became very small' and 'humbled himself before death, in order to raise mankind up'.

But not all medieval authorities believe in the joint-less elephant. The thirteenth-century theologian Albertus Magnus claims that elephants' large legs are almost the same width from top to bottom, like pillars, and that nature joined their toes together to give better support. Albertus does say, however, that elephants do in fact have leg joints or they would be unable to walk 'in the ordinary way'. These leg joints are stiff rather than supple, so 'the ignorant' do not believe they exist. Suzanne Lewis points out that the thirteenth-century drawing by Matthew Paris depicts an elephant with 'pronounced articulation of the knee joints, accurately placed very low, just above the massive feet'. Meanwhile Bartholomaeus Anglicus seems to contradict his own belief that elephants lack leg joints when he claims the creatures can bow down. He says that elephants recognise a king when they see him and will pay their respects properly, bending the 'knees' in worship of him.

While beliefs about the elephant vary from one authority to another, perhaps more so than the *dēor* from earlier chapters, one thing remains constant: the animal's extraordinary nature. It is an *or-mǣte* creature, the size of a *munt*. It's brave enough to carry soldiers into battle but is frightened of pigs. Its keen intelligence is paired with a generous and compassionate nature. Instead of hunting the *ylp*, why not feed it some *mōr-berian* before politely asking for directions? And if it doesn't like you, have a good think about your own behaviour – maybe that is the true *elpend* in the room.

Elephant's Wordhord

bera, noun (BEH-ra / ˈbɛ-ra): Bear (plural: *beran*).

be-swīcan, verb (beh-ZWEE-kahn / bɛ-ˈzwiː-kan): To deceive, seduce, evade, betray.

elpend, noun (EL-pend / ˈɛl-pɛnd): Elephant (plural: *elpendas*).

elpend-bān, noun (EL-pend-BAHN / ˈɛl-pɛnd-ˌbaːn): Ivory (elephant-bone).

Engla þēod, noun (ENG-gla-THAY-od / ˈɛŋ-gla-ˌθeːɔd): Country or nation of the English.

ge-scēad, noun (yeh-SHAY-odd / jɛ-ˈʃeːad): Reason, discretion.

gram, adjective (GROM / ˈgram): Angry, wrathful; hostile, fierce.

hūs, noun (HOOS / ˈhuːs): House.

lāð, adjective (LAWTH / ˈlaːθ): Hostile, malign, bearing hate toward another.

mōr-berige, noun (MOR-BEH-ri-yuh / ˈmoːr-ˌbɛ-ri-jə): Mulberry
(plural: *mōr-berian*).

munt, noun (MUNT / ˈmʌnt): Mountain, hill (plural: *muntas*).

nīten, noun (NEE-ten / ˈniː-tɛn): Animal; cattle.

nīten-cynn, noun (NEE-ten-KUEN / ˈniː-tɛn-ˌkyn): Kind of animal.

or-mǣte, adjective (OR-MAT-uh / ˈɔr-ˌmæː-tə): Immense.

pard, noun (PARD / ˈpard): Leopard or panther (plural: *pardas*).

rȳung, noun (RUE-ung / ˈryː-ʌŋ): Grunting, groaning, roaring.

syllic, adjective (SUEL-litch / ˈsyl-lɪtʃ): Strange, wonderful.

tiger, noun (TIH-gur / ˈtɪ-gər): Tiger (plural: *tigras*).

wīg-hūs, noun (WEE-HOOS / ˈwiːj-ˌhuːs): Battle-house, war-house, a
tower or fortification.

ylp, noun (UELP / ˈylp): Elephant (plural: *ylpas*).

The Good

THE ELEPHANT CAN represent Jesus Christ as well as the failure of God's Law in the Old Testament. The eagle's swooping descent can signify humanity's fall from innocence or Christ rescuing souls from the depths of hell. Raccoons are both city pest and beloved mascot, foxes both screeching nuisance and beautiful garden wonder. In other words, most animals come with associations that are both positive and negative, and many more are neutral.

But certain animals in medieval bestiaries are very clearly aligned with the 'good' side or the 'bad'. We have this today with certain animals, usually linked to how they positively or negatively affect the lives of humans. I don't think there are many people who would think of the mosquito as anything but bad – at best they give us itchy bites on summer nights and at worst they spread deadly diseases like malaria. Bees used to have a bit of a bad rap, paired with wasps as frightening creatures that sting; this has changed in more recent decades as people have been educated on the bee's important role of pollinator. Fables and children's stories sometime echo the positive or negative associations we have with certain animals, like the Big Bad Wolf or Wile E. Coyote.

During the Middle Ages, 'good' and 'bad' are largely determined by religion rather than by fairy stories or global health concerns.

Christianity is a religion of the book, but even those who couldn't read were exposed to the Bible's messages and stories through a church's artwork and sculpture, carved into wooden pews and stone baptismal fonts. People of early medieval England would also have heard the stories of these animals repeated in oral poetry as well as in the sermons and saints' lives, which became increasingly accessible as they were translated from Latin into the vernacular, Old English. Certain animals show up again and again in church iconography and allegory and, as in our cartoons and fairy tales, they were inevitably 'good' or 'bad'.

8

Lion (*leo*)

MOST PEOPLE IN England would have had little reason to encounter a lion, so there's no reason for a lion to be seen as particularly helpful or beneficial to them. Yet the lion is one of the 'good' animals, one of the *dēor* whose attributes – whether based on reality or pure invention – are compared to those of God, Christ, the Holy Spirit or the saints.

The lion often appears first in medieval bestiaries; it is, after all, the 'king of beasts'. Its name in Old English, **lēo**, derives directly from Latin *leo*, which comes from the Greek word for 'king'. This word has cognates in all Germanic languages, probably because the creature would have been unknown to people in northern Europe prior to Latin influence; outside of the Bible, encountering such a creature would have been unlikely.

The good king

St Mark, one of the four evangelists, has a *lēo* as his symbol. This could be due to the special focus of the Gospel of Mark on Christ's resurrection and kingship. Ælfric provides another reason in his *Lives of Saints*, saying that the *lēo* belongs to Mark because he begins his gospel with a reference to St John the Baptist, who

> ... <u>cried out</u> (*clypode*) loudly, as the <u>lion roars</u> (*leo grimmeteð*), greedy in the desert ... A voice <u>crying</u> (*clypiende*) in the desert: Prepare God's way, make straight his paths.

It's true that I said John the Baptist was associated with the dove in Chapter 4, but a saint needn't be limited to one symbol. John's association with baptism (and thus the Holy Spirit) makes the dove a suitable symbol, but the lion is equally apropos for the saint's 'roaring' style of evangelising. Similarly, an animal like the lion can be symbolic of more than one person, Mark as well as John, in addition to (as we shall see) other saints and forms of divinity.

Grymettan can mean 'roar', 'bellow', 'cry out' or 'howl', depending on whether the sound is produced by an animal like a lion, bear or wild boar or by a human, demon or tormented soul. It's slightly more bestial than the verb **clipian** (to cry, call out). In the quotation above, Ælfric references the Gospel of Mark, which has nearly identical wording: 'A voice of one crying in the desert: Prepare ye the way of the Lord; make straight his paths.' In manuscripts like the Lindisfarne Gospels, produced in Northumbria around the year 700, the *lēo* appears beside Mark, illustrating how the evangelist could not get John's 'roaring' out of his mind.

Despite its fearsome **grymettung** (roaring), the lion is generally portrayed as intelligent and non-confrontational in the *Physiologus* and bestiary lore, not fierce and aggressive. Lions are powerful and benevolent, like Christ the king. They roam the mountain tops, and the art historian Margaret Haist explains that the mountain is seen as 'God's seat on earth'. This concept appears in the Old Testament, when Isaiah

St Mark and his lion in the Lindisfarne Gospels (England, *c.*700)

says, 'the mountain of the house of the Lord shall be prepared on the top of mountains, and it shall be exalted above the hills'. When lions smell hunters they retreat into caves, cleverly using their tails to wipe away their tracks. Bestiaries compare this behaviour to that of Christ, who hides his tracks from Satan when he comes down to earth. When the lion sleeps its eyes remain open, in the way that Christ's divinity keeps watch while his body lies 'asleep' on the cross. The myth that lions sleep with their eyes open may have come about because they can be quite still while resting but awake. The idea goes back at least as far as the early second century, to an observation made by the Greek philosopher and historian Plutarch. Although this idea is present in ancient pagan literature, medieval Christians use it to compare the lion to Christ. In the Song of Songs, Christ says, 'I sleep, and my heart watcheth,' and Psalm 120 states, 'Behold he shall neither slumber nor sleep, that keepeth Israel.' Many medieval bestiaries describe how lions will spare humans who lie helpless on the ground, lead captives back to their homes and attack men instead of women. They say that the thoughtful lion only kills children if it is exceptionally hungry and only becomes angry when humans threaten them with harm. It is true that lions are aggressive only to humans they perceive as a threat.

Fierce yet helpless, wild yet tameable

Yet it seems the lion is not universally adored by Christians. In his *De Proprietatibus Rerum* (*On the Properties of Things*), Bartholomaeus Anglicus draws upon the negative way in which lions are often depicted in the Bible, claiming that the lion is cruel when angry, biting in indignation and gnashing its teeth in hunger. In the Psalms, for instance, the creature seems far from 'good'. In the Old English verse translation of Psalm 56, even the **hwelp** (cub) of a *lēo* is dangerous and **rēðe** (fierce). King David compares his enemies to lion cubs, saying:

> Mighty God has sent his merciful thought and his true spirit, both together, and he at once saved my soul from <u>lion cubs</u> (*leon hwelpum*), <u>fierce</u> (*rēðe*) fellowship.

Don't underestimate a *hwelp*'s ferocity. More than simply 'fierce', Old English *rēðe* also means 'cruel' or 'savage'. As early as the fifth century BCE, lionesses were believed to suffer terrible pregnancies, despite the fact that, according to Herodotus, the lioness is 'the strongest and most courageous of creatures'. Herodotus attributed this to the cubs' sharp claws, which tear and scratch at their mother's womb. Given the incredible pain a lioness supposedly suffered during pregnancy, perhaps it's not surprising that the bestiary Bodley 764 claims that the lioness gives birth to fewer and fewer cubs each year. According to the bestiary, the first time a lioness gives birth she produces five cubs, then each subsequent year this number diminishes by one until one year she has zero, having lost her fertility. (In another example of fact-checking the past, I can confirm that this is not the case according to the *Encyclopaedia Britannica*, which says that in the wild lionesses usually produce a litter of one to six cubs every two years, two to four cubs being the norm.)

Despite their ferocity in the womb, lion cubs enter the world truly helpless – 'dead', according to the *Physiologus* (tired out from all that womb-bound scratching?). And this time it's closer to the truth, since while they are clearly not born 'dead', newborn lions are born blind and vulnerable – according to Pliny in an 'unfinished' state, needing to be warmed and licked into shape by their parents. Some medieval bestiaries say that the cubs enter the world dead, others just asleep, but either way they remain like that for three days. (In actuality, lion cubs don't open their eyes until three to eleven days after birth.) Medieval bestiaries say that the father lion comes on the cubs' third day of life and breathes into their faces, which wakes them up or brings them to life (depending on your opinion). This extraordinary behaviour does not reflect reality – aside from the delayed eye opening – but makes a lovely metaphor for the resurrection of Christ, who ascends to heaven three days after his crucifixion (licked back to life, so to speak, by God the Father).

Even the great **mægen** (power) of lions is weak against that of God. An Old English translation of Psalm 57 says:

> God will furiously shatter the great teeth that they have in their mouths;
> the Lord will speedily dissolve the <u>power of lions</u> (*leona mægen*).

The Psalms also say that God can walk over the **aspide** (asp), tread boldly upon the **basilisca** (basilisk), and subdue with cunning the *lēo* and the **draca** (dragon). Asps, basilisks and dragons are all related to

Lions licking their cubs in a bestiary (England, *c.*1200–1210)

serpents, and serpents generally symbolise Satan, so it might seem strange for a creature that symbolises Christ to be included with them. This psalm is more of a commentary on Christ's omnipotence – the creatures are similar not in their morality but in their might.

The Old English translation of one of Boethius' *Metres* describes a lioness's inherent savagery. You might chance to meet a *lēo* (lioness) who is pleasant and well tamed, when she loves and fears her master. But Boethius warns:

If it ever happens that she tastes any blood, no one needs to ponder what will happen, whether she will keep her tameness afterwards. I determine that she will not be mindful at all of this new <u>tameness</u> (*taman*) but will wish to remember the <u>wild</u> (*wildan*) habits of her elders. She will begin in earnest to tear her fetters, to rage and <u>roar</u>

(*grymetigan*), first biting the keeper of her own house and soon afterwards every man that she can seize.

According to Boethius, the **tama** (tameness) of the *lēo* goes only so deep, and it is counter to her base instincts to be **wilde** – to rage, roar, bite and kill.

St Daria and the lioness

Although Boethius doubted their tameability, some lions and lion-esses could be made truly gentle by God's great power. And not only can their *mægen* be vanquished by God, it can be governed by saints. In the fourth century, St Mary of Egypt befriends a lion while living in the desert. The fifth-century saint Gerasimus allegedly removes a thorn from a lion's paw, and the lion becomes his friend and personal assistant. Later on this story is ascribed to Jerome, a better-known fifth-century saint than Gerasimus, and consequently St Jerome is often depicted in the company of a lion. In his Old English saints' lives, Ælfric tells the story of St Daria and her own helpful lioness. During the third century CE, Daria and her husband Chrysanthus lived together in a celibate marriage and spent their time convert-ing pagans to Christianity. Eventually Numerian, the wicked Roman emperor, grows tired of the couple's pious activities and decides to torture them in a variety of ways. It is during this torture that Daria has a unique experience with a lioness sent by God.

Numerian begins his torture of Daria by sending her to live in a brothel against her will, thinking she will be forced to break her vow of celibacy. Confined to the brothel, Daria awaits her fate, kneeling in prayer. Fortunately, God comes to her rescue, sending a *lēo* (lioness) from the lions' enclosure. (Why such an enclosure would be part of or nearby a brothel remains unexplained.) The *lēo* lies down with limbs outstretched before the faithful **mǣden** (virgin), ready to serve her.

When the first **hǣþen** (heathen) goes to have his wicked way with Daria, unaware of her feline companion, the *lēo* seizes him, lays him down and looks to Daria as if to ask for further instructions. Daria says, 'I beseech you by Christ not to harm the young man, but let him listen to my speech without terror.' So the *lēo* releases the **un-gelēaful** (unbelieving) man but blocks the door so he is forced to hear Daria's words. Daria says to him:

> Now even this <u>fierce lioness</u> (*reþe leo*) honours God, while you, a <u>rational</u> (*gesceadwisa*) man, defile yourself! You rejoice in foul lust, you <u>unfortunate wretch</u> (*earmincg*), for which you shall weep and suffer torment.

The supposedly **ge-scēadwīs** (rational or intelligent) human falls short when compared to the *rēðe* lioness. The **earmincg** (unfortunate wretch) approaches Daria and fearfully begs her to let him depart safely. From now on he will worship her God, he promises, proclaiming him the saviour of men. Then Daria commands the *lēo* to move aside so the man can depart, and he runs out, honouring God and the holy *mǣden* and making her **miht** (power) known.

Other *hǣþenan* (heathens) ignore the proclamations of this changed man, however, and keep entering Daria's chamber, certain they will defeat the *lēo*. But the *lēo* always catches them through the Lord's *miht*, bringing them one at a time to Daria so she can lecture them properly. To these men Daria says, 'If you will believe in the living Christ, then you may all go from here uninjured. If you will not believe, I do not know if your gods can help you.' And so the men all agree to believe in Christ, and they depart, crying out to their fellow Romans and exhorting them to believe in no god but Christ.

The prefect of the city, enraged by this mass conversion, orders a *fȳr* (fire) to be kindled in front of the door of Daria's chamber, trapping the woman and lioness inside. The *lēo* is exceedingly frightened because of the *fȳr*. (As pigs are to elephants, so fire is to lions: in his *Etymologies*, Isidore claims that while lions fear the rattle of wheels, they fear fire even more.) Daria tells the *lēo*:

Don't be afraid, this <u>fire</u> (*fȳr*) will not harm you. Nor will you be slain before your time. Now go away, safe from danger. God will deliver you, whom you have honoured with your <u>actions</u> (*weorcum*) today.

The *lēo* walks away from the chamber unharmed, her head bowed respectfully. All those men whom she seized before are baptised, after acknowledging Christ *þurh ða leon* (through the lioness). God has worked a miracle through the *lēo's* **weorc** (actions).

We are told nothing more of the *lēo*, for she has done her part in God's interventions. The city prefect's other torments are equally unsuccessful. He tries to stretch Chrysanthus on a rack while burning his sides with flames, but the machinery breaks apart and the candles are extinguished. He orders men to injure Daria, but God makes their sinews shrink painfully whenever they try to touch her. The prefect eventually gives up, terrified by these signs from God, but Emperor Numerian, unfazed by what he thinks is merely a bit of sorcery, orders the couple to be buried alive in a sandpit. Chrysanthus and Daria finally die, but they still win in the end. Having maintained their chastity and faith, they are able to ascend to heaven to dwell with Christ.

Unlike inept city prefects continually thwarted by a saint's faith, lions are far from harmless. In the Bible especially they seem well known for their *rēðe* ways. The fact that they can be tamed says more about God's power than about an amenable, obedient nature. Yet overall, lions represent good things and help good people. When it comes to protecting a saintly woman from rape, they are there to make sure she is not only safe from but heard by her tormentors. They are companions of saints and manifestations of God's *miht* and *mægen*. Kingly and noble, their *grymettung* (roaring) cannot be ignored. And despite Boethius' reservations, as long as you aren't a tyrant or a persecutor of Christians, the medieval lion will most likely let you be.

Lion's Wordhord

aspide, noun (AH-spih-duh / ˈa-spɪ-də): Asp.

basilisca, noun (BA-zih-liss-ka / ˈba-zɪ-lis-ka): Basilisk.

clipian, verb (KLIH-pi-ahn / ˈklɪ-pɪ-an): To call, cry out.

draca, noun (DRAH-ka / ˈdra-ka): Dragon.

earmincg, noun (EH-ar-minj / ˈɛar-mɪndʒ): Miserable being, unhappy or unfortunate wretch.

fȳr, noun (FUER / ˈfyːr): Fire.

ge-scēadwīs, adjective (yeh-SHAY-odd-wees / jɛ-ˈʃeːad-wiːs): Reasonable, rational, intelligent.

grymettan, verb (GRUE-met-tahn / ˈgry-mɛt-tan): To roar, bellow; to cry out, howl.

grymettung, noun (GRUE-met-tung / ˈgry-mɛt-tʌŋ): Roaring, bellowing; loud outcry, howling.

hǣþen, noun (HATH-en / ˈhæː-θɛn): Heathen, pagan, person who is not Christian (plural: *hǣþenan*).

hwelp, noun (H'WELP / ˈhwɛlp): Cub of a lion or bear; (in other contexts) young dog.

lēo, noun (LAY-oh / ˈleːɔ): Lion, lioness (plural: *lēon*).

mǣden, noun (MADD-en / ˈmæː-dɛn): Virgin, maiden.

mægen, noun (MAE-yen / ˈmæ-jɛn): Power, might.

miht, noun (MI'HT / ˈmɪxt): Power, might.

rēðe, adjective (RAY-thuh / 'reː-θə): Fierce, cruel, savage, wild.

tama, noun (TAH-ma / 'ta-ma): Tameness.

un-gelēaful, adjective (UN-yeh-LAY-ah-vull / 'ʌn-jɛ-ˌleːa-vʌl): Unbelieving, incredulous.

weorc, noun (WEH-ork / 'wɛɔrk): Work, action, deed (plural: *weorc*).

wilde, adjective (WILL-duh / 'wɪl-də): Wild, not tamed.

9

Deer (*heorot* and *hind*)

In old english a deer is a *dēor*, but a *dēor* is not always a deer. Indeed, you can call a deer a *dēor*, but it wouldn't be clear whether you meant a deer or some other creature, like an *earn* or *ylp*. Better, then, to stick with an entirely unmistakeable word like **heorot.**

Heorot (from which we get 'hart') is believed to refer to the red deer that were one of the most common species of deer in early medieval England. It usually refers to a male deer, with **hind** as its female counterpart. **Hēa-dēor** (literally 'lofty animal') is a less common, more poetic word that means 'deer' or 'stag', which also probably refers to a red deer. The other most common species of deer was the roe, with the male called a **buc** or **rā** and the female a **dā** (which led on, or brings us back to, the modern English 'doe', a deer, a female deer).

Hedges, hunters and heath-steppers

In England today you can see deer in deer parks, like the royal park at Richmond. Richmond Park is now a national nature reserve, but the original purpose of deer parks was not wildlife conservation. In fact they were areas reserved for the hunting of deer. While a deer park would provide deer with a wide-open area to roam, its borders were enclosed by ditches, banks and walls, which prevented the animals from leaving. Some of these deer parks existed in early medieval England – a **ge-hæg** (yeh-HAIE) was a piece of land enclosed by **hegeas** (hedges or fences) – but it wasn't until the arrival of the Normans that they became popular among royalty and landed gentry. The Normans stocked their deer parks with fallow deer from France, which were better suited for reserve life than the indigenous *heorotas* and *bucas*. The Normans enjoyed killing deer for sport, and stockpiling their land with them made this much easier (why bother with the challenge of *hunting* them?).

In early medieval England, hunting **wild-dēor** (wild animals) was probably not crucial to the general food supply, which was more reliant on farming, but deer were undoubtedly hunted to some extent. Ælfric of Eynsham's *Colloquy* – a practice conversation for students learning Latin, with Old English glosses – indicates that the *heorot* is primarily associated with the hunt. In the *Colloquy*, a **hunta** (hunter) is asked what type of *wild-dēor* they catch the most. (This is a different sort of *hunta* from the spider in Chapter 2.) The *hunta* responds, 'I catch <u>harts</u> (*heortas*), boars, <u>roe deer</u> (*rann*), wild she-goats, and sometimes hares.' The *hunta* adds that just yesterday they caught two *heorotas* in a *nett* (net). You might have noticed that the *Colloquy* has *heortas*, not *heorotas*, for the plural of *heorot*. This is because Old English has no standardised spellings (as an aside, this can be quite helpful for determining the specific time and place a text was written – people spelled words how they said them, and there was much variation between regional dialects).

While some clearly found deer-hunting to be an entertaining pastime, not everyone was on board with it. The *Peterborough Chronicle*'s entry for 1067, the year of William the Conqueror's death, recounts the king's legacy, saying:

> He established great game preserves, and he laid down laws for them so that anyone who killed a <u>hart</u> (*heort*) or <u>hind</u> (*hinde*) would be blinded. He forbade the hunting of <u>harts</u> (*heortas*) and also of boars. He loved the <u>stags</u> (*headeor*) so very much, as though he were their <u>father</u> (*fæder*). He also made it so that hares might go free. His powerful men lamented it, and the poor men complained of it.

Chronicles were manuscripts written for the specific purpose of recording important events year by year – they were a kind of diary, rather than a historical analysis, written by multiple contributors over decades and sometimes even centuries. There is something rather endearing about the fact that this powerful king loved the *hēa-dēor* as though he were their *fæder* (father). It doesn't seem as if the anonymous scribe was particularly impressed by William's anti-hunting legislation, though; nor is it likely the hunt-loving Norman nobles were pleased with it.

While the fierce *lēo* fears little in this world (aside from fire and loud wheels), the gentle *heorot* is easily spooked – a rational response when you live in a society that sees you primarily as prey. Pliny claims that deer are surprised by everything. According to medieval bestiaries, if a deer hears the barking of hounds it will run with the wind, leaving no trace of its scent. In *Beowulf* we get an idea of just how frightening Grendel's lake home must be from a *heorot*'s reaction when it reaches the murky waters:

> If the <u>heath-stepper</u> (*hæðstapa*), the <u>strong-horned</u> (*hornum trum*) <u>hart</u> (*heorot*) seeks the forest, hotly pursued by <u>hounds</u> (*hundum*), put to flight from afar, it would rather give up its life and spirit at the shore than save its head in there. This is no pleasant place!

Hæþ-stapa (heath-stepper) is a poetic expression that appears only twice in extant Old English. In this case *hæþ-stapa* refers to a stag, but its second occurrence refers to a different animal, which we'll meet in a later chapter. The *heorot* may have **hornas** (antlers) that are **trum** (strong), but it knows it doesn't stand a chance against a pack of hunting dogs. Even so, the pool is so frightening – 'no pleasant place' – that it would prefer to sacrifice itself to the hunt rather than enter those cursed and dreary waters.

Placidas and the Christ-deer

While the *heorot* in *Beowulf* gives up its flight because entering the mere seems worse than certain death, other deer have more success fleeing, as we see in one of Ælfric's saints' lives, when Placidas, a pagan Roman general of the turn of the second century CE, goes out hunting one day with his companions, and they come upon a great **flocc** of deer.

Today 'flock' usually refers to a group of birds (especially geese) or sheep or goats. A modern English 'flock' is most often a group of animals that are domesticated rather than wild, creatures managed together under a human's charge. Old English *flocc*'s usage is more general, referring to any group of animals and even to a gathering of humans. Nowadays a pastor might refer to their congregation as their 'flock', or people might 'flock' to see something, but in Old English there is a greater variety of people 'flocks'. There might be a *flocc* of robbers or a *flocc* of military personnel. Today we usually use 'herd' for groups of deer; 'bevy' is another option in modern English but is far less common. It first appears as 'bevey' in Middle English in the fifteenth century, referring diversely to a flock of quail or larks, a herd of roe deer or a company of ladies.

But back to Placidas in Ælfric's saint's life. He and his companions are delighted to come across this *flocc* of deer and are busy hunting them when Placidas sees an *or-mǣte* (immense) *heorot*, bigger than all the others and **wlitig** (beautiful). He pursues it with some of his companions, but his friends eventually become weary; they fall back and he continues the chase alone. Ælfric says that it is only because of God's **fore-stihtung** (predestination) that Placidas and his horse have the stamina to keep up the pursuit, for this is no ordinary *heorot*. Eventually the *heorot* ascends a high rock where he stands still. Placidas stops and stares. Despite his proximity to the prey he has been chasing for hours he doesn't draw his bow, but, frozen in awe, he marvels at the creature's greatness. Things become even more marvellous when God makes the glittering likeness of Christ's cross appear between the hart's *hornas* and gives it the power of human speech. The *heorot* says:

> Oh, Placidas, why are you chasing me? Truly, I come now for your sake, so that I might reveal myself to you through this <u>animal</u> (*nyten*). I am the Christ whom you worship <u>ignorantly</u> (*nytende*).

Christ, speaking through the hart, recognises that Placidas is a good person at heart (no pun intended), someone who gives money to the poor and needy. Because Placidas does good deeds he unknowingly serves Christ, even though he worships pagan gods, the 'unclean devils and unwitting idols'. Christ says that Placidas is **nyten** (ignorant) of his inherent Christian faith. Here Ælfric indulges in some wordplay, for Christ appears as a *nyten* (an alternate spelling of *nīten*, animal) to tell Placidas he is *nyten* (ignorant).

In the guise of a *heorot*, Christ offers Placidas **mildheortness** (mercy), but the pagan man, understandably terrified, goes home to consult his wife. His wife explains that Placidas has witnessed 'God who was crucified, whom Christian people worship'. She admits that she has seen him herself, for God had appeared to her the previous night to say, 'Tomorrow you, your husband and your sons shall come to me.' She says they must go that very night to be baptised as Christians, and Placidas agrees. When the bishop baptises them, each person in the family is given a new Christian name. Placidas becomes Eustace, and eventually he would become St Eustace.

Enemy of all that is evil

Why does Christ take the form of a *heorot* in this story? The *hæþ-stapa* in *Beowulf* is frightened and timid, but in the bestiaries of later centuries the deer is known for trampling and destroying snakes, its arch-enemy. This antipathy goes at least as far back as the first century BCE, when the Roman philosopher Lucretius writes about deer snorting snakes out of their lairs using breath from their nostrils. (Lucretius does admit that this idea seems rather fanciful.) According to medieval bestiaries, the deer fills its stomach with water at a stream, which it then expels from its nose to force a snake from its hole. This behaviour is likened to the Harrowing of Hell, when Christ pursues the Devil into the lowest reaches of the earth.

Deer, familiar and ordinary though they may be in early medieval life, clearly belong in the category of 'the good'. The deer's starring role in Old English saints' lives is not only as a disguise for Christ: there are stories about deer acting under divine influence, at the behest of God or a saint or command. In the Old English *Martyrology*'s entry for 15 November, the feast day of St Milus and St Sennius, a *hind* plays a role of vengeance. Milus, a fourth-century bishop, performed many miracles in his time, including walking across water while keeping his feet dry. He is in the city of Maheldagdar one day when he is approached by two **ār-lēas** (impious or dishonourable) brothers, who urge him to worship the sun, a **dēofol-gyld** (idol). Milus refuses, so the brothers

A deer faces off with a snake in the Rutland Psalter (England, *c*.1260)

pierce his body with their spears, one from the front and the other from behind. As he dies, Milus says:

> Tomorrow at this time each of you will kill the other at this same place. <u>Dogs</u> (*hundas*) will lick your blood, and <u>birds</u> (*fugelas*) will eat your flesh, and your wives will be widows on the same day.

Sure enough, the next day the *ār-lēas* brothers find themselves hunting in the same location. A *hind* runs in between the brothers, and they both shoot their arrows at it from either side.

And the arrow of the elder came to be in the younger one's innards, and the younger one's arrow in the breast of the elder, and they were dead at once in the same place where they had killed the man of God.

The *hind* doesn't kill the brothers herself, but she becomes an instrument of their death through God's predestination, his *fore-stihtung*.

Milk of mercy

The other *hind* from the *Martyrology* appears in the entry for 15 September, the feast day of St Mamilian, fifth-century bishop of Palermo, who is forced out of town by the Vandals. Mamilian lives in exile as an **ancor** (recluse), performing many miracles, healing the sick, and being so kind to guests that he even takes his meals with foreigners (eating with strangers apparently being a way to show appreciation 'for God's love'). One day a presumptuous bishop decides to test this famed hospitality and sends two of his soldiers to Mamilian. The recluse invites the soldiers to eat with him. One consents, but the other, older and more arrogant, refuses – it seems he cannot stomach a simple meal shared with a lowly recluse.

The three then go on their way together, because the soldiers have been instructed to conduct Mamilian to the haughty bishop, who wants to meet the humble *ancor* for himself. Before long, the older soldier begins to thirst to death and falls to the holy man's feet, praying for mercy – perhaps he was too quick to scoff at the recluse's repast. Then Mamilian, God's **þēow** (servant), sees a wild lactating *hind*, and he 'signs' to it. It's not any old sign: the verb **ge-sēnian** (to sign) specifically refers to making a sign of blessing or the sign of the cross. The *hind* stands still so the desperate man can drink her *meolc* (milk), alleviating his unbearable thirst. Rather than being grateful for this miracle the soldiers become fearful, for even though they have been treated with affection and generosity they have witnessed an extraordinary power, St Mamilian and the merciful deer as evidence of God's might.

In fact, it is the bishop who should have been afraid. When the three men finally arrive, he is about to baptise a newborn baby. The bishop claims it is the son of his prefect, but Mamilian asks the child directly, 'Who is your *fæder* (father)?' Demonstrating extraordinary early cognitive and linguistic ability, the newborn responds with 'The bishop who is standing here', and goes on to explain how he had been conceived through the bishop's illicit sex. The story concludes with Mamilian baptising the child and condemning the bishop for his **unriht-hæmed** (unlawful intercourse).

Another story of a *hind*'s merciful lactation appears in the Old English *Life of St Giles*. Like Mamilian, Giles lives the life of an *ancor* or **wēsten-setla** (wilderness-dweller), taking shelter in a cave and living off herbs, roots and spring water. God sees the hard life that Giles has chosen for himself, and so every day he sends him a *hind* to nourish him with her *meolc*. The *Life* even describes Giles as the *hind*'s **fostor-cild** (foster-child). One day the *hind* is being pursued by the king's huntsmen, and she comes to Giles's cave for protection. Giles gets down on his knees and prays to God that she who had been a **fostor-mōdor** (foster-mother) to him would be unharmed. Then a miracle occurs so that the hounds can come no closer to the *hind* than a stone's throw. Frustrated, the hunters leave. But they return another day, and this time they try a different tactic: an archer shoots at the *hind*, who is lying at Giles's feet. The arrow misses and hits Giles instead. Though the holy man is severely wounded, he continues to pray to God for the protection of his dear (deer) *fostor-mōdor*. At this point the king, who is among the hunters, realises that he is in the presence of someone with great power, and he approaches Giles with bare feet, begging his forgiveness. The king's men try to offer the injured *wēsten-setla* medicine, but he will have none 'except his lord's alone'. Giles becomes very ill from his wound but asks God not to bother healing him, thinking of the words of Christ to his apostle Paul: 'In sickness is God's glory fulfilled.' The text doesn't say what happens with this illness, but the saint goes on to found two monasteries with the wealth given to him by the apologetic king as well as perform miracles throughout his life. It seems that ill health didn't prevent him from accomplishing many things. The *Life of St Giles* doesn't tell us what became of the motherly *hind*, but the relationship between animal *fōstor-mōdor* and human *fōstor-cild* is truly touching. Each is concerned with protecting and nurturing the other, and their miraculous acts of love are enabled through God's power.

In both the *Life of St Giles* and the story of St Mamilian, a mother *hind* miraculously feeds a human being with her own *meolc*, but was *hind*'s milk really something that people drank? The *Lacnunga*, a book of Old English medical remedies, includes hind's milk (*hinde meolc*) as an ingredient for curing a pock or pustule of the eye. The historian Joyce Salisbury says that early medieval laws indicate 'more intense domestication' of deer and points out that multiple literary sources refer to deer that are 'sufficiently tamed to provide milk': Gerald of Wales sees cheese made from deer's milk, the Countess of Chester tames deer for their milk, and St Kevin allegedly nourishes an infant with doe's milk. Salisbury notes that people seem to have thought of milking a deer as 'remarkable but not impossible'. Even today deer milk is a product of a New Zealand agribusiness. The specific deer being milked is the red deer, which is one of England's native species (*hind*, in Old English). The main reasons why deer aren't typically milked is because they don't produce very much, and large numbers of deer are not domesticated in countries that don't consume a lot of venison (like the UK and the US). Giles's *hind* must have been miraculous in that it produced enough *meolc* to keep the saint well nourished year-round.

Domne Eafe and her leaping *hind*

In addition to the motherly deer of St Giles and St Mamilian and the vengeful deer of St Milus, Old English literature tells us about the trained deer of Domne Eafe. This special *hind* appears in a text about St Mildrith, which was likely composed for the monastic community of Thanet, in Kent, during the eighth century. Although the overall text is about Mildrith, the deer story comes in a section not about her but about Domne Eafe.

Domne Eafe was not a saint herself but belonged to the Kentish royal line, which produced quite a few saints (including Mildrith). Eafe married Merwald, king of Mercia (one of several independent kingdoms in what eventually became England), in the late seventh century. The royal couple eventually separated to lead holy (which is to say, celibate) lives, and Domne Eafe became an abbess. **Domne**, possibly a contraction of Latin *dominus* (lord) or *domina* (lady), is used for both lords and ladies in Old English. Here it is a courtesy title for the abbess.

But even an abbess could not expect to avoid palace intrigue. Domne Eafe's two younger brothers, Æthelred and Æthelbriht, were murdered while under the guardianship of their cousin, King Ecgbriht. The exact circumstances of their deaths vary according to the telling. Some accounts claim that Thunor, the king's man, murdered the boys in secret, while others say that he did so on King Ecgbriht's direct orders. Either way, Thunor killed the boys and hid their bodies.

The terrible crime is revealed, however, when God shines a beam of light upon the boys' secret graves. King Ecgbriht, alarmed and shaken by this miracle, figures he'd better do what's right and summon

Domne Eafe so she can choose her brothers' **wer-gild**. Wer-gild, literally 'man-price', is the recompense to which a victim's family is entitled in the case of wrongful death. The higher the victim's status, the greater the expected *wer-gild*. King Ecgbriht agrees to pay Domne Eafe the *wer-gild* in the form of land on the Isle of Thanet. Thanet is still a region in England today, though it is no longer an island: it was in fact separated from the mainland by the Wantsum Channel until the sixteenth century.

When the king asks Eafe which portion of the land she desires, she replies that she will take 'no more than her *hind* would run around', for her *hind* would always run in front of her when she was travelling. The king agrees to this, thinking he's got a good deal, but Eafe's *hind* keeps **hlēapende** (leaping) along in front of her, claiming more and more land. They eventually reach the land owned by Thunor, who, far from being amused by the situation, bows before the king, saying:

Dear sir, how long will you listen to this <u>dumb animal</u> (*dumban nytene*), which will run about all this land? Will you give it all to the lady?

But Thunor has worse things to worry about than losing his land to the deer. As soon as he speaks these words, the earth opens beneath him and swallows him up.

Thus a mere *nīten* (animal) who is **dumb** (unable to speak) obtains eighty hides of land for her mistress, enough for the *domne* to found her own monastery and leave a lasting mark on history. The deer, says the historian Eleanor Parker, is 'a personification of Domne Eafe's thought, or her will', so in a way, when Thunor calls the deer *dumb* or unable to speak, he may be implying that this woman does not have a voice worth hearing. But the hind's leaping is perhaps even more expressive than this. Whether or not this unlikely story is true, it is important in showing us how people imagined God's justice could be served, even by a *dumb* animal. Eafe's *hind*, whether by its own volition, as a symbol of Eafe's will or as a tool of God, ultimately punishes the evil-doer.

The *hlēapende* of Eafe's helpful *hind* explains why the Isle of Thanet was divided roughly in two, but it is also reminiscent of a verse referring to Christ in the Song of Songs: 'Behold he cometh leaping upon the mountains, skipping over the hills.' Christ can also be found leaping in an Old English poem creatively titled *Christ II* by modern editors. The poem describes significant moments in Christ's life as 'leaps': the first **hlȳp** (leap) is when he 'descends into a virgin', the second *hlȳp* is when he is born in a manger, and so on, with six *hlȳpas* in total. (Remember too that Christ himself appears to Placidas in the form of a leaping deer.) Christ's leaps come from a homily written by Gregory the Great in 591, which says, 'By coming for our redemption the Lord gave some leaps,' which are 'from heaven to the womb, from the womb to the manger, from the manger to the cross, from the cross to the sepulchre; and from the sepulchre he returned to heaven'. Gregory explains, 'Truth, having made himself known in the flesh, gave some leaps for us to make us run after him.' Christ, the embodiment of truth, takes leaps so we will follow, and Eafe's *hind* also takes leaps so that the royal court's justice will be upheld.

Leaping back to the St Mildrith legend, it's worth noting that Domne Eafe's authority is treated differently in the Old English account compared to the surviving Latin versions. In the three Latin versions of the text that survive, Domne Eafe relies more on the help of God or providence. The Old English version of the story makes it quite clear, however, that Domne Eafe has trained the *hind*, so it acts according to her will rather than God's. Thus Domne Eafe cleverly and intentionally exploits the king, for she knows ahead of time that her tame *hind* will do her bidding, claiming more land than Ecgbriht expects. King Ecgbriht underestimates both the *domne* and her deer to his own detriment. The historian Stephanie Hollis compares medieval monasteries ruled by royal abbesses to 'miniature kingdoms', for they were a means of transferring land and property through the female line, an option inaccessible to most queens of the secular world. The stag is a medieval emblem for kings, and Domne Eafe's *hind* is the female counterpart, symbolic of a woman's ruling power.

Both the *heorot* and the *hind* perform God's will, assisting and protecting worthy mortals. In Old English texts they generally help the 'good', the saints and abbesses. They leap through life, encouraging people to follow them, the way Christ leaps, encouraging people to follow the truth. Christ may even take the form of a *heorot*, not *dumb* but able to speak, capable of converting a hapless pagan. And in the bestiaries of later centuries a deer can overcome a serpent, the way in which Christ prevails over the Devil, good over evil. Easily spooked deer may be, but they are not easily defeated.

Deer's Wordhord

ancor, noun (AN-kor / ˈan-kɔr): Recluse, hermit, anchorite.

ār-lēas, adjective (AR-LAY-ahs / ˈaːr-ˌleːas): Impious, wicked; dishonourable, shameful.

buc, noun (BUCK / ˈbʌk): Buck, male deer, perhaps the roe deer specifically (plural: *bucas*).

dā, noun (DAH / ˈdaː): Doe, perhaps the roe deer specifically (plural: *dān*).

dēofol-gyld, noun (DAY-oh-voll-YUELD / ˈdeːɔ-vɔl-ˌjyld): Idol, statue of a pagan god.

domne, noun (DOM-nuh / ˈdɔm-nə): Lord or lady, referring to a person of high status.

dumb, adjective (DUMB / ˈdʌmb): Mute, unable to speak.

flocc, noun (FLOCK / ˈflɔk): Assembly of people; herd or flock of animals.

fore-stihtung, noun (FOR-uh-STI'H-tung / ˈfɔ-rə-ˌstɪx-tʌŋ): Predestination, preordination.

fōstor-cild, noun (FOH-stor-CHILLD / ˈfoː-stɔr-ˌtʃɪld): Foster-child.

fōstor-mōdor, noun (FOH-stor-MO-dor / ˈfoː-stɔr-ˌmoː-dɔr): Foster-mother.

ge-hæg, noun (yeh-HAIE / jɛ-ˈhæj): Enclosed piece of land.

ge-sēnian, verb (yeh-SAY-ni-ahn / jɛ-ˈseː-nɪ-an): To sign, mark with the sign of the cross, bless.

hǣþ-stapa, noun (HATH-STAH-pa / ˈhæːθ-ˌsta-pa): Heath-stepper, heath-wanderer.

hēa-dēor, noun (HAY-ah-DAY-or / ˈheːa-ˌdeːɔr): Stag, deer (lofty animal).

hege, noun (HEH-yuh / ˈhɛ-jə): Hedge, fence; boundary wall (plural: *hegeas*).

heorot, noun (HEH-o-rot / ˈhɛɔ-rɔt): Male deer, hart, stag (occasionally also used of the female), perhaps the red deer specifically (plural: *heorotas*).

hind, noun (HIND / ˈhɪnd): Hind, female deer, perhaps the red deer specifically (plural: *hinde*).

hlēapende, verb (H'LAY-ah-pen-duh / ˈhleːa-pɛn-də): Leaping, jumping, running.

hlȳp, noun (H'LUEP / ˈhlyːp): Leap, jump (plural: *hlȳpas*).

horn, noun (HORN / ˈhɔrn): Horn, antler (plural: *hornas*).

hunta, noun (HUN-tah / ˈhʌn-ta): Hunter.

mildheortness, noun (MILD-HEH-ort-ness / ˈmɪld-ˌhɛɔrt-nɛs): Mercy, compassion.

nyten, adjective (NUE-ten / ˈny-tɛn): Ignorant.

rā, noun (RAH / ˈraː): Roe deer (plural: *rān*).

trum, adjective (TRUM / ˈtrʌm): Strong, firm, sound.

þēow, noun (THAY-oh / ˈθeːɔw): Servant, enslaved person.

unriht-hǣmed, noun (UN-ri'ht-HAM-ed / ˈʌn-rɪxt-ˌhæː-mɛd): Unlawful cohabitation, illicit intercourse, adultery, fornication.

wer-gild, noun (WEHR-YILD / ˈwɛr-ˌjɪld): Man-price, recompense to which a victim's family is entitled in case of wrongful death, set according to the victim's status.

wēsten-setla, noun (WAY-sten-SET-la / ˈweː-stɛn-ˌsɛt-la): Wilderness-dweller, hermit, anchorite.

wild-dēor, noun (WILLD-DAY-or / ˈwɪld-ˌdeːɔr): Wild animal (plural: *wild-dēor*).

wlitig, adjective (W'LI-tih / ˈwlɪ-tɪj): Beautiful.

10

Phoenix (*fenix*)

THE HEOROT AND HIND may be hard to defeat, but the *fēnix* (phoenix) is impossible. The *fēnix* cannot truly die, for it is reborn again and again.

The earliest account of the phoenix is from the fifth century BCE, in Herodotus' history of the Greco-Persian wars. Herodotus claims that a young phoenix will nestle its dead parent within a ball of myrrh and carry it to Heliopolis, the Temple of the Sun, for burial. The Old English version of the phoenix's story appears in the tenth-century Exeter Book. The Old English *The Phoenix* is a reworking of a Latin poem, *Carmen de ave phoenice* (*Song on the Phoenix Bird*), attributed to a North African writer named Lactantius. Lactantius, advisor to the Roman emperor during the fourth century CE, was not born Christian but converted to Christianity. He is best known for his writing that explains and promotes Christianity to educated pagans. The literature scholar John Spencer Hill explains that Lactantius' poem is 'not overtly Christian in tone or imagery', but would inspire later Christian poets with 'an irresistible literary elaboration of the story'. A pagan story could thus be expanded and shaped to better represent Christian concepts and values.

The phoenix's home

Classical writers like Herodotus do not have much to say about the phoenix's home, but it was of greater interest to later writers, Christians who wished to imagine paradise. Medieval writers usually place paradise somewhere in 'Arabia' or 'India' (but remember how imprecise such terms can be). The Old English *fēnix* lives in **neorxnawang** (paradise), a distant and beautiful land set apart from the rest of the world yet still a part of it – not the same as **heofon** (heaven). The Old English poem says this *neorxnawang* is 'far from here in the east' in a place that is, rather confusingly, both 'well known' and 'inaccessible to many men'. It is not clear exactly which humans can enter this region, but it is 'removed from the wicked through the Lord's might'. The poem says it is an island and the location of the **dūru** (door) to **heofon-rīce** (the kingdom of heaven).

Though the etymology of the Old English word for paradise remains a mystery, **wang** almost certainly refers to a field or plain. The narrator of *The Phoenix* says:

> The entire <u>plain</u> (*wong*) is <u>beautiful</u> (*wlitig*), blessed with joys, with the sweetest <u>fragrances</u> (*stencum*) of the earth … That is a <u>pleasant plain</u> (*wynsum wong*), green woods spacious under the sky.

Wang appears repeatedly throughout the poem; here it is *wlitig* (beautiful) and **wyn-sum** (pleasant). *Neorxnawang* is a land of *stencas*, but that does not make it less *wyn-sum*. From Old English **stenc** (smell) we get modern English 'stench', but in Old English *stenc* might be defined as 'fragrance', not necessarily unpleasant in the way a 'stench' or 'stink' is today. Later in *The Phoenix*, the poet describes heaven as a place where 'souls journey together with bodies in blessedness with excellent fragrances'. The association of pleasant smells or perfume and the phoenix goes back to classical authors (as when Herodotus describes the phoenix's dead parent enclosed in a ball of myrrh). The medievalist J. Holli Wheatcroft notes that in pagan times, spices were important for preparing a body for the grave or funeral pyre (which is of course what the phoenix builds for itself). The higher the individual's status and the greater their family's wealth, the more spices were used. The fragrance of such spices symbolised triumph over death, and this pagan idea is later appropriated by Christian writers. One way in which medieval Christians determined whether a person was a saint was if their dead body remained uncorrupted after having been buried for some time. The uncorrupted body wouldn't just *not* smell bad, it would exude a beautiful fragrance.

The phoenix uses aromatic herbs and spices to build its nest – the Old English poem doesn't specify which ones, but ancient writers like Pliny specify cinnamon and frankincense. Other traditions explain that one can gather spices and herbs from the phoenix's nest, although it doesn't seem like an easy thing to find. No wonder importing these luxury goods to places like England was so expensive! With its herbs, spices, enticing smells and glorious heat, Arabia was also a possible location for Heliopolis. The perfect home for a sweet-smelling, sun-loving bird like the phoenix.

But *neorxnawang* remains a more nebulous place than real-life locations like 'Arabia' or 'India' (which are, after all, accessible to many people, counter to the Old English poem's description). It is an unchanging land with no rough edges, tranquil in both climate and landscape. The **weder** (weather) is always perfectly *wlitig*, beautiful, with no extremes of hot or cold:

> No rain or snow or breath of frost, no blaze of fire or falling of hail or dropping of rime-frost, no heat of the sun or constant cold, no warm <u>weather</u> (*weder*) or wintry shower can do any harm there.

Nor are there any extremes in topography:

There are no steep hills or mountains, no stone cliffs rising high ...
There are no glens or dales or ravines, no mounds or rough ridges,
never anything that inclines too sharply ... It's a tranquil <u>victory-plain</u>
(*sigewong*). The sunny grove glistens, bright-blossomed trees that
stand forever green, with leaves that never wither. Whether winter or
summer, the wood stays the same beneath the sky, laden with fruits.

Presumably the poet means when it is winter or summer in the *rest* of
the world, since they have already made clear that seasons don't exist
in *neorxnawang*. The medievalist Daniel Calder notes the poet's language of craftsmanship, imagining God's creation 'in terms of human
adornment', with **gehroden** (adorned) trees. This paradise is ornately
artificial, nature successfully sculpted to a creator's vision. It is a **sige-
wang** (literally 'victory-plain'), which might mean 'a plain where victory is won', like a battlefield; but in this context, where no physical
battle takes place, it could refer to 'a place in which evil is overcome'.

A uniquely crafted bird

After more than eighty lines describing paradise, the poem finally
introduces the *fēnix*:

> In that wood lives a <u>bird</u> (*fugel*) wondrously fair with strong <u>wings</u>
> (*feþrum*). It is called the <u>phoenix</u> (*fenix*). The <u>solitary one</u> (*anhaga*) holds
> the land, living bravely. Never will death harm it on that <u>delightful</u>
> <u>plain</u> (*willwonge*) while the world stands.

On that **wil-wang** (delightful plain), the *fugel* (bird) is a loner, an
ān-haga. This term may relate to a suggested etymology for the creature's name. Isidore says that the Arabs use *phoenix* to mean 'singular',

and the phoenix is itself 'singular and unique in the entire world' – a kind of solitary creature that could be called an *ān-haga*. Isidore suggests another (rather more convincing) etymology: that the bird gets its name from its scarlet or purple colour, which in Latin is *phoeniceus*. Modern etymologies reveal little more. According to the *Oxford English Dictionary* the word 'phoenix' comes from ancient Greek, but beyond that its origin is unknown. But regardless of the accuracy of Isidore's suggested etymologies, the phoenix's appearance is literally one of a kind, or **ǣnlīc** in Old English (literally, 'one-like'). There is only ever one phoenix in existence on earth.

There may be only one phoenix, but there are many variations on the bird's magnificent appearance. In the fifth century BCE, Herodotus writes that some of the bird's feathers are gold, some red, and its size and shape are similar to those of an eagle. In the first century CE, Pliny provides more details: 'It is as large as an eagle, and has a gleam of gold round its neck and all the rest of it is purple, but the tail blue picked out with rose-coloured feathers and the throat picked out with tufts, and a feathered crest adorning its head.' In the thirteenth century, Pierre de Beauvais, the creator of a French prose bestiary, says that the phoenix 'wears on its head a crest like a peacock; its breast and throat are resplendent with red, and it gleams like fine gold; towards its tail, it is blue as the clear sky'. Sir John Mandeville, born in England in the fourteenth century, whose *Travels* is supposedly the account of his journeys abroad, gives a similar description but adds that the bird has purple wings, a yellow neck and a tail barred with green, yellow and red, with a beak coloured 'blue as ind'. Mandeville notes: 'He is a full fair bird to look upon, against the sun, for he shineth full gloriously and nobly.' While these accounts give a sense of the wide variety of ways in which the phoenix was seen, at least one thing draws them together: the phoenix always seems to be red and gold, and any other colours it has are *bright*. No matter where it is found, or the specifics of its plumage, from classical to medieval lore the phoenix is always an impressive and colourful sight.

This is certainly the case in the Old English *Phoenix* poem, where the *fēnix* is described in terms that make it sound more like a constructed work of art than an animal. The poet uses words like **glæs** (glass), **gim** (gem) and **gold-fæt** (gold plate) to emphasise the bird's precious qualities:

> The front of the <u>bird</u> (*fugel*) is fair of hue, its breast marked with varied colours. The back of its head is green, wonderfully mingled and blended with purple. Its tail is beautifully varied, part brown and part crimson, skilfully covered with shining splotches. Its <u>wings</u> (*fiþru*) are white on the undersides, and its neck is green up and down. Its beak gleams like <u>glass</u> (*glæs*) or a <u>gem</u> (*gim*), its jaws bright inside and out. Its eye is piercing, very much like a sparkling stone set in <u>gold plate</u> (*goldfate*) – the <u>cunning work of smiths</u> (*smiþa orþoncum*). Around its neck is a feathered circlet, bright as the sun. The underside of its belly is <u>curious</u> (*wrætlic*), wondrously fair, bright and brilliant ... Its legs are scaly with yellow feet.

The word **wrǣt-līc** means wondrous, curious or excellent and often refers to created things. The *fugel*'s eye is an ingenious and cunningly made object, an **or-þanc** (skilful contrivance) that only the finest of **smiþas** (smiths) could have created. It's probably not a coincidence that in *The Lord of the Rings*, the Old English professor and author J. R. R. Tolkien gave the name 'Orthanc' to the tower of Saruman. Saruman, a wicked but highly skilled wizard, is all about cunning contrivances. But in the context of *The Phoenix*, the word *or-þanc* has none of the negative connotations of evil sorcery, only pure admiration of God's craftsmanship. The word **frætwe** appears several times throughout the poem and could mean 'fruits', 'ornaments' or 'good works' depending on the context. *Frætwe* is most often used to describe human-crafted ornaments and adornments. In addition to the beauty of divine creation, the *fēnix* is associated with brightness and wealth. The medievalist Heather Maring observes that the poem's description of the *fēnix* includes various similes 'that align light and treasure'. When the bird is newly born, its neck is like a **hring** (ring) of sunlight, the brightest of **bēagas** (necklaces). While we might admire the beauty of the natural world today, seeing it as the opposite of human-made creations, in early medieval England it is not unusual for nature to be made beautiful in its constructed-ness: a horse might be beautified by the elegant saddle it wears, while the bright eye of a bird might be compared to a carved gemstone. Plants and trees might be made beautiful by their cultivation, by making them belong within the bounds of human civilisation.

The *fēnix* is *ǣnlīc* for reasons beyond its striking appearance. While there is only ever one member of the species on earth at any time, the bird's gender is unknown to all but God. This is an addition to phoenix lore that may have been introduced by Lactantius in the fourth century CE. But it made its way into the Old English poem, which says:

> Only God knows, the Almighty King, what <u>gender</u> (*gecynde*) it is, <u>female</u> (*wif*) or <u>male</u> (*wer*). No one knows but the Creator alone, and such a wondrous thing that is – the beautiful, ancient decree of the <u>bird's</u> (*fugles*) birth!

I've translated the passage using the pronoun 'it', but the poet uses masculine pronouns. As with the raven and dove of Chapter 4, the poet's pronouns have to do with the gender of the noun, not the creature itself, and *fēnix* is a masculine noun. **Ge-cynd** can mean 'nature', 'kind' or 'condition', but here it means 'gender' – **wīf** (female) or **wer** (male). Today a 'wife' is specifically a married woman, but Old English *wīf* refers to a woman or female creature more generally. The *wer* can be found in modern English 'werewolf', which literally means 'man-wolf'.

Nourished by sun and water

The *fēnix* also has an *ǣnlīc* diet. All it requires for nourishment is **mele-dēaw** ('honey-dew'). **Dēaw** means 'dew', but *mele* is a little more contentious. The word for honey in Old English is **hunig**, not *mele*, and this word doesn't appear on its own anywhere else. Similar 'honey' words do, however, appear in other Germanic languages, like Old High German *mili-tou* and Gothic *miliþ*. It is also oddly like *miel*, the word for honey in both modern French and Spanish. In his edition of *The Phoenix* the Old English scholar N. F. Blake translates *mele-dēaw* as 'honey-dew' or 'nectar', but it's still not certain what this substance is. After all, the poem says *mele-dēaw* 'often falls at midnight', which is unlike the sweet liquid produced by plants and more like early morning *dēaw*. Perhaps *mele-dēaw* is meant to remind us of the honeycomb Christ consumes in his first meal after his resurrection, according to the Gospel of Luke. It seems that writers have debated the phoenix's diet for many centuries. According to Pliny the phoenix eats nothing at all, while Ovid, the first classical writer to describe the phoenix's food, claims that the bird is kept alive not by seeds and herbs but by drops of incense and the sap of the cardamom plant. Claudian, a pagan poet born in Alexandria in the late fourth century, says that the phoenix feeds on 'the sun's clear beam' and 'the sea's rare spray'.

Claudian's idea of feeding on sunlight is not so strange when you consider that the phoenix is a solar bird, naturally drawn to the sun. The phoenix of Greek mythology may have been inspired by the older

legend of the bennu bird, resembling a heron, which plays a prominent role in several Egyptian creation stories. The bennu is sometimes
associated with the Egyptian sun god Re, at whose temple the sun dies
and is reborn each day. At other times Bennu is the actual name of
the Egyptian sun deity, associated with creation and rebirth. In hiero-
glyphic writing the bennu bird represents the flooding of the Nile,
which is also associated with regenerative power.

In the legend of the phoenix, as well as that of the bennu, water
plays an important role, symbolic of rebirth and regeneration. In the
Old English *Phoenix* poem the *fēnix* fixes its gaze on the sun, eagerly
watching the 'noblest of stars' rise over the ocean waves in the east.
When dark night departs, the *fēnix* is drawn to the sun, God's **tācn**
(sign). And before that *tācn* appears the *fēnix* bathes twelve times in
the **burn** (stream), the gushing waters beside which the bird makes
its home. (*Burn*, which becomes 'bourne' in Middle English, gives us
place names like Bournemouth and the River Bourne, and 'burn' is
still used in some places like Yorkshire.) During each of its twelve
baths, the *fēnix* tastes 'the delicious, sea-cold well-springs'. Once the
sun has fully risen, the *fēnix* departs from the forest, flying through
the air, making music and singing.

After a thousand years of this supremely blissful life in *neorxnawang*
the *fēnix* is ready for a change of scene. By this point the *fēnix* has lost
its scarlet and gold plumage; the Old English poem calls the old and
wise bird **haswig-feþera** (grey-feathered one). As it grows more 'slow
and sluggish' the *fēnix* knows it is time to leave home, travelling westward to seek the vast realm of **middan-geard** (the earth, literally 'middle-dwelling'), where it rules over *fugel*-kind. Even though *middan-
geard* is the earth, the poem says it remains in a region 'where no man
lives' – only birds, it seems. (*Middan-geard* can also be translated as
'middle-earth', which Tolkien uses for the name of the continent in his
Lord of the Rings.) Once it has reached *middan-geard*, the *fēnix* wings its

way westward with many *fugelas* gathering around it, wishing to serve it. They eventually reach the land of the Syrians.

The phoenix tree

The *fenix* then leaves the other *fugelas* behind and finds a safe place to live in a secret forest:

> The <u>pure</u> (*clæna*) one abruptly hastens away, so that it inhabits a wood grove in shadow, a deserted place, concealed and hidden from the multitude of men. Then it lives and dwells on a tall, firm-rooted tree in the forest beneath <u>heaven's roof</u> (*heofunhrofe*), a tree that men on earth call <u>Phoenix</u> (*Fenix*) after the <u>bird's</u> (*fugles*) name. I have heard that the King, Ruler of mankind, mighty in glory, has decreed that of all the earth's lofty trees, this one has the brightest of blossoms. No bitter evil can harm it at all. It lives forever shielded, unharmed as long as the world stands.

The *fenix* is **clæne** (clean) – pure, purified or cleansed – but this is not due to the bird's twelve baths a day. The *fenix*'s soul is pure, unmarred by sin, which is why it is able to live so close to **heofon-hrōf**, 'heaven's roof' or the vault of heaven. It will remain here in the phoenix tree until its rebirth.

What tree is this with the brightest of blossoms? While the Egyptian bennu perches in any sort of tree, the phoenix has always been associated with a palm tree in Greek and Roman texts. According to Pliny, the phoenix bird was named after the phoenix tree or date palm (*Phoenix dactylifera*), which has been cultivated for its fruit for around 6,000 years. The *Oxford English Dictionary* points out that while Pliny believes the bird to be named for the tree, other ancient writers say it is the other way round, the tree was named for the bird, and it seems like the Old English poet agrees. Modern linguists do not believe that the two Greek words that refer to 'phoenix tree' and 'phoenix bird' are connected etymologically, but the notion could explain why the phoenix is often depicted in a palm tree.

Although the phoenix tree originates in pagan texts, like the phoenix bird itself, its allegorical significance is later shaped by Christian thought. Blake explains: 'If a man shelters in Christ nothing can harm him, as nothing could harm the phoenix in its nest ... To shelter in Christ man must build a nest by means of his own good works.' The Old English poem tells how the *fēnix* builds a nest in the tree's branches, gathering the sweetest things from near and far, *wyn-sum* plants and forest fruits. The bird makes itself at home in the nest's **solor**, the home's sunny upper chamber or solarium, surrounded on all sides by holy fragrances. These pleasant-smelling herbs and spices represent a human's good deeds in life, and it is by being enveloped in these that a human gains entry to heaven. Not simply nest-building materials, the forest fruits may also represent the good deeds by which humanity can redeem itself and be allowed back into paradise. Humans have not been permitted there since the fall of Adam and Eve. This fall, of course, happens when humans eat fruit from a tree in paradise, so humanity's fall and redemption are closely linked by forest fruits.

Rebirth in flames

When the summer sun, the *gim* of the heavens, is at its hottest, the house of the *fēnix* heats up from the radiant sky until it bursts into flame:

> Plants grow warm. The pleasant hall steams with sweet odours, then
> burns in flame, in fire's grasp, the <u>bird</u> (*fugel*) with its nest. The pyre is

kindled. Fire engulfs the house of the <u>disconsolate</u> (*heorodreorges*) one, hastening fiercely, pale flame consuming and burning the <u>phoenix</u> (*fenix*), who is wise with many years.

The *fenix* is **heoru-drēorig**, which means 'disconsolate' in this context but 'blood-stained' elsewhere. **Heoru** is a fairly uncommon word for 'sword' and **drēor** means 'blood', so the compound **heoru-drēor** usually refers to blood or gore spilled in battle. But there is no reason for the *fenix* to be bloody, no indication that it has been wounded and no mention of swords. The *fugel* has merely become 'old with years gone by' and has reached the end of its life. The Old English scholar Karl P. Wentersdorf argues that while **drēorig** (from which we get 'dreary') almost certainly derives from *drēor* (blood), there is no evidence that *drēorig* ever meant 'bloody' in Old English literature. According to the Toronto *Dictionary of Old English*, the adjective *drēorig* refers to something or someone that suffers from or causes anguish, grief, horror or misery, hence the translation of *heoru-drēorig* as 'disconsolate' (although the *heoru* element remains unexplained). Other translations use phrases like 'sad unto death' or 'deathly sick', possibly to emphasise the idea of mortality hinted at by the 'sword'. Nothing else in *The Phoenix* indicates that the bird is or ought to be 'disconsolate' or 'sad'. Perhaps the poet means *heoru-drēorig* to evoke Christ's suffering on the cross prior to his resurrection, a reminder of his sacrifice. If the *fenix* is to be reborn like Christ, the bird may first need to 'suffer' in some way.

The funeral pyre, the flames kindled by the heat of the sun, consumes the 'loaned body' of the phoenix, its flesh and bone, and it is at this point that we understand the real reason why the bird is *ǣnlīc*, one of a kind. Only one phoenix can exist on earth at a time. The phoenix's lifespan varies in medieval bestiaries – sometimes 1,000 years, sometimes only 500 – but regardless of the cycle's length, a new one can only be born once its predecessor burns to ash. In general, classical writers do not have much to say concerning the phoenix's self-immolation and rebirth. This part of the legend is far more significant to later pagan and Christian writers. For Christians the phoenix can represent Christ, who is resurrected after his death, but the funeral pyre may also represent the fire of judgement in which souls will be tested at the end of days.

Bestiary sequence showing the phoenix collecting twigs for its pyre and then burning up (England, *c*.1200–1210)

The Old English poem describes what happens as the fire burns away:

After some time, life returns anew, when the cinders, congealed into a ball, begin to join together again after the fury of the flame. That most resplendent of nests, the brave bird's dwelling, is clean, reduced by the blaze. The corpse, a broken <u>bone-vessel</u> (*banfæt*), grows cool, and the conflagration subsides. Then out of the pyre, among the ashes, something round is discovered, from which a <u>worm</u> (*wyrm*) grows, wondrously fair, as though it were brought forth from an egg, shining from its shell. In the shade it grows so that it is at first like an <u>eagle's fledgling</u> (*earnes brid*), a fair <u>young bird</u> (*fugeltimber*). It flourishes joyfully, so that it has the form of a grown <u>eagle</u> (*earne*), adorned with feathers as it was in the beginning.

Like *gange-wæfre* ('walker-weaver' or spider) in Chapter 2, **bān-fæt** is a kenning. By calling the body a *bān-fæt* or 'bone-vessel', the poem emphasises mortality. This vessel is empty without a soul to animate it, just a container of bones. It makes no difference that the *bān-fæt* is now broken since the soul will find a home in a new vessel soon enough. The newly hatched phoenix is compared first to a beautiful *wyrm* (in this case most likely referring to a 'worm'), then to the *earn*'s *bridd* (eagle's fledgling). Before growing to its full size, the young *fēnix* is **fugel-timber**. *Fugel-timber* is a hapax, a word that appears only once in extant Old English, that literally means 'bird-building-material'. Today 'timber' usually refers to the wood of trees to be used in construction, but the word's meaning still has more to do with its purpose (for building) than the actual material (wood). Thus *fugel-timber* or 'bird-timber' is the makings of a new bird.

Today the best-known quality of the phoenix is its ability to self-immolate and be born anew, and among medieval Christians this version of the story is by far the most popular. Virtually all accounts after the first century CE adopt this motif. However, there is a second, older version of the tale in which the phoenix dies and its flesh putrefies. A worm emerges from the decayed flesh and feeds upon it until eventually it grows into a new phoenix. The young phoenix then carries the (now fleshless) bones of its parent to Heliopolis to lay upon the sun altar. This older motif also appears in stories about the bennu bird, which doesn't self-immolate in any extant Egyptian sources. This earlier version of the story was short-lived, although it is found in the first century in the writings of Pliny and St Clement of Rome. St Clement may have been the first Christian to introduce a 'worm' into the story, perhaps to draw a parallel between the phoenix's death and that of humans, who are eaten by worms but will rise again on Judgement Day. The earliest Christian text that describes the phoenix rising from its ashes is the *Physiologus*. The *Physiologus* also introduces a waiting period of three days between the bird's death and resurrection, making the legend even more similar to the story of Christ's resurrection (likewise three days). (It also might remind you of the lion cubs of Chapter 8, who didn't come to life – or awaken – until three days after their birth.)

According to the Old English poem, the *fēnix* gathers up the crumbled bone and ashes, adorns them with plants and then carries them away in its talons. The bird flies eastward, back home to *neorxnawang*, and buries its predecessor's remains on that island. Death, even the painful agony of dying, does not concern the *fēnix* because it understands, the poem says, 'that after the fire's violence, life will always be restored to him, life after death'.

A certain wondrous bird

The phoenix is associated with Christ, resurrection and immortality. It can also represent humanity's rebirth through the power of Christ's sacrifice. It is for this reason that some scholars believe that the mystery third animal of the Old English *Physiologus* might be a phoenix.

If you recall from this book's Prologue, the Exeter Book (in which *The Phoenix* is preserved) has three sequential animal poems that have been described as the Old English *Physiologus*. The tricky thing is, this so-called *Physiologus* is really only two poems and one tiny fragment (a mere one and a half lines of verse). The fragment follows *The Panther* and *The Whale* poems (which we'll explore in future chapters) and says only:

> *Hyrde ic secgan gen   bi sumum fugle*
> *wundorlicne* . . .
> I have been told at length about a certain bird, wondrous . . .

The poem breaks off mid-sentence at the bottom of the page, and the following folio begins mid-sentence in what may or may not be part of the same poem. It's likely that at least one page is missing from the manuscript, and nowhere does the latter text mention a bird. Even if only a single folio has been lost, that could be seventy lines or so. We don't know how the folio or folios were lost. The fragment following the bird fragment seems to be part of a sermon, and there is no particularly compelling evidence for the two to be connected. The literature scholar Michael Drout argues that the fragments differ both in their palaeography (style of handwriting) and in their source material (older texts on which their ideas are based). That leaves us very little to go by in guessing what precisely **sum** *fugel* ('some bird' or 'a certain bird') is.

Aside from it being **wundor-līc** (wondrous), all we know about the creature is that it is some kind of *fugel*, yet scholars have been titling the fragment *The Partridge* since the nineteenth century. (Like the majority of Old English texts, the medieval scribe provides no title at all.) Old English doesn't have its own word for 'partridge' as far as we know, and the partridge theory relies upon the assumption that the Exeter Book scribe used a particular Latin translation of the *Physiologus* as a model. This translation, known today as the Bern *Physiologus* because it belongs to a library in Bern, Switzerland, was created in ninth-century Reims and is the oldest extant example of an illustrated *Physiologus* text. Some scholars believe that the Exeter Book must order its animals – panther, whale, partridge – in imitation of the Bern *Physiologus*. There is no proof, however, that the Bern *Physiologus* was a model or source for the Old English *Physiologus* poems, and there is no particular reason for the Exeter Book scribe to follow the Bern manuscript's order.

A sensible way to abridge a longer *Physiologus* is to have a representative from each of the traditional animal categories: beast (on land), fish (in water) and bird (in the air). These animals could also represent a spiritual triptych: the *panþer* signifying Christ in his human form on earth, the *hwæl* representing Satan dragging sinners down to hell, and . . . *sum fugel*? The literature scholar Frederick Biggs suggests that a partridge's behaviour could be compared to that of the Antichrist, 'who, like the partridge, gathers followers whom he did not beget'. In *Physiologus* lore the partridge is known for stealing the eggs of other birds to hatch them itself, but when the young birds are fully grown they return to their true parents.

A phoenix, however, is a far more likely choice for the mystery bird, forming a satisfying triptych with the panther and whale. The *fēnix*, like the panther and whale, is a solitary creature, an *ān-haga* (unlike the partridge, which kidnaps additional family members). As we have seen, the phoenix has the powerful ability to attract other animals – and, as we shall see in later chapters, so do the other two creatures in this triptych. Despite their charisma, all three prefer to keep their distance, seeming to enjoy a life of solitude. They are also all linked by the importance of *stenc* (fragrance) in their stories. Most convincingly, the allegories of these three creatures represent Christ's three-day journey at Easter: his death on earth (Good Friday), his Harrowing of Hell (Holy Saturday) and his resurrection into heaven (Easter Sunday). The first two parts of that journey belong to the panther and the whale (and the panther is our next chapter), but it should be clear at this point how the *fénix* represents resurrection.

Any of these theories requires a lot of assumptions to be made, for all we really know is that the fragment refers to *sum fugel* (a certain bird) which is *wundor-líc* (wondrous). By now we know that a wondrous bird need not be mythical – an everyday dove can represent the Holy Spirit and an eagle can soar as high as the sun. But if we are looking for a *fugel* that – like the panther and whale – is a sweet-smelling loner appropriate for an Easter weekend allegory, the *fénix* isn't a bad choice.

Éaster (Easter) is a day of celebration, and the death of the phoenix, rather than being a sorrowful event, is a recurring miracle, a fate worth celebrating. The death of this 'good' *fugel* is joyful in that it allows for rebirth. Long before the influence of Christianity, the phoenix inspired people with its legend of rebirth, and to medieval Christians the *fénix*'s story explores the *wundor-líc* (wondrous) mystery of Christ's resurrection. The *fugel* is goodness that never truly dies.

Phoenix's Wordhord

ān-haga, noun (AHN-HA-ga / ˈaːn-ˌha-ga): Solitary being.

ǽnlíc, adjective (ANN-leech / ˈæːn-liːtʃ): Unique, peerless, incomparable.

bān-fæt, noun (BAHN-VAT / ˈbaːn-ˌvæt): Bone-vessel, the body.

béag, noun (BAY-ahg / ˈbeːag): Circular ornament; necklace; crown, circlet (plural: *béagas*).

burn, noun (BURN / ˈbʌrn): Stream, brook, river.

clǽne, adjective (KLAN-uh / ˈklæː-nə): Pure, purified, cleansed.

déaw, noun (DAY-aw / ˈdeːaw): Dew.

dréor, noun (DRAY-or / ˈdreːɔr): Blood.

drēorig, adjective (DRAY-oh-rih / ˈdreːɔ-rɪj): Suffering from or
causing anguish, grief, horror or misery.

dūru, noun (DOO-ruh / ˈduː-rʌ): Door.

ēaster, noun (AY-ah-ster / ˈeːa-stɛr): Easter.

fēnix, noun (FAY-niks / ˈfeː-nɪks): Phoenix.

frætwe, noun (FRAT-wuh / ˈfræt-wə): Adornments, ornaments,
treasure; sometimes used figuratively to refer to 'fruits of the
earth'.

fugel-timber, noun (FUH-yell-TIM-ber / ˈfʌ-jɛl-ˌtɪm-bɛr): Bird material
(which forms the fledgling), the young bird which develops.

ge-cynd, noun (yeh-KUEND / jɛ-ˈkynd): Kind, gender.

gehroden, adjective (yeh-HˈROD-en / jɛ-ˈhrɔ-dɛn): Adorned.

gim, noun (YIM / ˈjɪm): Gem, precious stone, jewel.

glæs, noun (GLASS / ˈglæs): Glass.

gold-fæt, noun (GOLD-VAT / ˈgɔld-ˌvæt): Thin plate of gold.

haswig-feþera, adjective (HA-zwih-FETH-er-ah / ˈhaz-wɪj-ˌfɛ-θɛ-ra):
Having grey feathers; used as a substantive to mean 'the grey-
feathered one'.

heofon, noun (HEH-oh-von / ˈhɛɔ-vɔn): Heaven.

heofon-hrōf, noun (HEH-oh-von-HˈROAF / ˈhɛɔ-vɔn-ˌhroːf): Roof or
vault of heaven.

heofon-rīce, noun (HEH-oh-von-REE-chuh / ˈhɛɔ-vɔn-ˌriː-tʃə):
Kingdom of heaven.

heoru, noun (HEH-or-uh / ˈhɛɔ-rʌ): Sword.

heoru-drēor, noun (HEH-or-uh-DRAY-or / ˈhɛɔ-rʌ-ˌdreːɔr): Blood, gore
(caused by a battle).

heoru-drēorig, adjective (HEH-or-uh-DRAY-oh-rih / ˈhɛɔ-rʌ-ˌdreːɔ-rɪj):
Blood-stained, drenched in blood; very sad, disconsolate; used as
a substantive to mean 'the disconsolate one'.

hring, noun (HˈRING / ˈhrɪŋ): Ring, circlet.

hunig, noun (HUN-ih / ˈhʌ-nɪj): Honey.

mele-dēaw, noun (MELL-uh-DAY-aw / 'mɛ-lə-ˌde:aw): Honey-dew, nectar.

middan-geard, noun (MID-dahn-YEH-ard / 'mɪd-dan-ˌjɛard): Middle-dwelling (between heaven and hell), the earth, world.

neorxnawang, noun (NEH-ork-snah-WAHNG / 'nɛɔrk-sna-ˌwaŋ): Paradise.

or-þanc, noun (OR-thonk / 'ɔr-θɔnk): Skilful contrivance or work, artifice.

sige-wang, noun (SIH-yuh-WAHNG / 'sɪ-jə-ˌwaŋ): Victory-plain, a plain where victory is won, a plain where evil is overcome.

smiþ, noun (SMITH / 'smɪθ): Smith, usually someone who works in metals or wood (plural: *smiþas*).

solor, noun (SOLL-or / 'sɔ-lɔr): Upper chamber; sunny room, solarium.

stenc, noun (STENCH / 'stɛntʃ): Smell, scent, odour (plural: *stencas*).

sum, adjective (sum / sʌm): Some, one of many, certain.

tācn, noun (TAH-kun / 'ta:-kən): Token, sign.

wang, noun (WAHNG / 'waŋ): Field, plain.

weder, noun (WEH-der / 'wɛ-dɛr): Weather.

wer, noun (WEHR / 'wɛr): Man, male (plural: *weras*).

wīf, noun (WEEF / 'wi:f): Woman, female (plural: *wīf*).

wil-wang, noun (WILL-WAHNG / 'wɪl-ˌwaŋ): Delightful plain, pleasant land.

wrǣt-līc, adjective (WRAT-leech / 'wræ:t-li:tʃ): Wondrous, curious, excellent.

wundor-līc, adjective (WUN-dor-leech / 'wʌn-dɔr-li:tʃ): Wondrous, exciting admiration or surprise.

wyn-sum, adjective (WUEN-zum / 'wyn-zʌm): Pleasant, agreeable; joyous.

II

Panther (*panþer*)

I F   T H E   W O N D R O U S   P H O E N I X represents Christ's triumphant resurrection to heaven, the final scene of the Easter triptych, how does the panther contribute to the allegory? *The Panther*, the first of the three so-called Old English *Physiologus* poems, is about a colourful, lovable, big cat ... just what everyone associates with Christ (especially his death and burial)!

Before clawing our way too far into religious allegory, let's consider the salient characteristics of this fabulous feline. Like the word *fēnix*, the Old English word **panþer** probably derives from Greek via Latin. A popular but not necessarily accurate theory claims that Latin *panthera* comes from Greek *pan* (all) + *thero* (wild beast), and a variety of reasons have been invented for this particular etymology. In his book on animal symbolism in English church architecture, the clergyman Arthur Collins writes that the creature was given the name in antiquity because it supposedly had 'all manner of characteristics' and was 'decked with all manner of colours'. But in the seventh century, the Spanish scholar and cleric Isidore claims the panther got its name either because 'it is the friend of "all" animals, except the dragon' (more on this later), or because 'it both rejoices in the society of its own kind and gives back whatever it receives in the same kind'.

A unique and singular nature

Like the *fēnix* of the previous chapter, the *panþer* is *wrǣt-līc* – 'curious' or 'wondrous'. A **wrǣt** is an artwork, jewel or ornament, a beautiful object created by a skilled craftsperson. We have seen in previous chapters how a *wild-dēor* (wild animal) like a panther or phoenix can be beautiful in a constructed sort of way. In Old English poetry these carefully crafted creatures are the handiwork of the Creator, jewels of God's creation. Also like the *fēnix*, the *panþer* is adorned in many different colours. Pliny notes that the panther and tiger 'almost alone of beasts are distinguished by a variety of markings, whereas the rest have a single colour, each kind having its own'. We typically imagine panthers as black, but a black panther is actually a darker, melanistic variant of the leopard and jaguar, which have spots of different colours. Black panthers aren't really a solid black but have patterns of spots and rosettes; it's just that these can be harder to see because of their dark colour.

The Old English *Panther* poem describes the animal's unique appearance, comparing its fur to Joseph's famous multicoloured **tunece** (tunic or coat) from Genesis 37:

He is a <u>curious</u> (*wrætlic*) animal, shining wondrously in every colour. Heroes, holy-spirited men, say that just as Joseph's <u>coat</u> (*tunece*) was woven in shades of every colour, each gleaming brighter and <u>more unique</u> (*ænlicra*) than the others for the children of men, so is this animal's appearance: <u>dark</u> (*blæc*) in each of its hues, gleaming wondrously, brighter and more radiantly, so each hue is <u>more curious</u>

(*wrætlicra*) than the next, yet <u>more unique</u> (*ænlicra*) and more beautiful, dazzling with ornaments, always more extraordinary.

Both Joseph's coat and the *panþer's* fur are curious and beautiful, *wrǣt-līc* and *ǣnlīc* (unique), words also used to describe the *fēnix*. The creature's many colours may symbolise the countless, wondrous attributes of God. It may sound strange to describe something of many hues as **blæc** (from which we get modern English 'black'), but something dark, if also shiny and gleaming, can actually seem 'bright'. Within the dark hue of the panther's fur one can glimpse all the other colours dazzling in the light. Old English *blæc* is not necessarily a specific hue and can also refer to the way in which light reflects off a surface. Medieval bestiaries describe the panther as 'a beautiful beast', referencing Psalm 44, which says that Christ is 'beautiful above the sons of men', and this shining multicoloured cat's beauty is certainly one of a kind.

By his nature, Christ is separate from humanity, apart from and incomparable to other beings, and the *panþer* is also unique among animals in a positive way. *The Panther* says the animal has a **sundor-gecynd** (singular nature), a *ge-cynd* (nature) that is 'asunder' from others. The *panþer* is an **ān-stapa** – a lone wanderer, literally 'one-step-per' – always on its own, even when surrounded by those who love it. And this *dēor* has many admirers, for it is mild, modest, gentle, amiable and loving, the friendliest of animals.

As Isidore tells us when explaining its name, the *panþer* is in fact a **frēond** (friend) to all creatures except for the *draca* (dragon). This is because, of all the creatures, it cannot forgive the *draca's* evil deeds, and so the *panþer* remains forever **and-wrāþ** (hostile) towards it. The prefix *and-* means 'against', so to be *and-wrāþ* is to feel **wrāþ** (wrathful) towards something or someone, wishing to cause harm. The Old English poem says the *panþer* will harm no one except for the *draca*, but the *draca* is its **fyrn-geflita** (ancient foe). **Ge-flit** means 'contention', 'discord', 'dispute', 'quarrel' or 'altercation', separation that results from personal conflict, while **fyrn** is an ancient word for 'ancient', used up until the sixteenth century. We've seen how medieval bestiaries often depict the deer in opposition to its arch-enemy, the snake, and the same is true for the panther and the dragon. Bestiaries typically show a large cat-like creature surrounded by all different kinds of happy creatures except for the dragon, who either cowers before it or tries to hide in a hole. You can probably guess the dragon's symbolism – that *fyrn-geflita* of all that is good, Satan. Christ is friends with all the faithful, but Satan knows to cower in his presence.

A panther is loved by all animals but the dragon in this bestiary illustration
(England, *c.*1200–1210)

The holiness of food and a good nap

Our previous Christ-figure animal, the phoenix, lived on a simple diet – sunshine, sea spray and a bit of *mele-dēaw* (nectar). In *The Phoenix* it seems as though the *fēnix* simply eats to live, but does the subject of *The Panther* lead such an ascetic existence? No! The poem specifically tells us that the *panþer enjoys* its **foddor** (food, from which we get 'fodder'). But although we know that the panther takes pleasure from eating, its *foddor* of choice remains unspecified. The Old English scholar Michelle Hoek says that although it is possible that the poet did not know about or wished to hide the panther's carnivorous diet, its meal is more likely unspecified in order to (of course) encourage allegorical thinking. Hoek suggests that the *foddor* is really 'a spiritual repast like the Eucharist'. The Eucharist – bread and wine consumed at Mass, believed to be the body and blood of Christ – feeds the spirit rather than the body. Being overly interested in feeding the body may be a sin, but feeding the spirit can only be a good thing. Hoek compares the *panþer*'s meal to Christ's Last Supper, one of the holiest events in the Bible for medieval Christians.

When the *panþer* finishes its *foddor*, it seeks rest in a secret place, hiding away in its home in the **dūn-scræfu** (mountain gorges or caves). The word **scræf** means 'cave' or 'hollow place in the earth', but it can also refer to a 'den' or 'miserable dwelling', so the *panþer* does not live in luxury. 'Shraf' continued to be used during the Middle English period, but then 'cave' entered English via Old French – and we know which one survived into the modern period. In its secret, subterranean den, the *panþer* is 'swept away by slumber', completely overcome by sleep for three nights (three days/three nights – by this point we know what that symbolises . . .). But just as its appetite is not due to the sin of gluttony, the *panþer*'s long nap is not because of the sin of slothfulness. Instead, the *panþer*'s three-day sleep in a cave represents (you guessed it) the three days Christ lay in his grave before his resurrection. (Here is where we get the death and burial theme of the *Physiologus* triptych from the previous chapter.) *The Panther* says:

> Then on the third day the <u>brave</u> (*ellenrof*) one quickly rises from his sleep, endowed with <u>might</u> (*þrymme*).

Ellen is 'strength' or 'courage', while **rōf** means 'valiant' or 'brave', and together the words make a poetic compound that is doubly daring. But what is **ellen-rōf** (brave, strong) about a sleeping panther? The poet envisions Christ (and, by extension, the panther) as brave and strong in his sacrifice, a warrior instead of a victim. Christ willingly sacrifices himself to save humankind, and that is what endows him (and thus the panther) with **þrymm** (power or majesty). The thirteenth-century bestiary Bodley 764 says that Christ 'falls asleep and rests in the grave' before descending to the underworld, where he 'chains the great dragon', a reference, once again, to the Harrowing of Hell. This 'great dragon' is, of course, Satan, who fears Christ just as the *draca* dreads the *panþer*.

Sweet smells and sounds

The Panther recounts what happens when the *ellen-rōf* warrior awakes from his three-day slumber:

> A <u>sound</u> (*sweghleoþor*), the loveliest of songs, comes from the wild beast's <u>mouth</u> (*muð*). A <u>fragrance</u> (*stenc*) follows the <u>voice</u> (*stefn*), coming from that place, hot breath that is lovelier, sweeter and stronger than any scent, more than the blossoms of plants and forest fruits, nobler than all the earth's treasures. Then many bands of spear-

wielding warriors travel the earth from cities, royal thrones and castle halls, with forces of people and troops, hurrying hastily. <u>Animals</u> (*deor*) also travel towards that <u>voice</u> (*stefne*) and <u>fragrance</u> (*stenc*).

Like the *fēnix*, the *panþer* is associated with the finest fragrances, a beautiful *stenc*. The word **swēg-hlēoþor** (voice or sound) is also linked to these two animals, the melody of vocal music, like choirs of angels. So irresistible and enticing are the alliterative *stenc* (STENCH) and **stefn** (STEH-vun), fragrance and voice, that all kinds of people and *dēor* alike travel the earth towards their source, in this case the panther's **mūþ** (mouth).

In the context of the Old English poem, the panther's *stenc* and *stefn* are positive things, but that was not always the case. Hoek notes that in classical (pagan) natural histories, the ability of the panther to produce a tantalising scent is how it hunts down prey. Pliny writes that 'all four-footed animals are wonderfully attracted' by the panther's smell, although they become frightened at the sight of its head's 'savage appearance'. According to Pliny, a panther must hide its terrifying head and use its fragrance to attract prey. This luring technique of the panther appears as early as the writings of Aristotle and is repeated by other scholars of ancient Greece and Rome.

This more sinister reason for the panther's smell is repeated by Bartholomaeus Anglicus in the thirteenth century, but most Christian sources modify the material to make a more suitable allegory. The manuscript curator Ann Payne explains that medieval texts alter the classical tradition of the exploitative, killer panther, instead likening the irresistible breath to Christ's 'all-pervasive sweetness', with which he attracts humankind. Medieval bestiaries draw upon the wording in the Psalms, verses describing God's word as 'sweet' to the palate, like 'honey' in one's mouth. In the Old English *Panther* poem we are not told what happens to the people and animals once they reach the panther, only that they are drawn to him from far and wide. The eventual encounter with the panther may symbolise the Last Judgement, after which, Hoek says, 'those who were drawn by the *stenc* of Christ's goodness and sacrifice will dwell forever in paradise with him'.

Thus a dangerous beast is transformed by medieval Christian thought to signify Christ himself. The panther's breath, once a threat and form of deception, becomes the means of drawing humanity to goodness and truth. In the next chapter, however, we will see that not every classical creature gets this medieval makeover, and that one animal's goodness could be another *dēor*'s deception.

Panther's Wordhord

and-wrāþ, adjective (AND-WRAWTH / ˈand-ˌwraːθ): Hostile, antagonistic (towards something).

ān-stapa, noun (AHN-STAH-pa / ˈaːn-ˌsta-pa): Lone wanderer (one-stepper).

blæc, adjective (BLACK / ˈblæːk): Black, or of dark hue.

dūn-scræf, noun (DOON-SHRAFF / ˈduːn-ˌʃræf): Mountain gorge, mountain cave (plural: *dūn-scræfu*).

ellen, noun (EL-len / ˈɛl-lɛn): Courage, strength.

ellen-rōf, adjective (EL-len-ROAF / ˈɛl-lɛn-ˌroːf): Brave, strong.

foddor, noun (FOD-dor / ˈfɔd-dɔr): Food.

frēond, noun (FRAY-ond / ˈfreːɔnd): Friend.

fyrn, adjective (FUERN / ˈfyrn): Long ago, ancient.

fyrn-geflita, noun (FUERN-yeh-VLIT-ah / ˈfyrn-jɛ-ˌvlɪ-ta): Ancient enemy, long-standing foe.

ge-flit, noun (yeh-VLIT / jɛ-ˈvlɪt): Contention, discord; dispute, quarrel or altercation; separation (resulting from conflict).

mūþ, noun (MOOTH / ˈmuːθ): Mouth (plural: *mūþas*).

panþer, noun (PAHN-ther / ˈpan-θɛr): Panther.

rōf, adjective (ROAF / ˈroːf): Valiant, strong, brave.

scræf, noun (SHRAFF / ˈʃræf): Cave, hollow place in the earth; miserable dwelling, den.

stefn, noun (STEH-vun / ˈstɛ-vən): Voice.

sundor-gecynd, noun (SUN-dor-yeh-KUEND / ˈsʌn-dɔr-jɛ-ˌkynd): Peculiar or unique nature.

swēg-hlēoþor, noun (SWAY-H'LAY-oh-thor / ˈsweːj-ˌhleːɔ-θɔr): Sound, voice.

tunece, noun (TUN-eh-chuh / ˈtʌ-nɛ-tʃə): Tunic, coat.

þrymm, noun (THRUEM / ˈθrym): Power, might; glory, majesty, magnificence, greatness.

wrāþ, adjective (WRAWTH / ˈwraːθ): Angry, wrathful, incensed.

wrǣt, noun (WRAT / ˈwræːt): Work of art, a jewel or ornament.

The Bad

You've probably noticed by now that 'good' animals are often counterbalanced with 'bad' ones, and these arch-enemies all seem to have one thing in common – their association with Satan. The Christ-like deer hates snakes, and the friendly Jesus-panther loves everyone but the dragon. That great adversary of pagan stories – the dragon – became associated with Satan after early medieval England's conversion to Christianity. The name 'Satan' derives from the Hebrew word *śāṭān*, meaning 'adversary' or 'person who plots against another'. This next section will include those standard adversaries of medieval lore, snake and dragon, but there are plenty of other creatures who were in the bad books of Old English speakers.

Remember the beasts of battle in Chapter 1 – eagle, raven and wolf? Here, the wolf returns. While the eagle and the raven at least seem to communicate (or put up) with one another, the wolf is a real recluse, and not in a good way. Although we've seen holy hermits, the one-of-a-kind phoenix and that wandering loner, the panther, solitude is not always a good sign. A person with no companions in early medieval England was extremely vulnerable. If someone were accused of a crime – unless they were caught red-handed – they could prove their innocence by assembling credible friends and family to vouch for their good character. 'Friendless' (*frēond-lēas*) is a term that appears in law codes to refer specifically to people who lack those invaluable 'oath-helpers'. Exile from one's community was perhaps the worst non-capital punishment – you had no one to protect or support you, becoming an outlaw, someone 'who may be killed like a wolf, without fear of penalty'. If no one wants to be your companion, well . . . there may be a reason for that.

The 'bad' *dēor* have a negative image in Old English texts and also in the bestiaries of the later Middle Ages. They are cunning and deceitful, doing their best to make the unwary sinner take a wrong step. But is this always the case? The lioness, after all, was in the 'good' section, but she is known in some sources to be ferocious and untameable. And before the influence of Christianity, the 'good' panther's breath was a weapon of deception. If a 'good' creature can sometimes be 'bad', is the opposite true?

12

Whale (*hwæl*)

YOU MIGHT HAVE THOUGHT, given their bitter enmity, that the creature to follow the panther in the Old English *Physiologus* would be the dragon. But no: it is the fearsome, the terrible, the famously all-round bad guy... the whale. Like the *panþer*, the **hwæl** (whale) has a sweet-scented breath that is irresistible to other animals. But while Christian writers modified the panther's story so that this breath became a good thing, signifying the harmless and beautiful sweetness of Christ, the whale's sweet breath remains predatory and evil in medieval texts.

Deadly breath

The Old English poem describes the *hwæl*:

> When hunger troubles it in the ocean and the hostile fighter (*aglæcan*) lusts (*lysteþ*) for sustenance, then the sea-guardian (*mereweard*) opens its mouth (*muð*), its wide lips. A delightful smell (*stenc*) comes from its innards, a quality that deceives other sea-fish-kind (*sæfisca cynn*),

who swim <u>water-quick</u> (*sundhwate*) to where the sweet <u>smell</u> (*stenc*) emanates. There they go, an unwary throng, until the gaping maw is filled. Then suddenly savage jaws crash together around the <u>spoils of war</u> (*herehuþe*).

The *hwæl* is an **āglǣca**, a word that modern translators often gloss as 'monster' but is actually a more neutral term like 'hostile fighter' or 'fierce combatant'. (In *Beowulf* the word applies both to heroes like Beowulf and Sigemund as well as to villains of questionable humanity like Grendel.) Even though it plunders the **here-hūþ** (spoils of war) of the ocean, the *hwæl* is also known as the **mere-weard** (sea-guardian). This doesn't necessarily have caring connotations: the one who guards the sea takes what it wants from it, not exactly 'guarding' other sea creatures. The adjective **hwæt** means 'quick', 'active' or 'bold', usually a positive, but the **sund-hwæt** (water-quick) fish which rush towards the whale are in fact hastening to their doom.

While the *panþer* enjoys a good meal, it is never perceived as a glutton; but when the *hwæl* lures an 'unwary throng' of fish into its *mūþ* (mouth) it is representative of greed. The verb used in the context of the whale's hunger is **lystan** (to desire), from which we get 'to lust (for something)'. Lust, like gluttony, is one of the deadly sins. Michelle Hoek argues that the whale's image is even worse because it is 'undeniably portrayed as a cannibal'. The first line of *The Whale* identifies the *hwæl* as **fisca cynn** (fish-kind), while the passage quoted above says that he deceives and consumes **sǣ-fisca cynn** (sea-fish-kind). So, as far as the writer is concerned, the whale and fish are of the same family, the same fish kind (instead of distinguishing the whale as a mammal like we would today). This makes the whale's deceptive actions even more despicable, even cannibalistic as it's consuming its own kind. In Old English a **fisc** (pronounced FISH) could be any sort of animal that lives exclusively in the water, less specific than our 'fish' of today.

Here-hūþ refers primarily to wartime plunder, frequently appearing in historical chronicles. At other times, like in *The Whale*, it refers to an animal's prey. But *here-hūþ* may also refer to the souls of the damned, whom the unfortunate *fiscas* (the plural of *fisc*) represent. It is absent from the Old English poem, but the whale's victims are described in greater detail in later texts like the Middle English *Physiologus*, which explains: 'Although he deceives the small fish, the large ones he cannot seize.' The small fish represent humans of little faith, who are easily lured by the Devil to their doom, while the large fish, those of greater faith, have a better chance of resisting him. The whale's gaping maw signifies the entrance to hell, which medieval art often depicts as a beast's mouth opened wide and full of demons. The sinners (fish) are tempted inside by the Devil's deceiving words (the whale's sweet breath). The Old English poem compares the *fisc* that gets swallowed by the *hwæl* to a human who lives their **lǣne** (loaned or temporary) time without care. One's time on earth is fleeting, and if you lack the willpower or concern to avoid the Devil's temptations, you face the fate of the *fisc* who is deceived by a sweet *stenc*. Of such careless, hellbound sinners *The Whale* says: 'Those who enter there do not control their movement towards the deceitful one – an eternal exit – any more than the swimming fishes might turn from the whale's embrace.'

Beware the false island

The luring technique of the *hwæl* in the Old English poem extends from its mouth to its back. While its smell is a threat to fish, its appearance lures human victims. *The Whale* explains:

> Seafarers often meet it by accident ... Its appearance is like rough stone (*stane*), the greatest sea-bank, crumbling near the water's edge

(*ofre*), clothed in sand dunes, so that sea travellers think they are looking at some <u>island</u> (*ealond*).

The whale's rough grey back resembles **stān** (stone) at the **ōfer** (water's edge). *Ōfer*, a word with cognates in Old Frisian and Middle Dutch, is a margin or edge beside water, such as a riverbank or seashore. The word becomes obsolete by the end of the Middle Ages, surviving in only a few place names like Over (Cambridgeshire) and Wendover (Buckinghamshire). The *hwæl*'s back is a false **ēa-land** (island) that draws weary sailors with its tantalising promise of solid ground on which to rest. (We saw the *ēa* of *ēa-land* in Chapter 6, where it means 'river', although this *ēa-land* is in the sea.)

The *ēa-land* is in fact an **un-land**, land that is not land:

Men moor their tall <u>ships</u> (*scipu*) with anchor-ropes to the <u>false land</u> (*unlonde*), settling their <u>sea-steeds</u> (*sæmearas*) at the water's end and going boldly upon that <u>island</u> (*eglond*). Encircled by the current, the <u>ships</u> (*ceolas*) remain secure near the shore. The weary seafarers, expecting no danger, make camp on the <u>island</u> (*ealonde*), lighting a flame and kindling a great fire. The men are joyous but weary, ready for rest.

In this passage there are two different spellings for *ēa-land*: *eglond* and *ealonde*. These are all pronounced roughly the same (the 'g' is soft), and they demonstrate again how standardised spelling was not yet a thing. Even within the same text a scribe might spell a word in different ways! This passage also contains three words for 'ship', one of which has the same pronunciation in modern English, although its spelling has changed: **scip**. Another 'ship' word, **cēol** (pronounced CHAY-oll), frequently appears in poetic contexts. In Old English it is simply a seaworthy vessel, although as early as the fourteenth century a 'keel' is more specifically a flat-bottomed vessel, especially one for carrying charcoal, or the lowermost timber of a ship. The third 'ship' word is the kenning **sǣ-mearh**, literally 'sea-horse' or 'sea-steed'. (From *mearh* we get modern English 'mare', a female horse, but Old English **mearh** is any horse.) Ships, after all, are the steeds of sailors.

The unwitting, unfortunate sailors make themselves comfortable on the *un-land*. The *hwæl* may have been basking in the sun long enough for grass and shrubs to sprout from its back, adding to its disguise. But as soon as the *hwæl* feels the sailors' campfire burning, it plunges to the bottom of the sea:

> When the one who is crafty in deceit senses the travellers are secure, making camp and wishing for fair weather, all of a sudden it plunges down into the salty waves. The ocean's spirit (*gæst*) seeks the abyss (*grund*), delivering his plunder to the hall of death (*deaðsele*), ships (*scipu*) with their drowned men.

Here the whale is a *gǣst* of the ocean. **Gǣst** (also *gāst*) can loosely be defined as 'spirit', but it can be a variety of things: breath or air, one's vital spirit or the incorporeal part of one's being, a spiritual force, one's disposition or temper, courage or mettle, or the soul after death. Sometimes it is a ghost, a heavenly spirit like an angel, the Holy Spirit (or Holy Ghost), an evil spirit, demon or fiend, or the Devil. A *gǣst* might even be a natural phenomenon – like fire, frost or a tempest – personified as a living spirit. In the case of the whale, *gǣst* is probably meant to make us think of the Devil or a demon, since **dēaþ-sele** (hall of death) is a poetic term for **hell** (hell). **Grund** (from which we get 'ground') is the bottom, the deepest part of something, so it could be either the sea floor or *hell*, the great abyss.

Sailors mistake a whale for an island in the Harley Bestiary
(England, *c.*1230–40)

The Devil's deep dive

The *hwæl*'s deep dive is symbolic of the Devil's temptation of unwitting sinners, who are inevitably dragged down to *hell*. This dramatic episode is understandably one of the most popular subjects for whale illustrations in later medieval bestiaries. While there are no images of this scene in extant Old English manuscripts, the story of sailors camping out on the *hwæl*'s back is the focal point of *The Whale*. The Old English poem explains:

> When, from <u>eternal torment</u> (*cwicsusle*), the insidious and shameless <u>fiend</u> (*feond*) perceives that each living creature, each human, is confined securely within its circuit, it then becomes their life-slayer through cruel artifice, killer of the proud and the abject who sinfully perform its will. Among them, it is covered by its <u>helm of concealment</u> (*heolophelme*), and, deprived of good things, it seeks out <u>hell</u> (*helle*) at once, the bottomless surge beneath a <u>misty gloom</u> (*mistglome*). The great <u>whale</u> (*hwæl*) submerges those sailors, men and their <u>wave-steeds</u> (*yðmearas*).

In addition to *dēofol* (devil), Old English has the word *fēond* (fiend), which can refer to mortal enemies as well as supernatural ones (and to the Devil, the greatest enemy of all). The Old English scholar Jennifer Neville observes: 'Old English poets do not appear to have made a distinction between a "natural" and "devilish" whale; they mix epithets suitable for animals with those suitable for demons.' When something 'quickens' in modern English, it is animated or reanimated with life; **cwic-sūsl** then literally means 'living torment'. It can also mean 'eternal punishment' and is used to refer to hell (although hell is a place you might go when you are no longer alive, your experience of it is sure to be eternal and fairly lively). The torment 'lives' in that it never dies or never ends: it is eternal.

The *fēond*'s **heolop-helm** (helmet of concealment) is an intriguing accoutrement. The word appears only once in Old English, unless you count another instance in a poetic retelling of Genesis, where we find the very similar *hælep-helm* (literally 'hero-helmet'). A 'hero-helmet' might make sense here, but in the context of the whale it is worn by a demon, a force of evil rather than heroism, which makes it rather unlikely. The Toronto *Dictionary of Old English* defines *heolop-helm* as a 'helmet which makes the wearer invisible, helmet of deception'. Another Old English poem calls hell's inhabitants **heolop-cynn**, which could be translated as 'concealment-kind', a race living in darkness, again linking demons to concealment. Concealment is much more likely than heroism in the context of *The Whale*, since the *hwæl*, like the Devil, conceals itself until it is too late to escape its power. Both sinners and sailors are whisked down into the **mist-glōm**, 'mist-gloom' or 'darkness caused by mist'. Sailors and their **ȳþ-mearas** ('wave-steeds', another ship kenning) are taken to their own *cwic-sūsl*, a place of suffering, their punishment for trusting in the evil one and for letting down their guard on an unfamiliar shore.

Fastitocalon and other tricksters of the sea

Hwæl could refer to any whale (or indeed to any large marine animal – a dolphin, porpoise or walrus, for instance), not necessarily a cunning, false-island one. But the Old English *Whale* poem explains that this specific *hwæl* is named Fastitocalon, and he is a baddie for sure. The poem begins:

> Now with words, through thought and song-craft, I will tell a tale about a kind of fish (*fisca cynn*), the great whale (*hwale*). Seafarers often meet him by accident. Everyone gives him the name Fastitocalon, he who floats in the ancient streams.

Fastitocalon may be a corrupted form of *aspidochelon*, a word from Greek and Latin sources that means 'asp-turtle'. One medieval bestiary explains that Latin *aspido* means 'tortoise', which does seem rather un-whale-like. The Middle English *Physiologus* describes a whale in very similar terms to the Old English one, but this animal is instead called Cetegrande, which literally means 'big whale'. Today large aquatic mammals like whales and dolphins are called Cetaceans.

Fastitocalon, Cetegrande and the *aspidochelon* are not the only false islands of the Middle Ages. St Brendan, an Irish monk of the sixth century, encounters one during his wanderings in search of paradise. One night, after a long day sailing, Brendan's fellow monks disembark on an 'island' to rest, but Brendan himself remains on the boat. When the monks build a fire to boil water the next morning, much to their horror, the island starts to move. This is because it is in fact the giant fish Jasconius, a name deriving from Irish *iasc* (fish). The oldest extant account of this episode is from the tenth or eleventh century, which includes the rather bizarre detail that Jasconius has always wanted to join its head to its tail but cannot because of its extraordinary length. Perhaps it's about to attempt this feat that morning. Fortunately for the sailors, God reveals the island's true nature to Brendan in time for him to guide his monks to safety. Jasconius is somewhat unusual in his benevolence; he allows the fooled humans to escape. But maybe he didn't have a choice: the unwitting sailors do, after all, have a saint on their side.

The historian of cartography Chet Van Duzer thinks it likely that the Jasconius story was inspired by the *Physiologus* whale, but he points out many examples of the false-island narrative that surface across time and cultures. A similar tale appears in the fourth-century Babylonian *Talmud*, and the Arab writer al-Jahiz describes a whale-island in his ninth-century *Book of the Animals*. An island that is actually a giant sea turtle features in the work of the thirteenth-century Persian physician al-Qazwini. In the adventures of Sinbad in *One Thousand and One Nights*, sailors start a fire on a whale-island, which ends up drowning them all. The Swedish cartographer Olaus Magnus writes in the sixteenth century about the wonders of his homeland, one of which is a whale that looks like an island. The classicist Cornelia Coulter points out that Olaus's Scandinavian whale-island may have inspired the seventeenth-century English poet John Milton's description of the sea serpent Leviathan. In *Paradise Lost*, he writes:

> Leviathan, which God of all his works
> Created hugest that swim th' Ocean stream:
> Him haply slumbring on the Norway foam
> The Pilot of some small night-founder'd Skiff
> Deeming some Island, oft, as Sea-men tell,
> With fixed Anchor in his skaly rind
> Moors by his side under the Lee . . .

Later in the poem, Milton describes Leviathan's appearance:

> Hugest of living Creatures, on the Deep
> Stretcht like a Promontorie sleeps or swimmes,
> And seems a moving Land . . .

Each of these false-island tales warns that if something is too good to be true, it probably is.

The whale, it seems, is never to be trusted. Yet in the Old English *Whale* poem the wicked *hwæl*, like the Christ-like *fēnix* and *panþer*, is still *wrǣt-līc*. A monster is still wondrous, curious, excellent, even a work of art (*wrǣt*) in its own way. An animal is an example of God's craftsmanship, even when it is the creature 'created hugest' of all his works.

Whale's Wordhord

āglǣca, noun (AH-GLACK-ah / ˈɑː-ˌglæː-ka): Hostile fighter, fierce combatant, great opponent.

cēol, noun (CHAY-oll / ˈtʃeːɔl): Ship, sea-going vessel.

cwic-sūsl, noun (KWITCH-SOO-zull / ˈkwɪtʃ-ˌsuː-zəl): Living torment, eternal punishment; hell.

dēaþ-sele, noun (DAY-ath-SEH-luh / ˈdeːaθ-ˌsɛ-lə): Hall of death.

dēofol, noun (DAY-oh-voll / ˈdeːɔ-vɔl): Devil, demon; Satan, the Devil.

ēa-land, noun (AY-ah-LOND / ˈeːa-ˌland): Island.

fēond, noun (FAY-ond / ˈfeːɔnd): Fiend, devil; enemy.

fisc, noun (FISH / ˈfɪʃ): Fish; any animal that lives exclusively in the water (plural: *fiscas*).

fisca cynn, noun (FISK-ah KUEN / ˈfɪ-ska ˈkyn): Fish-kind.

gǣst, noun (GAST / ˈgæːst): Spirit.

grund, noun (GRUND / ˈgrʌnd): Bottom, lowest part of anything; solid bottom or earth underlying something; abyss; ground.

hell, noun (HELL / ˈhɛl): Hell.

heoloþ-cynn (HEH-oh-loth-KUEN / ˈhɛɔ-lɔθ-ˌkyn): Concealment-kind, the inhabitants of hell, possibly 'race living in concealment or darkness'.

heoloþ-helm, noun (HEH-oh-loth-HELM / ˈhɛɔ-lɔθ-ˌhɛlm): Helmet of concealment or deception.

here-hūþ, noun (HEH-ruh-HOOTH / ˈhɛ-rə-ˌhuːθ): Spoils of war, booty, loot, plunder.

hwæl, noun (H'WAL / ˈhwæl): Whale (also referring to any of various large marine mammals).

hwæt, adjective (H'WAT / ˈhwæt): Quick, swift; vigorous, active; bold, brave.

lǣne, adjective (LAN-uh / ˈlæː-nə): Loaned, not permanent, transitory, temporary.

lystan, verb (LUE-stahn / ˈly-stan): To desire, to lust for (something/ someone).

mearh, noun (MEH-ar'h / ˈmɛarx): Horse.

mere-weard, noun (MEH-ruh-WEH-ard / ˈmɛ-rə-ˌwɛard): Sea-guardian, one who keeps guard in the sea.

mist-glōm, noun (MIST-GLOAM / ˈmɪst-ˌgloːm): Mist-gloom, darkness caused by mist.

ōfer, noun (OH-ver / ˈoː-vɛr): Edge, border, margin; land that borders water, a bank or shore.

sǣ-fisca cynn, noun (SAE-FISK-ah KUEN / ˈsæː-ˌfɪ-ska ˈkyn): Sea-fish-kind, any creature that lives in the sea.

sǣ-mearh, noun (SAE-MEH-ar'h / ˈsæː-ˌmɛarx): Ship (sea-horse).

scip, noun (SHIP / ˈʃɪp): Ship.

stān, noun (STAHN / ˈstaːn): Stone, rock.

sund-hwæt, adjective (SUND-H'WAT / ˈsʌnd-ˌhwæt): Water-quick, active in swimming.

un-land, noun (UN-LOND / ˈʌn-ˌland): False land.

ȳþ-mearh, noun (UETH-MEH-ar'h / ˈyːθ-ˌmɛarx): Ship (wave-steed) (plural: *ȳþ-mearas*).

13

Snake (*nædre*)

ERHAPS A MORE FAMILIAR symbol for deceit today than the *hwæl* is the serpent, a creature that many Christian texts associate with the Devil. The Book of Genesis says that the serpent (Latin *serpens*) is 'more subtle than any of the beasts of the earth which the Lord God had made'. This serpent tempts Eve to taste the forbidden fruit, which leads to humanity's fall from God's grace and expulsion from paradise. It might make you wonder why God created such an animal in the first place.

In ancient (pagan) literature, the snake is well known for its subtlety. Pliny notes a snake's ability to camouflage itself, explaining that most serpents 'have the colour of the earth that they usually lurk in'. But despite their skill for deception, snakes in ancient Rome are not necessarily 'bad'. J. Holli Wheatcroft notes that they have 'a predominantly positive reputation', associated with fertility, healing and prophecy. They are seen as 'beneficent spirits of the dead' and are even kept as pets. It is unlikely that snakes in early medieval England were perceived in the same way.

The repentant sinner

Both ancient and medieval writers note the snake's ability to shed its skin, and in the case of the Christian *Physiologus* tradition this signifies a repentant sinner seeking spiritual renewal. The *Physiologus* explains that the snake renews itself by shedding its skin when it becomes weak with age. In one of his homilies, Ælfric says:

> The <u>snake</u> (*næddre*) each year <u>casts away</u> (*awurpð*) its old covering and is then clothed in a completely new <u>skin</u> (*felle*). Let us do likewise, <u>casting away</u> (*awurpan*) our sins and evil habits and learning good things, so that we, with God's grace, may be clothed within.

In this Old English text the snake is indeed a sinner, but a repentant one. Let us **a-wurpan** (cast away) our sins and bad habits as easily as the *nædre* casts away its **fell** (skin)!

In this passage Ælfric uses the word **nædre**, Old English for 'snake', from which we get modern English 'adder'. By the time the word reached Middle English, people were already starting to spell it without the initial 'n'. In the Middle English *South English Legendary* from the late thirteenth century, we find the word spelled with and without the 'n' within two lines of verse: 'An Addre it hadde bi-clupt a-boute al naked with-oute skinne— / Þat was þat treo and þe Naddre.' In this case, the 'n' has moved from the beginning of 'naddre' to the end of the preceding word, turning the indefinite article 'a' into 'an'. (The same thing happened with the word 'orange': when it entered European languages from Persian and Arabic, it originally had an 'n' at the beginning. In Italian *narancia* became *arancia* and in French *narange* became *orange* due to confusion when the word was combined with the preceding articles *una* or *une*. From there, the word made its way into English.) The most common word for 'snake' in Old English is not *nædre* but *wyrm*, although (as we saw in Chapter 2 with the spider, an 'air worm') a *wyrm* might be anything from an earthworm to a parasite to an insect to a dragon. In Latin it's easier to tell which animal is which: a *lumbricus* is an earthworm, a *serpens* is a snake, a *draco* is a dragon, a *parasitus* is a parasite (and also a guest!). With Old English *wyrm*, you have to figure out what the creature is from the context.

A less common word than both *wyrm* and *nædre* is **snaca**, from which we get 'snake'. A *snaca* could be a snake or a reptile. In the Gospel of Luke it is a scorpion. In the Latin translation of Luke's Gospel Christ tells his disciples, 'Behold, I have given you power to tread upon <u>serpents</u> (*serpentes*) and <u>scorpions</u> (*scorpiones*), and upon all the power of the enemy: and nothing shall hurt you.' But in the Old English translation of this verse, Christ presents the disciples with the power to tread upon *nædran* and *snacan* – snakes and more snakes, unless 'scorpion' is an alternative definition of *snaca*. There is another Old English word for 'scorpion' that could have been used instead – **þrowend** – so it's possible that the translator is simply more fixated on the dangers of snakes or doesn't know what a scorpion is.

Yet Christ's apostles need not trample on the *nædran* or *snacan* that are repentant sinners. The *Physiologus* explains that when it is ready to shed its skin the snake hides in a hole for ten days, and when it finally pushes itself out through the rough, rocky opening it leaves its old skin behind. The bestiary Bodley 764 says that we emulate the snake when we cast off the sins of Adam and seek Christ, 'the spiritual rock'. In this rock we must find 'a narrow fissure', a small, straight gate through which to pass to salvation. This draws on a passage from the Gospel of Matthew, which quotes Christ's sermon on the mount:

> Enter ye in at the narrow gate: for wide is the gate, and broad is the way that leadeth to destruction, and many there are who go in thereat. How narrow is the gate, and strait is the way that leadeth to life: and few there are that find it!

The Old English translation of this passage warns us, *Gangað inn þurh þæt nearwe geat* (Go in through the narrow gate). Because of this allegory, snakes passing through narrow gates are a popular subject of illustration in the bestiaries of later centuries (though they really do have to be *narrow*, snakes not being famous for their width). While Old English texts focus on the *nædre's* skin-shedding as a metaphor for the repentant sinner, later medieval bestiaries include another image for self-renewal: a snake drinking so much water that it spews out the venom it has accumulated in its breast since birth.

The wisest animal

The *nædre* is not only subtle in Old English texts, it is **snotor** (wise). In the same homily as before, Ælfric says you should be *snotor* like a *nædre* and *bile-wit* like a *culfre* (innocent like a dove). He writes:

> The snake (*næddre*) is the wisest (*snoterost*) of all animals (*nytena*), and through it the Devil deceived the first created humans. Now we must be wise (*snotere*) against the Devil's deceits, as the Saviour said, and consider wisely the Devil's wiles, so that he does not deceive us.

Ælfric is referring to the Gospel of Matthew, when Christ tells his apostles, 'Behold I send you as sheep in the midst of wolves. Be ye therefore wise as serpents (*serpentes*) and simple as doves.' Even though the *nædre* is *snotor* to an extent that it is used by the Devil, it seems God also means for humans to learn from its wisdom. With the snake's wisdom and the dove's innocence, one is best equipped against the Devil's deception.

There is one more quality of the *nædre* that Ælfric encourages Christians to emulate. The *nædre* always protects its **hēafod** (head), completely encircling it with its body so that predators cannot reach it. Ælfric says we should be *snotor* in this way, permitting nothing to harm our **hǣlend** (Saviour), who is our *hēafod*. As St Paul says in his first epistle to the Corinthians, 'The head of every man is Christ.' It's better to sacrifice our bodies to protect our faith in Christ, who is both our *hǣlend* and *hēafod*. Loss of the *hēafod* means damnation of the soul. The *nædre* is *snotor* in that it knows what is most important and guards it fearlessly.

How to deal with a snake

Although the snake does have a few admirable qualities such as wisdom, Old English texts generally portray the *nædre* as a threat. Even though there were few venomous snakes in early medieval England (indeed, the only venomous snake in England today is the adder), people would have been well acquainted with their dangers by reading texts from other lands and hearing the stories of travellers. Jennifer Neville explains that a snake's **attor** (venom) was seen as 'inherently magical', for even a small bite could be potent enough to kill a person. Two remedies for snake bites appear in the Old English *Medicina du quadrupedibus*:

1. Melt the **smeoru** (fat) and *tord* (dung) of a *gāt* (goat) together with wax. Have the patient swallow this mixture whole.
2. Seethe or boil the **brǣgen** (brain) of a **bār** (boar), and mix it with honey. (This recipe does not specify whether you are to swallow the resulting concoction or apply it topically.)

The leechbook also suggests a way to get rid of snakes that become unwanted neighbours: burn the horn of a **fear** (bull or ox) to ashes, and scatter these around where snakes dwell. (Pliny notes that snakes are driven away by the smell of a burnt stag's horn, and as we saw in Chapter 9 there is a well-established enmity between the snake and the serpent-trampling deer.)

Wondrous snakes of the East

But the snakes of distant lands could be far more intimidating, not easily scared away by ox-horn ashes or antler smoke. The Old English *Wonders of the East* refers to a place called Hascellentia, which is another name for Seleucia, an ancient city near modern Baghdad. According to *Wonders of the East*, this land is 'filled with all good things' but also *nædran*. The text does not actually say that these *nædran* are dangerous, but its description of them is rather unnerving: they have two *hēafdu* (heads), with **ēagan** (eyes) that shine at night as brightly as a lantern. Illustrations of two-headed snakes appear in both Old English manuscripts of *Wonders of the East*. Pliny does say in his *Natural History* that snakes mate by embracing, 'intertwining so closely that they could be taken to be a single animal with two heads'. Did Hascellentia really have two-headed snakes, or a lot of sexually entangled single-headed ones?

A snake that is not only threatening but also deadly is the *corsia*. *Corsia* is a Latin name deriving from Greek that has no Old English equivalent translation in either of the two *Wonders of the East* manuscripts. *Corsias* (as it is pluralised in the Old English texts) are *nædran* living in the desert south of Babylon. The *corsia's* horns are the same size as **weþer** (ram) horns, so large and intimidating that even donkeys with horns as big as those of an ox will flee them (though it's unclear what exactly these ox-horned donkeys are). The most frightening thing about the *corsia* is that merely touching one will immediately

Two-headed snake in the Tiberius manuscript's *Wonders of the East*
(England, mid eleventh century)

kill you. You might expect people to avoid such creatures at all costs,
but as it turns out some really great **pipor** (pepper) grows in their habitat. *Corsias* love this *pipor* and guard it fiercely. If you wish to get your
hands on the *pipor* you must set the area ablaze, which makes the *corsias* flee beneath the earth. This has the side effect of course of also
burning the *pipor*, but that's OK: it just turns it black. With the *nædran*
safely underground, you can cross the scorched earth to pick the *pipor*
and not feel too guilty about the decimated landscape: other than the

pipor plants, this land is agriculturally barren because of its abundant *nǣdran*.

If you travel even further east, you might encounter the *nǣdran* that appear in *Alexander's Letter to Aristotle*. Alexander the Great describes *Indea* (southern Asia) as a place of many kinds of *nǣdran*, which he says are **un-ārīmed** (countless), **missenlīc** (diverse) and **un-āræfnedlīc** (intolerable). Alexander calls one kind of snake a *cerastes*, which is a Latin word for 'horned snake', deriving from the Greek for 'horned'. As with the *corsia*, there does not seem to be an equivalent word for the creature in Old English.

The earliest known depiction of the *cerastes* is from Egypt, dating to as early as 3000 BCE. The creature later appears in Pliny's *Natural History*, which claims that the snake moves its horns 'like worms' to attract birds to their doom. Accounts differ on whether these horns are 'true horns' (permanent and made of live bone, not shed like antlers) and also on their number. If we assume that this is a real creature, and not imagined, then it is likely that there are two. The common name for the real-life animal *Cerastes cerastes* is the Saharan horned viper or desert horned viper, native to the deserts of northern Africa and the Middle East. This viper has two 'horns' (actually scales, not true horns) on its head, one above each eye. The animal typically grows to a length of one to two feet including its tail, and its colours vary, although sand-coloured is the most common.

The *cerastae* Alexander describes in his *Letter to Aristotle* are **hornede** (horned) *nǣdran* of many colours (red, black and white), shining with scales that glitter like gold. Unlike the *fēnix* and the *panþer*, however, the creature's multicoloured appearance definitely does *not* represent its numerous virtues. The *cerastes* appears in the Book of Genesis as a metaphor for a threat, although Douay-Rheims translates Latin *cerastes* simply as 'serpent': 'a <u>snake</u> (*coluber*) in the way, a <u>serpent</u> (*cerastes*) in the path, that biteth the horse's heels that his rider may fall backward'. Alexander notes that the land resounds with the creatures' **hwistlung** (hissing) and admits that he and his men have 'no little fear of them'. The *hwistlung* may not be the snakes hissing with their tongues but rather the sound of their scales rustling as they slither along. Alexander and his men shield themselves as best they can, fighting them for around two hours, attempting to burn them in fires. As fierce and threatening as the *cerastae* and other *wyrmas* appear, they depart once they are able to have a drink from the nearby watering hole, showing no further interest in or enmity towards the warriors. It seems that Alexander would have been better off keeping his distance, letting them reach the water unimpeded. (This, however, is not a conqueror's way.)

Today the horned viper's venom is known to be toxic but generally not lethal; an estimated lethal dose is 40–50mg, more than one typically gets from a single bite. Still, that's not what you would think from reading historical accounts of people's encounters with the creature. The English cleric Edward Topsell gives a truly horrific description in his *Historie of Serpents* published in 1608:

> When a horned Serpent hath bitten a man or beast, first about the wound there groweth hardnesse, and then pustules. Lastly, black, earthy and pale matter: the genital member standeth out straight and never falleth, he falleth mad, his eyes grow dim, and his nerves immanuable, and upon the head of the wound groweth a scab like the head of a Nail, and continually pricking, like the pricking of Needles: And because this Serpent is immoderately dry, therefore the poyson is most pernicious; for if it be not holpen within nine dayes, the patient cannot escape death.

If descriptions like this were also familiar to people of the fourth century BCE, it's no wonder Alexander was concerned.

But the *cerastae* are not in fact the most concerning creatures, or even the most concerning snakes that Alexander encounters that night, for more *nǣdran* soon arrive – more *wundor-līc* (wondrous) and **egeslic** (terrifying) than the last. (Remember *ege*, 'terror', from Chapter 4?) Unlike the *cerastae*, these *nǣdran* cannot be identified with a particular species, and sound highly improbable. Much bigger than the *cerastae*, if the *cerastes* is a horned viper, they are as large as columns, some even longer and thicker. Some of them have two *hēafdu* (heads), others three. When they open their mouths Alexander can see that their tongues have three slits. They get around by slithering on their backs, breast turned upwards, and as they move they tear up the earth with their mouths and scales. The verb used to describe their movement is **slincan** (to crawl or slink away). The most dangerous aspect of this *nǣdre* is its deadly **oroþ** (breath), which leaves its mouth like a burning **þǣcele** (torch). Similar, then, to a legless dragon.

Fifty people are killed in the protracted *wyrm* battle that follows. Again, these multi-headed *wyrmas* come to Alexander's camp because they wish to drink the water, and again Alexander's warriors get in the way. It seems Alexander is not 'the Great' for his wisdom, since he does not learn from recent past experience. But perhaps, when faced with such an *egeslic* opponent, it's hard to be as *snotor* as a snake.

Snake's Wordhord

attor, noun (AHT-tor / ˈat-tɔr): Venom, poison.

a-wurpan, verb (ah-WURP-ahn / a-ˈwʌr-pan): To cast away.

bār, noun (BAR / ˈbaːr): Boar.

brægen, noun (BRAE-yen / ˈbræ-jɛn): Brain.

ēage, noun (AY-ah-yuh / ˈeːa-jə): Eye (plural: *ēagan*, pronounced AY-ah-gahn).

egeslic, adjective (EH-yez-litch / 'ɛ-jɛz-lɪtʃ): Terrible, dreadful, frightening, terrifying.

fear, noun (FEH-ar / 'fɛar): Bull, ox.

fell, noun (FELL / 'fɛl): Skin, hide.

hǽlend, noun (HAL-end / 'hæ:-lɛnd): Saviour, Christ; healer.

hēafod, noun (HAY-ah-vod / 'he:a-vɔd): Head (plural: *hēafdu*).

hornede, adjective (HORN-eh-duh / 'hɔr-nɛ-də): Horned.

hwistlung, noun (H'WIST-lung / 'hwɪst-lʌŋ): Hissing, whistling.

missenlīc, adjective (MISS-sen-leech / 'mis-sɛn-li:tʃ): Different, diverse, various.

nǽdre, noun (NADD-ruh / 'næ:-drə): Snake, serpent, adder, viper (plural: *nǽdran*).

oroþ, noun (OR-oth / 'ɔ-rɔθ): Breath, breathing.

pipor, noun (PIP-or / 'pɪ-pɔr): Pepper.

slincan, verb (SLINK-ahn / 'slɪn-kan): To crawl; to slink away.

smeoru, noun (SMEH-or-uh / 'smɛɔ-rʌ): Fat, grease, suet, tallow.

snaca, noun (SNAH-ka / 'sna-ka): Snake, reptile, perhaps even a scorpion (plural: *snacan*).

snotor, adjective (SNOT-or / 'snɔ-tɔr): Prudent, wise.

þæcele, noun (THATCH-el-uh / 'θæ-tʃɛ-lə): Torch, light.

þrowend, noun (THRO-wend / 'θrɔ-wɛnd): Scorpion.

un-ārǽfnedlīc, adjective (UN-ah-RAV-ned-leech / 'ʌn-a:-ˌræv-nɛd-li:tʃ): Intolerable, impossible to bear.

un-ārīmed, adjective (UN-ah-REE-med / 'ʌn-a:-ˌri:-mɛd): Unnumbered, countless.

weþer, noun (WEH-ther / 'wɛ-θɛr): Ram.

14

Dragon (*draca*)

WYRM IS A CATCH-ALL TERM for creepy-crawlies of all sorts, but there is another Old English word used exclusively for the dragon: ***draca*** (from Latin *draco*). And while some *wyrmas* are harmless enough, the sight of a *draca* never bodes well.

Look at a chronicle entry for the year 793, for instance. Things were looking grim up north during that year: the *Peterborough Chronicle* (which includes entries up to the mid twelfth century) refers to the *rēðe* (cruel) portents and fearsome ***fore-bēacen*** that had fallen upon the land of Northumbria. *Fore-bēacen* are ***bēacen*** (signs) that come before, 'beacons' of a sort, and in Northumbria they consisted of immense bolts of lightning and ***fȳrene*** *dracan* (fiery dragons). The historian Michael Swanton suggests that the fiery dragons which the chronicler is referring to are long-tailed comets, which were *fore-bēacen* of disaster. Isidore explains that the sight of a comet may portend pestilence, famine, war or a change of king. In 793 Northumbria had to deal with at least a couple of these disasters. The chronicler says there was a great ***hungor*** (famine) followed by the ***hergung*** (pillaging) of heathen men, who destroyed the church on the Isle of Lindisfarne through their plunder and slaughter. These men were the Vikings, whose raid on Lindisfarne struck the spiritual heart of the Northumbrian kingdom.

Monks behaving badly

Dragons tend to represent forces of evil in medieval literature, sometimes the Devil or one of his minions. Two of Ælfric's homilies tell stories about monks behaving badly who must face a *draca* as a consequence. In one story, a monk is unsatisfied with his life at the monastery and wants to leave, which goes against the will of the holy abbot St Benedict. The monk is determined, however, and Benedict eventually tells him to go. But as soon as he leaves the monastery, the monk comes face to face with a *draca* whose gaping mouth is ready to swallow him. Trembling and fearful, the monk cries out:

> *Yrnað, yrnað, for ðan ðe þes draca me forswelgan wile!*
> Run, run, for this dragon will swallow me!

The verb **for-swelgan** means to swallow entirely, to completely devour something or someone, and it is a common danger with dragons. The other monks emerge from the monastery, but all they see is the fearful monk – no *draca*. It turns out that the *draca* is an invisible *dēofol* (devil), whom the monk unwittingly followed from the monastery. (It had been the *dēofol* driving him to leave.) Benedict's prayers make the *dēofol* visible to the wayward monk in the form of a *draca*. The monk is thus able to see the evil that motivates his departure and amend his decision.

In his other homily, Ælfric refers to a story told by St Gregory about one of the monks at the monastery he founded. This monk has

several marks against him: he chooses the monastic life out of necessity rather than for the sake of bettering himself (or getting closer to
God), is fond of idle conversation, dresses well but behaves badly, and
is impatient whenever someone encourages him to do better. The
other monks find him irritating in the extreme, but they put up with
him as patiently as they can (they are monks, after all). One day the ill-
behaved monk becomes very sick, and the other monks gather to pray
for his soul. On the edge of death, the sick monk cries out suddenly,
saying:

> Leave me! Behold, here a <u>dragon</u> (*draca*) has come that will <u>swallow</u>
> (*forswelgan*) me, but he cannot because of your presence. He has
> seized my head in his jaws. Give way to him so that he will no longer
> trouble me. If I am given to this <u>dragon</u> (*dracan*) to be <u>swallowed</u>
> (*forswelgenne*), why must I suffer a delay because of your opposition?

The other monks ask him why he speaks so despairingly and instruct
him to mark himself with the sign of the cross. The ailing monk replies
that he would gladly do so, but cannot because the *draca* oppresses
him sorely. So the monks prostrate themselves upon the earth, weeping and praying earnestly to God for their brother's salvation, when
suddenly he recovers from his illness, saying:

> I thank God! Behold, now the <u>dragon</u> (*draca*) that would <u>swallow</u>
> (*forswelgan*) me is put to flight through your prayers. He is driven away
> from me, unable to stand against your intercession.

The man vows to behave properly as a monk from now on, abandon-
ing worldly ways, and so he does. Later on, when he eventually dies of
the same illness, the monk does not see the *draca* on his deathbed – 'he
had overcome him with the conversion of his heart'.

St Margaret's dragon

Dracan don't always appear as a warning to wayward monks; they also come to test the strength, faith and fortitude of saints. The most famous dragon-slaying saint is undoubtedly St George, patron saint of England since the fourteenth century (and of numerous other countries, including Ethiopia, Greece, Germany, Georgia and Lithuania). Although not as well known today, St Margaret, another dragon-slayer, was one of the most popular and revered saints during the Middle Ages, especially in England. Her legends are recorded in both Old and Middle English.

Margaret lived in Antioch (modern-day Turkey) during the late third and early fourth century CE. Despite being the daughter of a pagan priest, Margaret embraced Christianity at a young age. She had the misfortune of living during the reign of Emperor Diocletian, whose persecution of Christians is considered to be the most brutal undertaken by the Roman Empire. (Diocletian also persecuted Ananias, the saint visited by the Holy Spirit in the form of a dove in Chapter 4.) When a Roman governor asked for her hand in marriage and also demanded that she renounce Christianity, Margaret refused, which led to her torture, imprisonment and eventual martyrdom by decapitation.

The Old English *Life of St Margaret* includes a wonderfully descriptive passage about a *draca*. The creature appears to her in a dark prison, an *egeslic* (terrifying) *draca* of many colours. In fact it sounds like a beautiful example of fine craftsmanship, with its **loccas** (locks of hair) and **beard** (beard) that seem **gylden** (golden), **tēþ** (teeth) that are like sharpened **īsen** (iron), and *ēagan* (eyes) that shine like **searu-gimmas** (curious gems) – a great deal less pleasant than the good *fēnix*'s gleaming gem-like beak and eyes that resemble jewels set in gold plate. Out of the *draca*'s **nosu** (nose) comes a great **smoca** (smoke), and he pants with his **tunge** (tongue). He fills the prison cell with a great *fūlnes* (foulness or stench). The *draca* rears up, hissing fiercely, and the darkness is made bright all of a sudden because of the *fȳr* (fire) that emerges from his *mūþ* (mouth).

Margaret, quite understandably, is very frightened by this creature's appearance, and she bends her knees, stretching out her hands in a prayer to God:

> God Almighty, subdue the might of this great <u>dragon</u> (*dracan*) and take pity on me, needy and wretched. Never let me perish, but protect me from this <u>wild animal</u> (*wilddeor*).

While Margaret is praying, the *draca* puts his *mūþ* over her head, swallowing her whole. But within the dragon's **innoþ** (innards), Margaret makes the sign of the cross and the *draca's* body splits in two so she can escape unharmed. (In other versions of this story she holds an actual crucifix, but in the Old English *Life* the hand gesture is sufficient.) After this unsettling experience, a *dēofol* (demon) appears before her and says:

> I sent Rufus, my brother, to you in the likeness of a <u>dragon</u> (*dracan*), so that he would <u>swallow</u> (*forswulge*) you, and your virginity and beauty would be lost, and your memory would be blotted out from earth.

But Margaret's faith is stronger than the *dēofol's* brother Rufus, even when he takes the form of a powerful *draca*. The saint thanks God for his help.

Because she escapes the *draca's innoþ* unharmed, by the twelfth century Margaret had become the patron saint of women in childbirth. Even in her Old English *Life* there is evidence of Margaret's association with parturition, since one of the manuscripts that contains her *Life* also includes prognostics for pregnant mothers and their caregivers. As the art historians Sherry C. M. Lindquist and Asa Simon Mittman point out, St Margaret's symbolism is rather confusing. Does Margaret represent a baby, leaving the dragon to represent the mother? If so, it doesn't turn out well for the 'mother' killed in the process of 'giving birth'. Lindquist and Mittman note that with high rates of maternal mortality during the medieval period, 'the gory horror of the image was likely not lost on its female viewers'. The other issue with the story's symbolism is that the dragon is an evil creature, representative of a devil. How then can it also represent a mother? The symbolism attributed to saints' lives is not always perfect.

Where a dragon belongs

All the *draca* encounters so far have been those of individuals, and it's not always clear whether anyone besides the individual can actually see the creature. Sometimes, however, an entire community is threatened by a *draca*, which does real physical harm to human beings. In another of his homilies Ælfric tells the story of St Philip, one of Christ's apostles, who preached the gospel to heathens in the land of Scythia for twenty years after Christ's death. Heathens capture Philip and try to force him to worship their idol, but when they arrive at the idol they also find an *or-mǣte* (immense) *draca*. This *draca* kills the son of an idolater who brings incense as an offering, as well as two prefects, and everyone becomes very ill from the creature's foul **blǣd** (breath). Philip tells the heathens that things can only be made right if they cast down their idol and raise the sign of Christ's cross in its place. After the heathens agree to this, Philip says to the troublesome *draca*:

> In the name of Christ the Saviour, I command you to leave this place and go to the <u>wilderness</u> (*westene*), where you will have no interaction with humans, and you must not trouble any human on your way there.

The only good place for a *draca* is the *wēsten* (wasteland), a desert or wilderness where people rarely go unless they're testing their strength or faith. The fierce *draca* obeys the saint's command and departs, never to be seen by humans again. Philip then brings the three dead men back to life and heals everyone of the sickness caused by the *draca's blǣd*.

If a *draca* is on its own in the *wēsten*, be sensible and leave it be. An Old English maxim includes the wisdom:

> A <u>dragon</u> (*draca*) shall be in a <u>barrow</u> (*hlǣwe*), old and wise, proud with <u>treasures</u> (*frætwum*).

A wise person who wants to live to a ripe old age knows better than to touch a dragon's *frætwe* (treasure), and to stay out of its **hlǣw** (barrow). Sometimes a barrow is a burial mound, although it can also be a corpse-free, low rounded hill. Still, when you consider the most likely fate of a person who dares to enter a *draca's hlǣw*, 'burial mound' doesn't seem far off the mark.

Beowulf's dragon

Even an intruder who manages to escape a *hlǣw* doesn't necessarily escape a *draca's* wrath. In the poem *Beowulf*, it is an unwise thief who enters the *draca's* treasure hoard that sets off a chain of death and destruction in the formerly prosperous kingdom. This part of the story was badly damaged by the eighteenth-century library fire, but enough of the text remains to tell us that a **þēof** (thief) sneaks into a *draca's* lair and 'out of necessity' steals a **sinc-fæt** (costly vessel), perhaps a gold or silver cup.

The poem explains how the dragon originally took possession of the *hord* (hoard), describing the creature with a variety of evocative names: **ūht-sceaþa** (pre-dawn-robber), **nīþ-draca** (hate-dragon), **lyft-floga** (air-flier). According to the poem:

> An old pre-dawn robber (*uhtsceaða*) found 'hoard-joy' (*hordwynne*) available to him, the one who seeks out cities, a burning, naked hate-dragon (*niðdraca*), he who flies by night enveloped in fire (*fyre*). Earth-dwellers greatly fear him. He seeks a hoard (*hord*) in the earth where, old in winters, he guards heathen gold; he is none the better for it.

Hord-wynn, literally 'hoard-joy', refers to treasure that delights. After the pre-dawn robber is himself robbed he makes his way to human settlements, spewing flames and burning down dwellings. In his anger, and spurred by a vengeful nature, 'the cruel flier in the air (*lyftfloga*) did not wish to leave anything there alive'. The *ūht-sceaþa* returns to his secret hall, the barrow, before daybreak, the countryside ablaze in his wake.

King Beowulf goes to fight the *draca*, trusting in his strength alone to take it down. He calls out to the *āglǣca* (hostile fighter), stirring up hate with his battle-clear voice. The **hord-weard** (hoard guardian) hears him and breathes out hot **hilde-swāt** (battle vapour) from the cave. *Hilde-swāt*, a hapax or word appearing only once in Old English, literally means 'battle-sweat' and is reminiscent of St Philip's dragon's foul breath. With the assistance of Wiglaf, his faithful warrior, Beowulf manages to slay the *draca* but not without receiving a mortal wound himself. In this vengeful *āglǣca*, Beowulf has finally met his match.

The history of dragons (and other fire-breathers)

Although people often think of dragons as particularly 'medieval', they have in fact been around for millennia, and they've never really lost popularity. Medieval maps are sometimes associated with the legend 'Here be dragons', since the cartography of the time includes illustrations of strange and marvellous creatures. But the earliest example of *Hic sunt dragones* appears on a map from *c.*1480, the very end of the medieval period and long after Old English had been replaced with Middle. The only other cartographic item which includes the phrase is a globe from *c.*1510. Drawings of dragons do show up on medieval maps, but not necessarily because people believed they lived in certain places. On a world map from the thirteenth century a pair of dragons sits in the lower frame, below the map of the world, to contrast with Christ and his angels, who appear in the upper frame. This map metaphorically depicts the state of the world, floating somewhere between sin and salvation.

Beowulf's dragon may be the earliest example of a fire-breathing dragon, although flame-free dragons have been around for a very long time. The oldest known example of a dragon is in the form of a statue discovered in Henan, China, that dates to the fifth millennium BCE. Mesopotamian mythology dating back to the sixth century BCE tells of a scaly dragon called *mushussu*. Dragons appear in ancient Egyptian mythology and ancient Hindu texts, as well as in early Judaic and Christian traditions. The earliest dragons are depicted as giant four-legged serpents. By the first century CE, the dragon already had a reputation as a treasure-guardian and force of destruction in Roman literature. It wasn't until the early medieval period that dragons acquired wings and often sported two legs instead of four. It is also when the fire-breathing ability first appeared. Throughout the medieval period, dragons were less intelligent and more ferocious, antagonists for heroes to fight rather than powerful creatures to respect and admire.

There were, of course, other fire-breathing creatures before the early medieval dragon. Homer's *Iliad*, from the eighth or seventh century

Dragon with a knotted tail in a bestiary (England, early twelfth century)

BCE, features the chimaera of Greek mythology, a creature with a lion's head, a goat's body and a serpent's tail. The Old Testament's Book of Job has a giant sea creature known as the Leviathan, which was discussed in Chapter 12. The Book of Job describes the fish/serpent/whale:

> His sneezing is like the shining of fire, and his eyes like the eyelids of the morning. Out of his mouth go forth lamps, like torches of lighted fire. Out of his nostrils goeth smoke, like that of a pot heated and boiling. His breath kindleth coals, and a flame cometh forth out of his mouth.

Such a description would have been familiar to medieval Christians and undoubtedly influenced the way in which they imagined fire-breathing dragons.

The gateway to hell

Why does the dragon's fire-breathing ability first appear in early medieval Britain? It may be due to the *draca*'s association with **helle-fyr** (hell-fire). During this period, manuscript artists begin to illustrate

A hell-mouth illustration from the Guthlac Roll (England, 1175–1215)

the gates of hell as a beast's mouth, what's known as a **helle-mūþ** (hell-mouth). (Remember how unsuspecting fish swam into the *hwæl*'s gaping *mūþ* in Chapter 12, the way in which sinners unwittingly stumble into hell?) The *helle-mūþ* resembles the gaping jaws of a dragon, not unlike the *dracan* that threaten to swallow Ælfric's monks or the *draca* that swallows St Margaret.

Dragons are frequently associated with hell in Old English poetry, as the literature scholar Margaret Goldsmith explains. In a poem called *Elene*, Judas speaks to God about the fall of the rebellious angels, using the phrase 'in the dragon's embrace' (*in dracan fæðme*) to say that they are in hell. **Fæþm** means 'bosom' or 'embrace', but also 'grasp', 'clutch' or 'possession'. (The length of a *fæþm* – 'fathom' in modern English – can either be the distance from the end of one outstretched arm to the other or the length of a forearm.) In another poem, Satan refers to the *dracan* who dwell forever 'at the doors to hell' (*æt helle duru*), which might be associated with a *helle-mūþ*. *Draca* is sometimes used as a poetic variation of *dēofol*. Another poem describes fire coming from Satan's mouth as he speaks, which accords with the idea of a fire-breathing *draca*:

> He <u>emitted sparks</u> (*spearcade*) when he began to speak, <u>fire</u> (*fyre*) and <u>poison</u> (*atre*).

Later, the poem says:

> Words flew in <u>sparks</u> (*spearcum*) much like <u>poison</u> (*attre*) when he drove them out.

It seems that *fyr* and *attor* (poison) go hand in hand. The pestilential breath of dragons like the one St Philip encounters might as well be fiery too. Satan's **spearcan** (sparks) – his words – contain both *fyr* and *attor*, just like the Old English *draca*'s deadly breath.

Both Beowulf and St Margaret face fire-breathing dragons and ultimately defeat them, but their victories differ substantially. Beowulf goes to his battle armed with sword, shield and helmet, but still sustains a mortal injury. Margaret faces her *draca* armed only with her faith in God, and her killing blow is making the sign of the cross with her hands. Goldsmith explains that in Old English literature there is an important difference between secular and hagiographic dragon fights: 'The saint needs no weapons, or rather, his spiritual weapons are so powerful that the monster can make no defence against them.'

(She does admit one exception to this rule: St Michael, who defeats a dragon with a flaming sword.) When we see depictions of St George today, he is usually portrayed as a warrior holding a lance. Goldsmith explains that this is 'a chivalric modification' of older versions of his story, in which the dragon is defeated merely by the sign of the cross or by the saint's command. Similarly, none of the Old English stories about monks who encounter dragons have the heroes fighting with weapons; their faith and prayers alone are enough.

The idea that dragons represent the Devil and can thus be conquered by faith continues throughout the medieval period, reimagined in various ways in the bestiaries of later centuries. Given that the panther and deer (and sometimes the elephant) represent Christ in these texts, it is no surprise that they are the dragon's mortal enemies. Although dragons often have deadly breath, they themselves fear the panther's breath, which is particularly poisonous to them. A dragon might be able to take down an elephant, but it will probably be crushed in the process. As if these holy foes weren't enough, dragons have another enemy in doves, which often represent the Holy Spirit. In this case it's not the dove's stature or its breath that threaten the dragon – instead it's their choice of refuge. Doves take shelter in the mythical peridexion tree (which represents God the Father), and it is this tree's looming shadow that terrifies the dragon (because, of course, it represents Christ). Bestiaries say that the dragon bides its time near the tree, watching for when the birds leave – a reminder that the Devil lies in wait for those who make the mistake of leaving the Church. This sneaky tactic is typical of dragons, and is another reason why they are compared to the deceitful Devil – just as the dragon will kill its prey by tripping, lashing, suffocating and swallowing, so does the Devil trip people up and drag them to their doom by deceiving them with lies.

Whether it's by tripping with its tail or spitting out flames or simply showing its face at your deathbed, the Old English *draca* is there to remind humans of the world's many dangers. In the stories of this chapter, *dracan* threaten one's physical well-being, but in the end it's really one's spirit or soul that is in peril. A hero might find *hord-wynn*, or delightful treasure, within a *draca*'s impressive *hord*, but such worldly wealth is meaningless at their life's end – and finding it in the first place might even precipitate the end of their life. A warrior might slay a *draca* with a sword, but it's the saint armed only with their faith who lives to tell the tale.

Dragon's Wordhord

bēacen, noun (BAY-ah-kun / ˈbeːa-kən): Sign, portent (plural: *bēacen*).

beard, noun (BEH-ard / ˈbɛard): Beard.

blǣd, noun (BLADD / ˈblæːd): Blowing, breath, breathing.

draca, noun (DRAH-ka / ˈdra- ka) : Dragon (plural: *dracan*).

fæþm, noun (FATH-um / ˈfæ-θəm): Bosom, embrace; grasp, clutch, possession; fathom (a unit of measurement).

fore-bēacen, noun (FOR-uh-BAY-ah-kun / ˈfɔ-rə-ˌbeːa-kən): Foretoken, portent, sign (plural: *fore-bēacen*).

for-swelgan, verb (for-SWELL-gahn / fɔr-ˈswɛl-gan): To swallow (something/someone) entirely, devour (something/someone) utterly.

fūlnes, noun (FOOL-ness / ˈfuːl-nɛs): Foulness, stench.

fȳrene, adjective (FUE-reh-nuh / ˈfyː-rɛ-nə): Fiery, flaming with fire, fire-producing.

gylden, adjective (YUEL-den / ˈjyl-dɛn): Golden.

helle-fȳr, noun (HELL-uh-VUER / ˈhɛl-lə-ˌvyːr): Hell-fire.

helle-mūþ, noun (HELL-uh-MOOTH / ˈhɛl-lə-ˌmuːθ): Hell-mouth, the entrance to hell.

hergung, noun (HER-gung / ˈhɛr-gʌŋ): Plundering, pillaging, looting, ravaging.

hilde-swāt, noun (HILL-duh-SWAHT / 'hɪl-də-ˌswaːt): Hostile vapour (battle-sweat).

hlǣw, noun (H'LAEW / 'hlæːw): Barrow, burial mound; low rounded hill.

hord-weard, noun (HORD-WEH-ard / 'hɔrd-ˌwɛard): Hoard-guardian, guardian of treasure.

hord-wynn, noun (HORD-WUEN / 'hɔrd-ˌwyn): Delightful treasure (hoard-joy).

hungor, noun (HUNG-gor / 'hʌŋ-gɔr): Hunger; famine.

innoþ, noun (IN-noth / 'ɪn-nɔθ): The inner part of the body, innards (stomach, womb, bowels, etc.).

īsen, noun (EE-zen / 'iː-zɛn): Iron.

locc, noun (LOCK / 'lɔk): Hair, lock of hair (plural: *loccas*).

lyft-floga, noun (LUEFT-FLO-ga / 'lyft-ˌflɔ-ga): Flier in the air.

nīþ-draca, noun (NEETH-DRAH-ka / 'niːθ-ˌdra-ka): Hate-dragon, a hostile or malicious dragon.

nosu, noun (NO-zuh / 'nɔ-zʌ): Nose.

searu-gim, noun (SEH-ah-ruh-YIM / 'sɛa-rʌ-ˌjɪm): Curious gem, precious stone (plural: *searu-gimmas*).

sinc-fæt, noun (SINK-VAT / 'sɪnk-ˌvæt): Costly vessel, vessel of gold or of silver.

smoca, noun (SMOCK-ah / 'smɔ-ka): Smoke.

spearca, noun (SPEH-ar-ka / 'spɛar-ka): Spark (plural: *spearcan*).

tōþ, noun (TOATH / 'toːθ): Tooth, tusk (plural: *tēþ*, pronounced TAYTH).

tunge, noun (TUNG-guh / 'tʌŋ-gə): Tongue.

þēof, noun (THAY-off / 'θeːɔf): Thief.

ūht-sceaþa, noun (OO'HT-SHEH-ah-tha / 'uːxt-ˌʃɛa-θa): One who robs in the time just before dawn.

15

Wolf (*wulf*)

YOU WERE UNLIKELY to encounter a deadly *wyrm* in early medieval England, whether a venom-less *nædre* or a legendary *draca*. Jennifer Neville notes that the only animals that really posed a physical threat to humans at that time would have been wolves, bears, wild boars and possibly some wild cats. (There are no Old English descriptions of wild cats, but there is evidence in place names for their lairs – Lostford in Shropshire, for instance, may mean 'ford of the lynx', the Old English for 'lynx' being **lox**.) Neville points out, however, that none of these animals were likely to have been responsible for many human deaths, not even the wolf.

The **wulf** (wolf), one of these few legitimately dangerous animals, seems to have been universally feared in early medieval England. Wolves do not live in England today, but they did not become rare until the end of the medieval period. Though certainly capable of violence, *wulfas* were more of a threat to livestock than to humans, but that was reason enough for humans to dislike them. During the thirteenth century, King Henry III, followed by King Edward I, actively commissioned their extermination. Wolves lasted a bit longer in Scotland, but human activities such as deforestation contributed to their demise in the sixteenth century. The last wolf in Britain is thought to have been killed in 1621.

The wolf is the Devil

The *wulf*'s negative image in the early medieval period goes beyond fear of physical injury or even death. In one of his homilies, Ælfric of Eynsham makes it clear that the *wulf* is a danger to one's soul:

> *Se wulf is deoful.*
> The wolf is the Devil.

For Ælfric, the *wulf* is unambiguously 'bad'. He explains that the *wulf* 'lies in wait among God's congregation and observes how he can corrupt the souls of Christian men with sins'. The job of the good **hyrde** (shepherd) – a bishop or other teacher – is to withstand the *rēðe* (fierce) wolf, shielding God's people with doctrine and prayers.

In Ælfric's homily, Christ says:

> I am a good shepherd (*hyrde*). The good shepherd (*hyrde*) gives his own life for his sheep (*sceapum*). The hireling (*hyra*), who is not the right shepherd (*hyrde*), sees the wolf (*wulf*) come, and he abandons the sheep (*sceap*) and flees. And the wolf (*wulf*) seizes one and the others scatter. The hireling (*hyra*) flees because he is the hireling (*hyra*), and the sheep (*sceap*) do not concern him.

A **hyra** is someone who works for pay, a hired servant, and because their pay is their sole motivation, they turn tail and run when faced with a threat. Too steeped in **weorold-þing** (worldly things), the *hyra* cares more about transitory rewards than the eternal reward of heaven. But you can only distinguish *hyrde* from *hȳra*, Ælfric warns, when the *wulf* shows up. Christ, a good *hyrde*, cares so much about the people of the world that he considers all of them his *scēap* (sheep), even non-believers. A *wulf*, it seems, has its uses, even as a threat. The danger of its presence brings out the best and the worst in humankind, and reveals who your real friends are.

Whether the context is real sheep or Christ's flock, the wolf is always accompanied by slaughter and violence. It was first added to the *Physiologus* in the seventh century by Isidore, who claims that *lupus* (Latin for 'wolf') derives from the Greek for 'rage'. Known for being vicious, violent and cruel, the wolf always represents the Devil in medieval bestiaries. Bodley 764 says that the wolf is strong in its forequarters (muzzle and chest) but weak in its hind legs, to remind us that the Devil was originally an angel in heaven (strong) but then became an enemy of God (weak). Bestiaries also say that the wolf cannot turn its head backward, since the Devil cannot turn back to repent.

Like the Devil, the wolf as portrayed in medieval bestiaries has unholy desires, a voracious appetite for both food and sex, but it can also be incredibly patient while waiting for the fulfilment of those cravings. Bestiaries explain that the wolf can survive for a long time without eating, sometimes even living off earth or wind instead of animal flesh. If it is very hungry it might fill its stomach with a ball of clay, using its paw to vomit it up again once there is food to be had. The usual victim of the wolf, both in Old English texts and later medieval bestiaries, is the hapless sheep. This prey is easily spooked, and so the wolf must creep up quietly. Sometimes patience gives way to the rage referred to by Isidore, for the bestiary wolf will bite its own foot to punish it if it makes too much noise when sneaking up.

In medieval lore, both the wolf and the Devil are too clever for their own good, sneaky and deceitful. The well-known warning to look out for a 'wolf in sheep's clothing' has a long history. The Old English Gospel of Matthew warns Christians to beware of false prophets who come to you in the clothing of *scēap* but are **rēafigende** (ravening) *wulfas* inside. (*Rēafigende* is related to the verb **rēafian**, which means 'plunder', 'rifle', 'spoil', 'waste' or 'rob'.) Later medieval bestiaries say that the mother wolf is crafty in her hunting, seeking food for her cubs only in the faraway sheepfolds so her enemies won't find her lair. This behaviour is likened to the way in which the Devil particularly enjoys victories over humans who have tried to distance themselves from him.

A wolf faces three sheep in a bestiary (England, c.1170)

Though not all the behaviours of later medieval bestiaries appear in Old English texts, the wolf remains consistent in its symbolism. The *wulf* represents the *dēofol* in Old English literature, a great danger, with a patience for seizing prey that should never be underestimated. One Old English poem calls Satan the *awyrgda wulf*, the word **a-wyrgda** meaning 'cursed one' or 'the Devil'. Jennifer Neville notes that in the poem *Daniel*, the evil King Nebuchadnezzar may be associated with demonic powers because of his **wulf-heort** nature. (Literally 'wolf-heart', this adjective means 'cruel'.)

A wretched solitary being

Old English wisdom poetry is a genre that imparts wisdom through maxims, precepts and other concise statements of truth – and it certainly has nothing positive to say about the *wulf*. One maxim says: 'A <u>wolf</u> (*wulf*) must remain in a forest, a wretched <u>solitary being</u> (*anhaga*).' An *ān-haga* (one-dweller) is a loner, like the *fēnix* of Chapter 10 (also an *ān-haga*) or the *panþer* of Chapter 11 (an *ān-stapa* or 'lone wanderer'). But the *fēnix* and *panþer* are 'loners' in that they are unique and special above all human-kind, representative of Christ who alone must die for the world's sal-vation. The *wulf* is a loner of an entirely different nature. It is society's hatred, not innate superiority or personal sacrifice, that separates the *wulf* from its fellow *dēor*, cursing him with a lonely life. According to a twelfth-century Latin law code from the East Midlands, the English once used the term 'wluesheued' (wolf's head) to mean 'outlaw', a person who could be killed 'like a wolf, without fear of penalty'. There is no Old English text to support this, but the concept certainly fits with the gen-erally hostile view of wolves that we see in Old English poetry.

Wulfas must live alone because they make treacherous companions, grieving for nothing but their own hunger. *Fortunes of Men*, another Old English wisdom poem, says:

> To some unfortunate men who go forth in their youth a woeful conclusion will come. One might be eaten by a <u>wolf</u> (*wulf*), the grey <u>heath-stepper</u> (*hǽðstapa*); then his mother will mourn his <u>journey hence</u> (*hinsiþ*). Such is not in a man's control!

Hin-sīþ, literally 'journey hence', is an Old English word for 'death', and it is death that awaits the unfortunate person who wanders alone across the **hǣþ** (heath), the outskirts of civilisation, far from cultivated land and relative safety. The 'heath-stepper' preys upon you if you yourself become a *stapa* of the *hǣþ*, someone condemned to live in the margins of society. We saw the word *hǣþ-stapa* in Chapter 9 describing the stag who refuses to enter Grendel's mere in *Beowulf*, even to save its life. Here *hǣþ-stapa* refers to a *wulf*, again in the context of a bleak outcome and certain *hin-sīþ*. It's always best to avoid the *hǣþ*.

Another Old English maxim reminds us of the importance of having faithful companions at your side in a threatening world:

> It is good for one to have a friend on each journey. Often one will avoid a town if he knows friendship is uncertain there. The friendless, unblessed man takes <u>wolves</u> (*wulfas*) as his <u>companions</u> (*geferan*) – very treacherous <u>animals</u> (*deor*). Quite often that <u>companion</u> (*gefera*) will rip him apart.
>
> There shall be fear for the grey ones and graves for dead men. The creature moans in hunger, not at all bothered by grief. Indeed, the grey <u>wolf</u> (*wulf*) will never weep for the slaughtered, the murder of men, but always wishes for more.

Never trust a *wulf* – you need a better **ge-fēra** (companion) than that. Whether you're visiting a new town or fighting on the battlefield, a *ge-fēra* remains beside you to support you no matter what. The only thing to which the *wulf* is loyal, it seems, is its stomach, always concerned about feeding its insatiable appetite.

We first encountered 'beasts of battle' in Chapter 1, a common poetic trope in Old English descriptions of warfare. Accompanied by the *hræfn* (raven) and the *earn* (eagle), the *wulf* stays near the battlefield to pick over the slaughtered corpses, and it always wants more.

The poem *Elene* paints a picture of impending bloodshed: a *wulf* in the **weald** (woodland) chanting a **fyrd-lēoþ** (battle-song). Later in the poem, as the fight begins, the *wulf* again has a voice: *Wulf sang ahof* (A wolf raised a song). This *fyrd-lēoþ* must be a truly chilling sound, a wolf howling in anticipation of its meal of slaughtered warriors.

Wolves are considered incredibly dangerous, but they can be useful – and not just for cleaning up the battlefield or revealing the good *hyrde* in your midst. An Old English leechbook contains a variety of remedies that make use of *wulf* by-products. The wolf's **flǣsc** (flesh), **hrycg-hǣr** (back hair), **tægl-hǣr** (tail hair), right *ēage* (eye), **mearh** (marrow, not to be confused with the equine *mearh* of Chapter 12), and even *meolc* (milk) have specific uses. It's possible that wolf's *meolc* isn't milk at all, since in modern English there's a slime mould called 'wolf's milk', though the *Oxford English Dictionary* doesn't cite this particular usage until the nineteenth century. As early as the sixteenth century, an English medical text refers to 'woulfes milke' as a kind of spurge, a plant with an acrid milky juice. Questionable *meolc* aside, the other ingredients definitely come from a *wulf*, with remedies for ailments ranging from eye pain to unwanted hair to possession by devils. There's even a recipe for repelling wolves:

If you see a <u>wolf's trace</u> (*wulfes spor*) before you see the wolf, it will not harm you if you have with you on your journey <u>hair from a wolf's back</u> (*wulfes hrycghǣr*) and <u>hair from the tip of the tail</u> (*tæglhǣr þa ytemǣstan*). You may go about your journey without fear, but the <u>wolf</u> (*wulf*) will be anxious about its journey.

Perhaps the *wulf* worries that you'll go after its own *hrycg-hǣr* and *tægl-hǣr*.

The **spor** of an animal is its track or trace. In Old English *spor* can also mean 'wound' – a weapon's *spor*. The word is related to the verb

spyrian, to 'track', 'make a track', 'investigate', 'inquire', 'search after' or 'seek to attain'. 'Spoor' is still used in modern English with the same meaning, mainly for the track of wild animals pursued as game but also for those of people, currents, glaciers and vehicles. *Spyrian* survives in modern English 'speer', which is used mainly in Scotland and northern England to mean 'put to a question' or 'make inquiries'. The poem 'The Tarbolton Lasses', written by the Scottish poet Robert Burns in the 1770s, instructs the reader to 'spier in for bonie Bessy', suggesting she is a more worthy subject of romantic inquiries than Peggy, Sophy, Mysie and Jenny.

But are they always bad?

Although homilies compare them to the Devil and leechbooks provide remedies for repelling them, wolves appear in quite a few Old English personal names – perhaps meaning 'don't mess with me'. The most famous of *wulf* names is Beowulf (bee-wolf, possibly a reference to a bear). Other male names include Cynewulf (bold-wolf), Wulfstan (wolf-stone), Wulfsige (wolf-victory), Wulfwine (wolf-friend), Coenwulf (fierce-wolf), Deorwulf (bold-wolf), Eadwulf (riches-wolf), Wulfnoth (wolf-daring), Wulfgar (wolf-spear), Wulfhere (wolf-army or wolf-greatness), Wulfhelm (wolf-helmet), Æthelwulf (noble-wolf), Rædwulf (counsel-wolf), Wulfræd (wolf-counsel), Ecgwulf (sword-wolf), Frithuwulf (peace-wolf, rather paradoxically) and plain old Wulf. (Names like Æthelwulf and Rædwulf may be related to the modern names Adolf and Ralph.) *Wulf* names are far more popular among men in extant historical records, although this isn't helped by the fact that the names of men are recorded far more frequently than those of women. There is at least one *wulf* name for a woman: Wulfgifu (wolf-gift). (Whether that's a gift to a wolf, from a wolf, or of a wolf is unclear.)

Despite all the *wulf* names, being called a *wulf* in Old English texts is generally not complimentary. Ælfric uses it for the antagonist in his story of St Edmund, king of East Anglia from around 855 till his death in 869. Edmund reigned during trying times, for a coalition of Vikings invaded England in 865, with the intention of conquering and occupying East Anglia as well as Northumbria, Mercia and Wessex. The villains of Ælfric's narrative are Hingwar and Hubba, a pair of Danish captains who are 'united by the Devil'. After successfully laying Northumbria to waste, Hingwar sails eastward to East Anglia. Ælfric says:

> Suddenly Hingwar, <u>like a wolf</u> (*swa swa wulf*), stalked across the land and killed people, men and women and unwitting children, shamefully harassing innocent Christians.

The comparison to a *wulf* is particularly apt, since Ælfric has already mentioned Hingwar's unsavoury ties to the *dēofol*. King Edmund refuses to fight Hingwar with violence. He says he will never bow to Hingwar unless Hingwar first bows to Jesus Christ, converting to the Christian faith. Hingwar, the metaphorical *wulf*, orders Edmund to be tortured and eventually beheaded.

Yet *wulfas* are somewhat redeemed later in this story. After Hingwar beheads Edmund he orders his men to hide the head in the forest, so it cannot be properly buried with the rest of the king's body. Edmund's people search desperately for it, but at first there is no *spor* to be found. While the fruitless search for the head is on, God sends a *wulf* to protect it from other animals. The *wulf* stands guard over Edmund's saintly head day and night. This is followed by another miracle, for when Edmund's people call out, *Hwær eart þu nu gefera?* (Where are you now, companion?), the head answers them, *Her, her, her* (Here, here, here). They continue playing this game of Marco Polo until the searchers successfully locate the head:

> The grey <u>wolf</u> (*wulf*) who presided over the head lay there, with his two feet embracing the head, <u>greedy</u> (*grædig*) and <u>hungry</u> (*hungrig*). Because of God, it did not dare to taste the head and guarded it from other <u>animals</u> (*deor*).

With God's guidance, the *wulf* miraculously overcomes its natural instinct to devour a tantalising piece of flesh. The *wulf* is still *grædig* (greedy) and **hungrig** (hungry), as wolves usually are in medieval literature, but it does not act upon its desire. This time, patience wins out.

The Old English *wulf* is typically the opponent of the *hyrde* (shepherd or guardian), but in St Edmund's story the *wulf* becomes a *hyrde* itself. The people who find Edmund's head are astonished by the wolf's **hyrd-ræden** (guardianship), the **ræden** (condition) of being a good *hyrde*. The *wulf* even follows along behind the head until the people make it back to town – as if it were **tam** (tame) – before returning to the forest. In this case the potential danger presented by the wolf is used to illustrate the miraculous power of God.

In the end it seems the Old English *wulf* only breaks out of its 'bad' nature through God's omnipotence. When a *wulf* behaves well, it's more of a credit to God or holy men and women than to the animal itself. But the wolf must also have been admired in early medieval England for there to be so many personal names with a *wulf* component. The wolf is never really a threat to humans, only to their sheep. More than the wolves themselves, perhaps it is the people and devils with 'wolf-like' qualities that are truly feared – those who are *wulf-heort*.

Wolf's Wordhord

a-wyrgda, noun (ah-WUERG-da / a-ˈwyrg-da): The cursed, the Devil.
flæsc, noun (FLASH / ˈflæːʃ): Flesh.

fyrd-lēoþ, noun (FUERD-LAY-oth / ˈfyrd-ˌleːɔθ): Battle-song.

ge-fēra, noun (yeh-VAY-ra / jɛ-ˈveː-ra): Companion, comrade (plural: *ge-fēran*).

hǣþ, noun (HATH / ˈhæːθ): Heath; open, uncultivated ground.

hin-sīþ, noun (HIN-SEETH / ˈhɪn-ˌsiːθ): Departure (journey hence), death.

hrycg-hǣr, noun (H'RUEDG-HAER / ˈhrydʒ-ˌhæːr): Hair on the back of an animal.

hungrig, adjective (HUNG-grih / ˈhʌŋ-grɪj): Hungry, famished.

hȳra, noun (HUE-rah / ˈhyː-ra): Hireling, one who works for pay, a hired servant.

hyrde, noun (HUER-duh / ˈhyr-də): Shepherd, herdsman; keeper, guardian.

hyrd-rǣden, noun (HUERD-RADD-en / ˈhyrd-ˌræː-dɛn): Guardianship, care, keeping.

lox, noun (LOCKS / ˈlɔks): Lynx.

mearh, noun (MEH-ar'h / ˈmɛarx): Marrow.

rǣden, noun (RAD-en / ˈræː-dɛn) : Condition.

rēafian, verb (RAY-ah-vi-ahn / ˈreːa-vɪ-an): To plunder, rifle, spoil, waste, rob.

rēafigende, adjective (RAY-ah-vi-yen-duh / ˈreːa-vɪ-jɛn-də): Ravening, rapacious.

spor, noun (SPOR / ˈspɔr): Track, trace; mark left by anything.

spyrian, verb (SPUE-ri-ahn / ˈspy-rɪ-an): To track; to make a track; to inquire, investigate, search after, seek to attain.

tam, adjective (TAHM / ˈtam): Tame, the opposite of wild.

tægl-hǣr, noun (TA-yull-HAER / ˈtæ-jəl-ˌhæːr): Hair of an animal's tail.

weald, noun (WEH-ald / ˈwɛald): High land covered with woods, forest.

weorold-þing, noun (WEH-oh-rold-THING / ˈwɛɔ-rɔld-ˌθɪŋ): Worldly thing, matter or affair (plural: *weorold-þing*).

wulf, noun (WULF / ˈwʌlf): Wolf (plural: *wulfas*).

wulf-heort, adjective (WULF-HEH-ort / ˈwʌlf-ˌhɛɔrt): Wolf-hearted, cruel.

The Baffling

U P TO THIS POINT, the *dēor* of this *hord* have been – for the most part – identifiable. Some have been more extraordinary than others, and we might question their existence, but at least it's clear which *dēor* we mean when we talk about a *fēnix* or *draca*. While the creatures thus far have been far from straightforward, none are truly baffling like the final *dēor* in this book. We cannot say with certainty what any of the creatures in this section actually are.

Many of the animals we've encountered so far have been associated with religious allegory or symbolism. We've had lions that assist the saints and deer that speak in God's voice. We've seen whales that deceive the unwary like Satan and birds that are born again from flames. Such stories provide good preaching material, and many of them make their way from Old English sermons, poems and saints' lives into the bestiaries of the later Middle Ages.

But not every *dēor* needs a moral lesson. The griffins and self-immolating hens have brief, extraordinary descriptions – entertaining, but unlikely to feature in a Sunday sermon. These creatures appear in travel narratives rather than religious texts – *Alexander's Letter to Aristotle* and *Wonders of the East*.

These travel narratives are home to some 'baffling' creatures too, as well as other texts that prove more diverting than didactic. Some come from riddles, poems that are intentionally puzzling, so it makes sense that their identities are obscured. Old English riddles can be quite bawdy and humorous, more double entendre than moral wisdom. Other *dēor* appear in poems that describe the epic adventures of pagan heroes, brave warriors who fight monsters and win worldly wealth. Although these texts were mostly copied down in monastic scriptoria, it is clear that monks and nuns found a variety of genres worth preserving.

We are left wondering if the unidentifiable creatures in these stories and narratives would have similarly baffled contemporary readers. Do they flummox us merely because of our separation of a millennium or more from those who wrote about them? Did everyone in early medieval England simply know what a *nicor* was, and that's why no writer felt the need to describe it? Did people struggle to imagine creatures of Alexander's campaigns like the teeth tyrant and moonhead? Were the solutions to riddles more obvious than they are today? Whatever the answers to these questions, the 'baffling' *dēor* present us with a *hord* of shining puzzles, a treasure trove for the imagination.

16

Water-monster (*nicor*)

T HE NICOR, THE FIRST of our baffling *dēor*, is defined by
Bosworth Toller's *Anglo-Saxon Dictionary* as a 'hippopotamus' or 'water
monster'. Cognates of the Old English word include Old Norse *nykr* (sea
goblin) and Old High German *nihhus* (crocodile, sea monster). Obviously,
hippos, goblins, crocodiles and sea monsters are all quite different.
Should we simply take dictionaries as the true arbiters of language and
go with *Bosworth-Toller*'s 'hippo' (potentially a kind of 'water monster' as
well)? An Old English–Latin glossary uses *nicor* to define Latin *hypopotami*,
so at least one contemporary scholar would have agreed.

But what is a hippo? Or rather, has the idea of a 'hippo' always been
the same? In ancient Greek, *híppos* means 'horse' and *potamós* 'river'.
Herodotus describes this 'river-horse' in the fifth century BCE, a creature sacred to certain people of the Nile Delta. Some of its qualities
resemble what we call a hippo today: it has four feet, teeth that resemble tusks (at least the large canines) and a very thick hide, and it's as
large as the largest ox. But other characteristics cited by Herodotus
make his 'river-horse' sound rather different. For instance, the hippo's
feet aren't really cloven like the hooves of an ox; it has knobbly toes

An assortment of sea creatures (*pisces*, or 'fish' according to the label), some more realistic than others, in the Harley Bestiary (England, *c.*1230–40)

that are slightly webbed. Nor does the hippo have a horse's mane and tail or make a sound like a horse.

When they came up with the word *nicor* to define the Latin *hypopotami*, was the Old English glossator thinking of Herodotus' 'river-horse' – or even the creature we call a hippo today? Or did they imagine something completely different? Was it an animal they'd ever seen, or was it something they'd only heard stories about? Given that hippos are native to Africa, it is unlikely that the English scribe ever saw one. Although this might also be true for lions and panthers, hippos don't seem to have loomed large in the early medieval imagination; at least, they are not included in the *Physiologus* tradition. Let's be honest, the glossator probably had no idea what *hypopotami* meant, and even less inkling of what one looked like. Perhaps *nicor* – a dangerous, water-dwelling creature – was simply deemed close enough to what the animal must be, and the scribe just shrugged and slotted it in.

Beowulf's *nicoras*

What, then, is a *nicor*? Old English texts never describe *nicoras* in much detail, but while its form might be uncertain, two *nicor* qualities remain constant: it is aquatic and it is ferocious.

In *Beowulf*, the hero encounters ferocious *nicoras* multiple times (and, given the poem's setting is early medieval Scandinavia, it's highly unlikely that they are hippos). The first encounter is during a swimming contest Beowulf undertakes in his youth, in which he competes against another young man called Breca. He narrates the story as an adult:

We remained together at sea for five nights, until the flood, the raging waves, drove us apart. In the coldest weather, in the darkening night, the north wind turned <u>battle-grim</u> (*heaðogrim*). The waves were rough.

The temper of the <u>sea-fishes</u> (*merefixa*) was stirred up. My coat of mail, hard and hand-linked, protected me against the loathsome creatures. My battle-garment, woven and ornamented with gold, lay across my breast. A fierce foe drew me down to the bottom, grimly gripping me fast in its <u>grasp</u> (*grape*). But I was granted a hit to that hostile fighter with the point of my battle-blade. By my hand, a storm of war slew the mighty <u>sea animal</u> (*meredeor*).

The <u>evil-doers</u> (*laðgeteonan*) were a harsh threat, but I served them with a bold sword as was fitting. The <u>wicked destroyers</u> (*manfordædlan*) who wished to partake of me took no joy in their fill as they settled down to a feast near the sea-floor. The next morning they lay upon the shore, left bare by the waves. Wounded by weapons, they had been put to sleep by a sword. Never again would they hinder seafarers from passing on the high water-way.

A light shone from the east, God's bright beacon, and the sea settled so I could see the sea cliffs, windy walls. <u>Fate</u> (*wyrd*) will often save a man not doomed to die when his bravery avails. So did it happen that I slew nine <u>water-monsters</u> (*niceras*) with my sword. I have heard of no fiercer fight beneath heaven's vault, nor of a man <u>more wretched</u> (*earmran*) upon the ocean currents. Yet <u>weary</u> (*werig*) from the venture, I escaped with my life from the <u>grip</u> (*feng*) of foes.

Beowulf is no ordinary warrior. It seems he can survive for an inhuman length of time underwater, and it is with little concern that he undertakes a swimming contest in the cold, stormy sea, battling not only the **heaþu-grimm** (battle-grim) waves but many a moody **mere-fisc** (sea-fish). But despite his supernatural strength and endurance, Beowulf finds the nine *nicoras* to be no small threat. He is **earm** (wretched – remember *earmincg* from Chapter 8?) and **wērig** (weary) after fighting them, and it is not so much his strength as it is **wyrd** (fate) that aids his survival – he is not yet doomed to die.

Beowulf calls the creatures he fights **mere-dēor** (sea animals), but his dramatic encounter with them doesn't give us much of an idea of what they look like. The *nicoras* have a **grāp** or **feng**, a 'grip' or 'grasp', but they could be grasping their victims in a number of ways – with teeth, with claws or even with the length of their bodies like a serpent. Rather than the animals' physical forms, Beowulf focuses on their fierce hostility and cruelty. The creatures are *lāð-getēonan* and *mān-fordǣdlan*. The verb **ge-tēon** means 'to do' or 'to cause', while **lāð** is anything hateful, harmful or evil. A **lāð-getēona** is thus an evildoer. **Mān-fordǣdla** is a compound of **mān** (wicked) and **for-dǣdla** (destroyer) – 'wicked destroyer', someone or something that destroys with evil intent. To be both an evil-doer and a wicked destroyer is to be pretty emphatically bad.

Beowulf encounters these creatures again when he visits the underwater dwelling of his enemy Grendel and Grendel's mother, a place described as the pool or lake of *nicoras*. Modern-day translators of *Beowulf* have called these *nicoras* 'monsters', 'water-monsters', 'demons', 'water-demons' and 'sea-monsters' (notably, none have translated them as 'hippos'). At least one translator avoids taking a stand on what a *nicor* is by keeping the Old English word and using a modern style of pluralisation – 'nicors'. In the water, Beowulf and his companions observe many *wyrmas* (snakes, dragons, reptiles or worms) and even strange **sǣ-dracan** (sea-dragons). Reachable only via a narrow path along precipitous bluffs, the pool is a place of many **nicor-hūs** (homes of *nicoras*). Some *nicoras* lie dead on the sloping headlands, although the poem does not explain how they ended up there. Humans don't normally journey to this place, so it's unlikely they were responsible. Perhaps the beasts were killed by the Grendelkin, or by some other kind of even more fearsome creature that lives in the treacherous waters. The presence of their corpses adds to the grim, fearful and foreboding atmosphere of Beowulf's descent deeper and deeper into the murky waters. Whatever normally goes on at this forest pool is best avoided.

The Grendel-kin's mere bears an uncanny resemblance to a pool in a vision of St Paul. An Old English homily describes St Paul's vision of the damned at the entrance to hell. Under a stony cliff in an icy forest is the **eardung** (dwelling) of *nicoras*, a pool of water wreathed in dark mists. This place is the punishment for the souls of people who sinned without ceasing during their lives and didn't repent before their deaths. The damned hang from the cliff's trees, twelve miles above the water. Even though this pool is described as the *eardung* of *nicoras*, no actual *nicoras* appear in St Paul's vision. Instead, Paul sees 'fiends in the likeness of *nicoras*' in the pool, greedily waiting for the tree branches high above to break so their victims will fall down into the water. We might imagine these fiends swimming around the dreadful pool, faces eagerly turned towards the creaking canopy of the trees – but when we try to imagine *how* they move, or what those faces look like, Paul's comparison is not very helpful, since we still don't know what a *nicor* looks like.

The creatures in *Beowulf* actually are *nicoras*, not fiends that look like them, but this poem is no more helpful in giving us a sense of what kind of animal they are or what they look like. Perhaps we don't need to be able to identify them as a specific species. Jennifer Neville says that the *nicoras* are simply 'a test for Beowulf' and are 'described fully enough for that purpose'. Does it really matter whether the *nicoras* more closely resemble hippos or crocodiles or water-horses or toothy deep-sea fish? In modern horror movies, directors know the power of the half-glimpsed threat: monsters are often most frightening while they remain mere shadows in the darkness, bloody tracks upon the ground, an unexpected movement at the edge of a frame. A CG monster rarely lives up to what our own imaginations can conjure.

We don't need to know what a *nicor* looks like to find it frightening, and perhaps that's the point – its mystery allows us to fill in the blanks with our own nightmares. This may even add to the horror of the creature, making it a worthier opponent for a brave hero.

Alexander's *nicoras*

Beowulf is not the only renowned warrior who must contend with *nicoras*. Alexander the Great and his army are walking along a river in the early afternoon when they come upon an unnamed town. The town is constructed on an island in the centre of a river. In his *Letter to Aristotle*, Alexander says:

> We saw that town and observed a few half-naked Indian men dwelling there. When they saw us, they immediately hid in their houses. But I wanted those men to be visible, so they could take us to fresh, sweet water. We waited a long time, but no one would come out, so I ordered a few arrows to be shot into the town. If they would not come to us willingly, then it must happen by necessity, out of fear for a fight. But the men were all the more afraid because of the arrows and all the more determined to remain hidden.

Eventually, Alexander (whose 'great'-ness is clearly not in diplomacy) decides that the only way to force the Indian men to help him is to send his men over to their island town. He commands 200 soldiers from his army to equip themselves with light weapons and approach the town by water, swimming across the river to the island.

The town that Alexander believes to be vulnerable to his whims ends up having a highly effective, natural defence system. When his men have swum a quarter of the way across the river, an **on-grislīc** (dreadful) thing befalls them. (**Grislīc**, incidentally, describes something that inspires terror, horror or awe, becoming 'grisly' in modern English.) It's the perfect word for what is about to happen. Alexander explains:

> There was a great number of *nicoras*, bigger and <u>more savage</u> (*unhyrlicran*) than <u>elephants</u> (*elpendas*). They dragged the men to the bottom of the river, between the water's waves, tearing apart and bloodying their bodies with their <u>mouths</u> (*muðe*). They carried these men away so that none of us knew what had become of them.

The stature of Herodotus' ox-sized 'river-horse' pales in comparison to these creatures' *elpend*-like enormity – and remember that elephants are compared to mountains in medieval texts. Imagine the horror of seeing the river turn blood-red, bodies ripped asunder by mysterious creatures barely glimpsed just beneath the surface. The *nicoras* can tear men apart using only their *mūþas* (mouths), so they must have sharp teeth or powerful jaws (or both). The thrashing about in the foaming waves would have made it hard for those on shore to get a good look at the attackers. Alexander (or the Old English translator) gives us the perfect example of how withholding details about the *nicoras*' appearance – whether intentionally or not – can increase the fear factor for the reader. Alexander says that he doesn't know what became of his men, but it's pretty clear they didn't survive. The horror here is of not even having bodies to bury after the slaughter, unlike the aftermath of a battle – no chance of a formal burial, or a corpse to grieve. **Un-hīrlīc** means 'fierce' or 'savage' and can refer to animate beings like the *nicoras* as well as inanimate aspects of creation, like the wind or a storm. Like a fierce storm, these *un-hīrlīc* creatures are as sudden, powerful and inescapable as a force of nature.

Alexander is furious with his guides for leading his soldiers into such danger, and they quickly become his scapegoats. The general commands that 150 of them (apparently he has many guides) be shoved into the water, sharing in the fate of the 200 soldiers:

> As soon as they entered the water, the *nicoras* were ready. They pulled them to pieces as they had done to the others before. Then the *nicoras* <u>swarmed</u> (*aweollon*) in the river as thickly as <u>ants</u> (*æmettan*), a countless number of them.

A few hours and 350 avoidable deaths later, Alexander orders his surviving troops to sound their trumpets and depart. (His 'great'-ness is clearly not in leadership either.)

The verb used to describe the creatures' movement is **a-weallan**, which can mean 'well up', 'surge' or even 'boil' in the case of liquids. In the case of *nicoras* and *æmettan* (ants), the verb means 'abound in numbers' or 'swarm'. *A-weallan* can also apply to burning or fervent thoughts and passions – heated emotions – or to overheating due to illness. The verb can even refer to a bad smell arising, a stench welling up from unsavoury origins. The river of welling, seething *nicoras* in *Alexander's Letter to Aristotle* is not unlike Beowulf's surging, monster-ridden mere. In both contexts the *nicoras* are there as a terrifying threat, something we never get a good look at, whether it's because they lurk too deep in murky waters or because their killing sprees are a frantic, writhing mess. It's impossible to single out one from the mass, and our imaginations must fill in the missing details.

Terrifying and timeless

Nicoras certainly haunt the imaginations of writers in the early medieval period, but what became of them after Old English? This strange creature makes an appearance in early Middle English: Layamon's *Brut* (*c*.1190) refers to 'nikeres' bathing in a hideous pool, creatures believed to be water-monsters or demons. Eugene Mason's translation of the Middle English says:

> That is a marvellous lake, set in middle-earth, with fen, and with reed, and with water exceeding broad; with fish, and with fowl, with evil things! The water is immeasurably broad; nikers therein bathe; there is play of elves in the hideous pool.

Despite the pool's hideous nature, the 'nikeres' (as they are called in Middle English) do not seem particularly threatening, bathing alongside playful elves. In the Middle English romance *Kyng Alisaunder*, Alexander the Great visits Meopante, a place vaguely located somewhere between Egypt and India. Alexander descends beneath the waves, in a way similar to Beowulf's dive into the Grendel-kin's mere. The people of Meopante use a special material for their buildings that hardens in water, and they dwell underwater 'with eker and fysch'. In this context, Middle English 'eker' refers to some kind of demon or sea monster. The creatures also appear in place names, like 'Nikerpoll' (*nicor* pool) and 'Nikersmadwe' (*nicor*'s meadow), in documents from the thirteenth and fourteenth centuries. Fourteenth- and fifteenth-century texts use 'nykeres' to translate the Anglo-Norman word *seraines* (sirens). Beware the 'myry song' of the 'Nykeres', who take pleasure in sending you the wrong way! The *nicor*'s latest appearance is in a dictionary from 1568, after which the word seems to drop out of use until the nineteenth century, when scholars revive it in their discussions of Old English texts.

Although the word falls out of use in English, the *nicor* never vanishes completely from modern lore. The term survives in modern German as *Nix*, a mythical creature – half-human and half-fish – that lives in an underwater palace. The *Nix* can assume a variety of disguises, appearing as a beautiful maiden or an old woman, or even turning invisible. The *Nix* is usually malevolent; stories tell how it kidnaps human children and lures people into deep water to drown. Germany also has the *Nickel*, a goblin that dwells underground in mines.

The UK has its share of *nicor*-esque creatures as well. In Cornwall the 'knocker' is another mine-dwelling creature, though it's a bit friendlier in nature than the *Nickel* or *Nix*. Sussex has the legendary 'knucker' (some kind of water-dragon), whose bottomless hidey-hole is said to be an entrance to hell. Scotland is home to the 'nuckelavee', a kind of sea-devil, which is described as looking rather like a horse with fins but with a head like a man's (only ten times bigger). It has a wide mouth that projects like a pig's snout and a single eye as red as fire. Its breath steams from its mouth, and like venom is deadly to plants and animals. Most curious of all, the nuckelavee has no skin, its muscles and sinews visible beneath black, oozing blood. In the words of a nineteenth-century folklorist, 'What a study for an anatomist!'

Perhaps the most similar name to *nicor* is 'necker', a creature that is supposed to reside in Deptford Creek in London. According to the website *Portals of London*, it came to the area years ago: '[W]hen the Thames and its tributaries spread wide and unhindered into ancient bog and marshland, the thing swam down from the north, and became trapped here by the encroaching city'. A resident mudlarker notes that local wildlife avoids the area, yet there are still piles of animal bones, and also that the location gives him a certain 'desperate, draining feeling'. This mudlarker claims it is not out of fear of being 'chomped on' that he keeps away from that part of the creek but rather that he's 'scared of feeling that feeling again'. Like the Old English *nicor*, the Deptford Creek 'necker' exudes malevolence towards intruders.

After a thousand years of stories about it, the *nicor* remains as baffling as ever. Did Alexander the Great actually encounter hippos during his campaign, which transformed into *nicoras* in the Old English translation of his narrative? There were definitely no hippos in medieval Scandinavia, so what 'real-life' creature could Beowulf have met? Encounters with this creature in more recent centuries hint at something a bit more supernatural, something mythical and mysterious. The only real constant about this *dēor* is its grisly, terrifying effect on all who meet it . . .

Water-monster's Wordhord

a-weallan, verb (ah-WEH-al-lahn / a-ˈwɛal-lan): To well up; to abound in numbers, swarm; to be hot, burn, well up with heat.

eardung, noun (EH-ar-dung / ˈɛar-dʌŋ): Habitation, dwelling.

earm, adjective (EH-arm / ˈɛarm): Wretched, miserable.

feng, noun (FENG / ˈfɛŋ): Grip, grasp, clasp; the act of seizing.

for-dǣdla, noun (for-DAD-la / fɔr-ˈdæːd-la): Destroyer.

ge-tēon, verb (yeh-TAY-on / jɛ-ˈteːɔn): To do, effect, cause; to determine a course of action.

grāp, noun (GRAWP / ˈgraːp): Grasp, grip.

grislīc, adjective (GRIZZ-leech / ˈgrɪz-liːtʃ): Grim, horrible; inspiring terror, horror or awe.

heaþu-grimm, adjective (HEH-ah-thuh-GRIM / ˈhɛa-θʌ-ˌgrɪm): Battle-grim, fierce (as the fray of battle).

lāð, noun (LAWTH / ˈlaː θ): What is hateful or harmful, harm, evil, injury, hurt, trouble, grief, pain, enmity.

lāð-getēona, noun (LAWTH-yeh-TAY-on-ah / ˈlaː θ-jɛ-ˌteː ɔ-na): Evil-doer (plural: *lāð-getēonan*).

mān, adjective (MAHN / ˈmaːn): Wicked, false.

mān-fordǣdla, noun (MAHN-vor-DAD-la / ˈmaːn-vɔr-ˌdæː d-la): Wicked destroyer (plural: *mān-fordǣdlan*).

mere-dēor, noun (MEH-ruh-DAY-or / ˈmɛ-rə-ˌdeːɔr): Sea animal
(plural: *mere-dēor*).

mere-fisc, noun (MEH-ruh-FISH / ˈmɛ-rə-ˌfiʃ): Sea-fish.

nicor, noun (NICK-or / ˈnɪ-kɔr): Water-monster (plural: *nicoras*).

nicor-hūs, noun (NICK-or-HOOS / ˈnɪ-kɔr-ˌhuːs): Home of a *nicor*
(plural: *nicor-hūs*).

on-grislīc, adjective (ON-GRIZZ-leech / ˈɔn-ˌgrɪz-liːtʃ): Horrible,
dreadful.

sǣ-draca, noun (SAE-DRAH-ka / ˈsæː-ˌdra-ka): Sea-dragon (plural:
sǣ-dracan).

un-hīrlīc, adjective (UN-HEER-leech / ˈʌn-ˌhiːr-liːtʃ): Fierce, savage.

wērig, adjective (WAY-rih / ˈweː-rɪj): Weary.

wyrd, noun (WUERD / ˈwyrd): Fate, fortune, chance; event,
occurrence, circumstance; what happens (to a person), lot,
condition.

17

Moon-head
(*heafod swelce mona*)

THE NICOR IS FAR from being the only baffling creature that Alexander the Great encounters in his exploration of *Indea* ('India'). In the Old English translation of his *Letter to Aristotle*, Alexander tells of a mysterious and threatening creature he and his army meet while journeying through a dried-up **fenn** (marsh), where cane and reeds grow. The *dēor* emerges all of a sudden from its **fæsten**. *Fæsten* (from which we get 'fastness') means 'fortress' or 'fortified town', a place built by humans to resist attack, intrusion or siege, but the word can also refer to a natural fortification, a place made secure by its nature. In this case, the *dēor's fæsten* is a *fenn*, overgrown and not easily navigable by humans. Alexander describes the marsh-dwelling creature:

> The animal's <u>back</u> (*hrycg*) was all <u>studded with pegs</u> (*acæglod*). That same <u>animal</u> (*deor*) had a <u>headdress</u> (*snoda*). Its <u>head</u> (*heafod*) was <u>round</u> (*seonowealt*) <u>like the moon</u> (*swelce mona*), and it was called a *quasi caput luna*. Its <u>breast</u> (*breost*) was similar to that of a *nicor*, and it was <u>equipped</u> (*gegyred*) and <u>toothed</u> (*geteþed*) with big, hard teeth.

Alexander lists far more physical characteristics for this animal than he does for the *nicor*. Clearly, this animal is so strange that Alexander doubts whether even his highly educated tutor Aristotle will recognise it. But although he gives a detailed description of it, it is far from obvious what this baffling *dēor* is meant to be.

The Old English translation of the *Letter to Aristotle* does not provide a vernacular (Old English) name for the creature, only a Latin one: *quasi caput luna*, which means 'head-like-the-moon'. And so I have cheated slightly and given it my own Old English name: I call the creature a *hēafod* **swelce mōna** (head-like-the-moon or moon-head), since it is a direct translation of the Latin name, and the Old English text does include those words in the description: *hæfde þæt deor seonowealt heafod swelce mona* (that animal had a round head like the moon).

The *hēafod swelce mōna* has a back that is **a-cǣglod**, a hapax. **Cǣg** means 'key' in Old English, so some scholars have suggested that *a-cǣglod* means something like 'studded with many little keys' or maybe 'studded with pegs'. Perhaps we're meant to imagine a creature covered with differently sized ridges, like the teeth of a key. The corresponding word in the Latin version of the text is *serratus*, meaning 'serrated' or 'toothed like a saw'. **Hrycg** (pronounced H'RUEDG) is Old English for 'back' and survives in modern English as 'ridge'. By the Middle English period, 'rigge' also could refer to the ridge of a roof, the keel of a ship, a rocky ledge or elevation, or the ridge between two furrows of a ploughed field. This makes sense if you think about it, since the *hrycg* (back or spine) is a sort of 'ridge' (elevated or upper part) of the body of animals that move about on four legs, parallel to the ground. Also, the *hrycg* of a vertebrate has 'ridges' of its own in the form of bumpy vertebrae. The moon-head's *hrycg* is bumpy or rough, and we are told its hide is so thick it cannot be wounded with spears.

The creature's head is, of course, **seonu-wealt** (round) 'like the moon'. **Wealte** is a word for 'ring', and the verb **seonuwealtian** means 'to reel' or 'not stand firmly' – if you are reeling and unable to stand, you may find yourself spinning around in a ring (though modern English 'reel', a device on which you can wind thread, cable, film or fishing line, comes from Old English **hrēol**, a spool). The round *hēafod* of this creature also sports a **snōd** (headdress). From *snōd* we get 'snood', the decorative hair net you might find for sale at a Renaissance fair. (Knitted snoods have recently come back into fashion, and if you thought the new trend's name is a portmanteau of 'hood' and 'scarf' with a rogue 'n' slipped in, consider yourself freshly corrected.) You can find snoods all over Etsy, both as a historical costume accessory and a modern fashion trend, but what might a *snōd* look like on an animal's body? No feathers or hair are mentioned in Alexander's description, so perhaps it refers to something like the neck frills found on the heads of some lizards. Alexander's observation that the animal's **brēost** (breast) resembles that of a *nicor* is not very helpful to us, since there are no physical descriptions of this unidentifiable creature and so we have no idea what it looked like. The *nicor* comparison simply adds to the animal's generally threatening vibe.

The final detail in the moon-head's description further emphasises its fearsome nature, for it is 'equipped' and 'toothed' with big, hard teeth. The verb **ge-gyrwan** means 'prepare', 'make ready', 'dress', 'clothe' or 'adorn', so the past participle *ge-gyred* in the quotation above means 'prepared' or 'adorned'. In *Alexander's Letter to Aristotle*, *ge-gyrwan* is used specifically for arming or girding oneself with weapons. Before arriving at the river full of *nicoras*, for instance, Alexander knows he is entering perilous terrain and orders his men to equip themselves with weapons – *mid wæpnum gegerwan* (an alternate spelling of *ge-gyrwan*). When his soldiers prepare to enter the river's deadly waters, Alexander again commands them to gear up with weapons – *wæpnum gegyrwan*. The use of *ge-gyrwan* alongside the adjective **ge-tēþed** (toothed) emphasises that the moon-head's teeth are not merely for biting and chewing – more importantly, they're for fighting.

A new kind of beast

The Old English moon-head description is based on the *quasi caput luna* of the earlier Latin version of Alexander's *Letter*, but, surprisingly, the name *quasi caput luna* doesn't appear in the Latin version at all. It only crops up in the Old English translation. The Latin *Letter* simply calls the animal *belua noui generis* (a new kind of beast). With this significant difference revealed, we might ask how else did this creature transform in translation? Both the Old English moon-head and the Latin *belua* (beast) have rough, serrated backs and live in dried-up swamps with abundant reeds, but beyond this it turns out that the two animals differ significantly. The Latin *belua* has two heads: one 'like the moon' with the breast of a hippopotamus (or a *nicor* perhaps: see Chapter 16), the other like a crocodile's with hard teeth. Some scholars have noted that these two heads don't appear in every manuscript containing the Latin *Letter*, which seems odd. Surely such a strange and unique characteristic as two heads is worth mentioning! It has also been suggested that the moon-head should really be a lioness-head, assuming that the Old English scribe mistook the Latin dative *leaenae* (lioness) for *lunae* (moon) when writing their translation. The *Liber Monstrorum*, a Latin catalogue of fantastic beasts compiled in the late seventh or early eighth century, contains yet another variation on the moon-head. The literature scholar Edward Pettit translates the passage:

And they say that in India there was a beast which had two heads, one bearing the image of a two-horned moon (believe it!), the other of a crocodile. And armed with serrated back and savage teeth, it is described as once having rushed forward and killed two soldiers of Alexander.

But what does a 'two-horned moon' (*lunae bicornis*) look like? Perhaps a round face with two horns, or a face shaped like a crescent moon?

Never trust a crocodile

Because of the reference to a crocodile head in the Latin *Letter to Aristotle* and to a rough back in both the Old English and Latin translations, some scholars have theorised that the *hēafod swelce mōna* is in fact a crocodile. It's tempting, and you can imagine it – the big teeth, the terrifying habit of lurking in water and rushing out, the knobbly back. But this idea loses its allure if you take even a moment to look closely at the letters. The Latin *Letter* contrasts the crocodile-like head to the moon-like head – the two are not the same. And if the Old English animal is a crocodile, why not use the Latin word *crocodilus* instead of making up your own Latin name? Old English scribes would have known about this creature from Latin, even if there was no word for it in their own language (there not being much need in Britain to yell 'look out, a crocodile!'). According to Isidore, the *crocodilus* gets its name from Latin *croceus* (saffron, yellow), supposedly referring to the animal's yellowish hue. English doesn't have a word for this animal until the thirteenth century, but that yellow hue is present in the Middle English 'cocodril', which comes from Latin via French.

As you can probably tell, I think it highly unlikely that the *hēafod swelce mōna* is a crocodile, but if it *were* we might learn about its appearance and behaviour from the earlier *Physiologus* or later bestiaries. The earliest versions of the *Physiologus* do not include the crocodile; Isidore adds it in the seventh century, along with the wolf, ibex, dog, owl and dragon. The thirteenth-century Norman cleric Guillaume Le Clerc claims that the crocodile is 'somewhat like an ox' and 'as big around as the trunk of a tree'. In some bestiary illustrations the crocodile resembles a dog, while in others it looks more like a lion. Although it is never depicted with two heads, the crocodile's head does appear to be attached upside-down in some illustrations. The medieval bestiary scholar Florence McCulloch says: 'The only consistency in the portrayal of the crocodile is that it usually has four legs; beyond that point the artist's fantasy is at play.'

One could potentially connect the two-headedness of the Latin *Letter's belua* to the famously two-faced nature of the crocodile. In bestiaries the crocodile is known for weeping with contrition after eating a human being, so the animal is symbolic of hypocrisy – since it was so eager for the kill beforehand. Both Bartholomaeus Anglicus and Guillaume Le Clerc write that when a crocodile finds a human to eat it will slay him, swallow him and weep over him, although the order of events in the scenario differ slightly. According to Bartholomaeus, a crocodile will weep after it kills a man and before finally swallowing him. Guillaume's crocodile gets all the swallowing out of the way first, gulping the man down so that nothing remains and only then lamenting it for the rest of its life. Another 'two-faced' behaviour of the bestiary crocodile is its alleged habit of spending daytime as a land animal and night-time as a water animal. A crocodile supposedly moves only the upper part of its mouth because it presents God's teachings to others without practising what it preaches. The bestiary Bodley 764 says that the crocodile signifies the hypocrite, who is puffed up with pride and greed but likes people to see them as a faultless ascetic. By the late sixteenth century, a weeping crocodile was used figuratively to refer to a person who weeps or makes a show of sorrow hypocritically or with malicious intent, and today English speakers still refer to a false, insincere display of emotion as 'crocodile tears'. The general message across the centuries is pretty consistent: never trust a crocodile.

The hypocrisy of the crocodile in later medieval bestiaries even extends to one of its by-products: its dung is used to make an ointment that makes ageing women appear young and beautiful. However, this ointment isn't really an effective anti-ageing cream since it only works until sweat washes it away. Bodley 764 compares the ointment to inexperienced people's praise of the wicked, which serves as 'a salve which makes their misdeeds heroic acts'. The bestiary warns: 'When the just judge is moved in his wrath to strike them for their evil deeds, then all the splendour of this praise vanishes like smoke.' Or like face-dung.

Despite the possible association of two heads with being 'two-faced', neither of these characteristics is relevant for the Old English moon-head. No matter how the Latin *belua* is described, the *hēafod swelce mōna* clearly only has one head, one that is 'like the moon', whatever that might mean. Both moon-head and crocodile are *a-cǣglod* on their backs and well *ge-tēþed* in their mouths, but there the similarities end. Crocodiles are semi-aquatic, but the moon-head lives in a dried-up *fenn*. With its long, narrow snout, the crocodile's head isn't *seonu-wealt* (round) by any stretch of the imagination. Built for battle, the crocodile sports talons and a hide that Pliny describes as 'invincible against all blows', but Alexander is able to kill the moon-head with iron **hameras** (hammers) and **slecga** (mallets). The bestiary crocodile has one vulnerable spot, the soft, thin skin on its belly – something against which a spear would be a fairly effective choice of weapon. The Old English *Letter to Aristotle* notes, however, that **speru** (spears) are useless against the moon-head's thick hide. If Alexander had been fighting a crocodile, *speru* would have been far more effective weapons than *hameras* and *slecga*.

Though undoubtedly an extraordinary creature and a dangerous opponent, the medieval crocodile just doesn't have enough in common with the *hēafod swelce mōna* for them to be the same animal. But what is even more strange is how different the moon-head is from the creature in the Latin text upon which the Old English description is based. Is this merely a case of scribal error, an Old English translator whose knowledge of Latin was somewhat lacking or who simply mistook *leaenae* for *lunae*, a lioness for a moon? Is the description based on some other text lost to the ages? Or is this just a case of an Old English scribe drawing on their imagination, enjoying themself, someone whose – in the words of Florence McCulloch – 'fantasy is at play'?

Moon-head's Wordhord

a-cǣglod, adjective (ah-KAG-lodd / a-ˈkæː-glɔd): Pegged, studded with pegs; serrated (definition uncertain).

brēost, noun (BRAY-ost / ˈbreːɔst): Breast, chest.

cǣg, noun (KAG / ˈkæːg): Key.

fæsten, noun (FAST-en / ˈfæs-tɛn): Fastness; place by its nature fortified against incursion.

fenn, noun (FEN / ˈfɛn): Fen, marsh.

ge-gyrwan, verb (yeh-YUER-wahn / jɛ-ˈjyr-wan): To prepare, make ready; to clothe, equip; to ornament, adorn.

ge-tēþed, adjective (yeh-TAY-thed / jɛ-ˈteː-θɛd): Toothed, provided with teeth.

hamer, noun (HA-mer / ˈha-mɛr): Hammer (plural: *hameras*).

hrēol, noun (H'RAY-ol / ˈhreːɔl): Reel, spool.

hrycg, noun (H'RUEDG / ˈhrydʒ): Back, spine.

mōna, noun (MO-na / ˈmoː-na): Moon.

seonu-wealt, adjective (SEH-on-uh-WEH-alt / ˈsɛɔ-nʌ-ˌwɛalt): Round, circular, spherical.

seonuwealtian, verb (SEH-on-uh-WEH-all-ti-ahn / ˈsɛɔ-nʌ-ˌwɛal-tɪ-an): To reel, not stand firmly.

slecg, noun (SLEDGE / ˈslɛdʒ): Mallet, sledgehammer (plural: *slecga*).

snōd, noun (SNOAD / ˈsnoːd): Headdress, snood.

spere, noun (SPEH-ruh / ˈspɛ-rə): Spear, lance (plural: *speru*).

swelce, adverb (SWELL-chuh / ˈswɛl-tʃə): As, like.

wealte, noun (WEH-all-tuh / ˈwɛal-tə): Ring.

18

Teeth Tyrant
(*dentes tyrannum*)

Y OU MIGHT BE NOTICING a pattern now in our baffling creatures; both the *nicoras* and the *hēafod swelce mōna* feature in Alexander the Great's adventures, as described in his *Letter to Aristotle* – and so does this next mysterious monster. The man meets his fair share of puzzling *dēor*, which are hard to picture even with his descriptions. During his adventures in the east, before he encounters the moon-head, Alexander comes upon a *swīðe micel dēor*, a very great animal, one that is bigger than any of the creatures he has observed thus far. At this point in his campaign, Alexander has seen **eoforas** (wild boars), *tigras* (tigers), *lēon* (lions), *pardas* (leopards or panthers), *beran* (bears) and *elpendas* (elephants), not to mention the *nicoras* (water-monsters) that he says are 'larger than elephants'. But the size of this new *dēor* dwarfs all of these.

A very great animal

Old English **swīðe** continues to mean 'very' until the end of the medieval period, at which point the definition becomes more specific – 'very rapidly' or 'very quickly'. Today 'swith' survives as a rare archaism and in Scots dialect. The Scottish writer James Lumsden, who went by the nom de plume Samuel Mucklebackit, writes in 1892 that the hours sped on 'far too swith'. This 'swith' may resemble 'swift', but really it goes back to *swīðe*. Modern English 'swift' comes from another Old English word: **swift**, which means the same as it does today.

The word 'mickle' may also be familiar to people living in Scotland and northern England. This regional term has exactly the same meaning that it did a thousand years ago – great or large – deriving from Old English **micel**, which is pronounced slightly differently (MIH-chell). If you're from the UK, you may be familiar with the Scottish proverb 'Many a mickle makes a muckle'. 'Mickle', as we know, means something large, but what is a muckle? It's just a variant of 'mickle'. In 1793 George Washington, first president of the United States, recorded the 'Scotch addage' of 'many mickles make a muckle', but it seems that he, or whoever he heard it from, garbled the saying. The phrase, which appears as early as 1614, is actually 'Many a little makes a micle,' which makes a lot more sense, as we know that a 'micle' or 'mickle' must be something large. This mistake caught on in the UK as well as the US, and pretty soon people were under the impression that a 'mickle' must be a *small* amount of something, while a 'muckle' was a large amount, otherwise the proverb made no sense. By the early twentieth century, pickles creep into the saying – 'Many a pickle makes a muckle.' Whether you have a mickle of pickles or a mistaken muckle, the truth is that *micel* and mickle have always been a lot, not a little.

But back to Alexander's *micel dēor*. The Old English translation of *Alexander's Letter to Aristotle* does not give a vernacular name for the *swīðe micel dēor*, saying only that the people of *Indea* ('India') call it *dentes tyrannum*, which is Latin for 'teeth tyrant'. One Old English word for 'tyrant' is **folc-sceaða**, literally 'people-harmer' or 'nation-harmer', another is **lēod-hata**, 'people-hater' or 'nation-hater', and the word for 'teeth' is *tēþ*. Technically, the Old English translator could have called the animal a *tēþ folc-sceaða* or a *tēþ lēod-hata*, but, unlike *hēafod swelce mōna*, those words don't appear in the text. I don't know if the scribe ever thought of the 'teeth tyrant' as a *tēþ folc-sceaða*, so I've stuck with the Latin name. Strangely, aside from the Latin name *dentes tyrannum*, there is no mention of either teeth or tyranny in the creature's description.

So what is the mysterious *dentes tyrannum*, the fearsome teeth tyrant? Alexander says the creature has three *hornas* (horns) on its **foran-hēafod** (forehead), which make it terrifyingly **ge-wǣpnod** (equipped with weapons), armed and ready for a fight. The creature's head resembles that of a *hors* (horse), and its colour is *blæc* (black or dark-hued). All in all, this *dēor* doesn't sound like any animal I've ever seen.

The *dentes tyrannum* is discussed on the blog *A Book of Creatures*, a kind of modern Internet bestiary that brings together an encyclopaedic collection of 'entities [that] have shared our world ever since we earned the capacity to wonder'. The bestiary's entries include everything from the the Witkəś (a tusked water-dweller of Russia 'known to invite guests underwater to drink tea') to the Sazae-oni (a Japanese demon with a 'sinuous sluglike' body and 'humanoid arms' coming out of a shell) – though, as of yet, there is no post about a moon-head or *nicor*. In his blog post on the *odontotyrannus*, Emile Marc Moacdieh lists many variant names for the *dentes tyrannum*, including *dentityrannus* and *arine hayant le tirant*. He explains that 'medieval reading errors led to a variety of increasingly awkward alternate names and direct translations'. Moacdieh's own artistic depiction of the creature is absolutely massive, at least five times the height of the average human being. It certainly fits the Old English *Letter*'s description of it being a *swīðe micel dēor*!

Giant worms and rhinos

Some scholars suggest that this 'teeth tyrant' may have been confused with another Indian animal, the Indus worm or *skōlex*, an enormous carnivorous worm from the works of the classical writers Ctesias and Aelian. In his history of India, Ctesias writes about a worm so thick that 'a child of ten could scarcely clasp it round in his arms'. In each of its jaws is a single four-foot-long tooth, strong enough to tear anything within its grasp with ease, 'be it a stone or be it a beast'. During the day these (most likely mythical) worms hide in the muddy bottom of the River Indus, but at night they leave the river in search of prey. The worm is difficult to kill because of its very thick skin, 'two finger-breadths thick'.

Maybe the Indus worm's teeth were mistaken for horns by Alexander. Or maybe he encountered a different horned creature. Another suggestion for the teeth tyrant's identity is the rhinoceros. The Old English scholar R. D. Fulk suggests that *dentes tyrannum* is the Old English-writing scribe's attempt to Latinise the Greek word *odontotyrannos*, which he claims means 'rhinoceros'. (*Odontotyrannus* – with a 'u' – is also listed as a variant name on *A Book of Creatures*.) But did the ancient Greeks really call the rhinoceros an *odontotyrannos*? The modern English word 'rhinoceros' derives from Greek – *rhino* (of the nose) + *kerato* (horn), and the modern word for the creature is *rinókeros*. *Rinókeros* appears in the writing of Strabo, the geographer and historian who lived from around 64 BCE until sometime after 21 CE. While Strabo's Greek is not as old as Alexander's (from the fourth century BCE), I can't help but wonder if the same term was used for 'rhinoceros' all along. I have found no compelling evidence for the Greeks calling the animal an *odontotyrannos* – a 'teeth tyrant'.

Another issue with the rhino theory is the number of horns, since the *dentes tyrannum* of the Old English *Letter* has three *hornas*. Real-life African Sumatran rhinos have two horns, while Javan rhinos have only one. That said, the Rhino Resource Center's website features a photo of a 'mutant', three-horned black rhino, supposedly photographed in Namibia in 2015, and the existence of other three-horned black rhinos has been recorded elsewhere. So three *hornas* doesn't necessarily rule out the rhino as a potential identification – it would just have been a very special one.

Mad beast or mad man?

Alexander repeats his mistake from previous animal encounters by obstructing the path to the local watering hole. Despite it being completely normal for animals to seek drinking water, the phenomenon seems to get the better of the general again and again. The fact that these *dēor* must search for water is in fact a reason why the creature cannot be the same as the *odontotyrannos*. The Greek writings of Palladius of Galatia (fifth century) and George the Monk (ninth century) claim that the *odontotyrannos* lives in the water, and there would be no reason to come searching for water if it already lives there. Unlike the *cerastes*, the horned snake of Chapter 13, the *dentes tyrannum* doesn't leave Alexander's men alone after satisfying its thirst, perhaps (correctly) identifying them as a continuing threat to its well-being. In the Old English *Letter*, Alexander says:

> When this <u>animal</u> (*deor*) had drunk the water, it then beheld our encampment ... and all at once it <u>rushed</u> (*ræsde*) upon us and our encampment. It did not flinch from the burning of hot <u>flame</u> (*leges*) and <u>fire</u> (*fyres*) that faced it but trampled it all <u>enraged</u> (*wod*).

The teeth tyrant has no concern for the soldiers' campfires and seems to be immune in its rage to *līg* (flame) and *fȳr* (fire).

The Old English *Letter* does not describe the *dentes tyrannum*'s means of movement (on four legs perhaps? Or no legs?), but we do know that it moves very quickly. The verb used to describe its movement is **ræsan** (to rush). The creature, Alexander says, rushes and tramples his men's campfires without care, completely *wōd*. **Wōd**, like modern English 'mad', can mean both 'angry' and 'insane', and it survives in modern English in the rare, archaic word 'wood'. From as early as the thirteenth century, the word 'woodman' referred to a madman or lunatic, not taking on the meaning of 'one who hunts game in a wood or forest' until the fifteenth century. ('Woodsman', which appears at the end of the seventeenth century, becomes the more commonly used word for 'huntsman'.) Alexander considers the *dentes tyrannum*'s violence to be *wōd* – insane and unreasonable – probably because it continues to attack his men when it could simply leave. But the creature's single-minded determination to fight anything and everyone in its path is not unlike Alexander, so arguably the man is rather *wōd* himself.

It's fortunate for Alexander that there is only one *dentes tyrannum*, because that animal alone results in many casualties. Even though it's up against Alexander's sizeable army, the teeth tyrant kills twenty-six men and wounds another fifty-two before it is taken down. Alexander's soldiers shoot it **un-sōfte** (with difficulty) with **stræla** (arrows) and *speru* (spears). More common definitions for *un-sōfte* are 'not at ease', 'in discomfort' and 'not gently', but an action done **sōfte** is one performed 'easily' or 'without opposition'. Granted, the men fighting the *dentes tyrannum* are probably not 'comfortable' or 'gentle' in their shooting either.

Medieval teeth tyrants

Unlike the mysterious moon-head or the enigmatic *nicor*, Alexander's teeth tyrant is depicted in medieval illustrations. The creature appears in two different manuscripts that date from several centuries after the Old English period. (It must be noted that neither illustration is of a creature that remotely resembles a rhinoceros.)

The older of the two examples is in a fourteenth-century manuscript, made in England and written in French, that describes how the Macedonians (Alexander's troops) are attacked by the *dent-tyrant*, or *odontotyrannos*. The creature in this manuscript is dark-grey, hairy and taller than a man (though not by much). It is four-legged, with four big claws on each foot, and has long pointed teeth, a long snout, long ears and three pointy horns that appear to join together on its forehead. The French description of the animal in this manuscript is not far off our Old English one: it is an appalling monster of horrifying ugliness, as large as an elephant, and it has a black head like a horse's but with three horns.

The second illustration is in a manuscript produced in fifteenth-century France. According to the text written in French, a history of Alexander the Great, the creature is called *arine* 'in the Indian language', which is one of the names listed for the *odontotyrannus* on the *A Book of Creatures* blog. The illustration itself depicts a hairy, brown- or tan-coloured animal with three horns rising straight up from its head like a crown. It has the long snout and ears of a dog, fearsome teeth and a swishing, hairy tail. It walks on four legs, but its foreleg appears to have the dexterity of a hand, for it grasps a warrior's spear that is lodged in its neck. Each foot is slightly webbed, with three claws extending forward and one at the back. This illustration does not closely resemble the animal described in the accompanying text; clearly the scribe and the artist worked separately. Like the textual description says, the depicted creature is 'a beast of marvellous size, stronger than an elephant' with 'three horns on its forehead', but the illustrated creature lacks the 'completely black head' to which the text refers.

Alexander fighting an *arine* (France, early fifteenth century)

Some qualities are common across all versions of the teeth tyrant. Whatever kind of animal it might be, the teeth tyrant is always fierce, fearless and aggressive. Alexander loses many men in a battle against just one of them. While all texts refer to the creature's teeth in its name, they don't comment on them in the descriptions. Depictions of the teeth tyrant always feature horns, so it seems that 'horn tyrant' would have been a better name. Or 'tricorn' perhaps? No matter what you call it, this creature doesn't run from a fight, so if you have the misfortune of meeting one, it's best to run and hide in a very un-Alexander-like way. Don't be *wōd*.

Teeth Tyrant's Wordhord

eofor, noun (EH-ov-or / ˈɛɔ-vɔr): Wild boar (plural: *eoforas*).
folc-sceaða, noun (FOLK-SHEH-ah-tha / ˈfɔlk-ˌʃɛa-θa): Tyrant (people-harmer).

foran-hēafod, noun (FOR-on-HAY-ah-vod / ˈfɔ-ran-ˌheːa-vɔd):
Forehead.

ge-wǣpnod, adjective (yeh-WAP-nod / jɛ-ˈwæːp-nɔd): Armed,
equipped with weapons.

lēod-hata, noun (LAY-od-HA-ta / ˈleːɔd-ˌha-ta): Tyrant (people-hater).

līg, noun (LEE / ˈliːj): Flame.

micel, adjective (MIH-chell / ˈmɪ-tʃɛl): Great in size, in quantity, or in
a metaphorical sense.

rǣsan, verb (RAZ-ahn / ˈræː-zan): To rush, move violently or
impetuously.

sōfte, adverb (SOAF-tuh / ˈsoːf-tə): Softly, without disturbance; at
ease, without trouble; gently; without discord; easily, without
opposition.

strǣl, noun (STRAL / ˈstræːl): Arrow, shaft, dart (plural: *strǣla*).

swift, adjective (SWIFT / ˈswɪft): Swift, moving or capable of moving
quickly.

swīðe, adverb (SWEE-thuh / ˈswiː-θə): Very, much, exceedingly.

un-sōfte, adverb (UN-SOAF-tuh / ˈʌn-ˌsoːf-tə): With difficulty, with
trouble; (in other contexts) not at ease, in discomfort, not gently.

wōd, adjective (WOAD / ˈwoːd): Mad, raving, raging, furious.

19

Street-maker
(*stræt-wyrhta*)

THE PREVIOUS BAFFLING animals may leave you thinking that mysterious *dēor* live only in distant lands, but familiar English creatures also have the potential to puzzle. These *dēor* creep and crawl throughout the tenth-century Exeter Book riddles. Modern English 'riddle' is related to Old English **rǣdels**, which has a much broader range of meanings: 'counsel', 'consideration', 'debate', 'conjecture', 'imagination', 'interpretation', 'enigma' and 'riddle'. **Rǣd** on its own means 'counsel', 'advice', 'prudence' or 'intelligence'. Riddles require careful consideration and an active imagination to solve. Their enigmatic descriptions provide a window into the riddler's own imagination, giving a unique perspective of everyday creatures.

The street-maker of *Riddle 15*

The Exeter Book offers no solutions to its riddles, so we can only guess what some of these creatures are meant to be. The alternately fearful and fierce *dēor* of *Riddle 15* is particularly baffling:

My neck is white and my <u>head</u> (*heafod*) is <u>tawny</u> (*fealo*), my sides the same. I am swift on foot, bearing a <u>battle-weapon</u> (*beadowǣpen*). Hair stands on my back, also on my cheeks. Two ears <u>tower</u> (*hlifiað*) above my <u>eyes</u> (*eagum*). I step with <u>spears</u> (*ordum*) in green grass.

My grief is certain if a <u>slaughter-grim</u> (*wælgrim*) warrior finds me in my home. I stay there, bold with my children, my young offspring. When a <u>guest</u> (*gǣst*) comes to my door, death is certain for them. <u>Timid in spirit</u> (*forhtmod*), I must carry my children from home, save them by flight, if ever he comes after me, bearing his <u>breast</u> (*breost*). I dare not await the savage one in my space – I will not consider such advice! Using my <u>forefeet</u> (*feþemundum*), I must bravely <u>make</u> (*wyrcan*) a <u>street</u> (*strǣte*) through a steep hill.

I can easily save the lives of the free, if only I can lead my family, my own relations, through the <u>hole</u> (*þyrel*) in the hill, a <u>secret</u> (*degolne*) way. Afterwards, I will have no need to worry about the attack of a <u>slaughter-whelp</u> (*wælhwelpes*).

If the <u>hateful foe</u> (*niðsceaþa*) follows my footsteps on the narrow trail, he will not lack a <u>battle-meeting</u> (*guþgemotes*) on the <u>hostile path</u> (*gegnpaþe*). Upon reaching the roof of the hill, I fiercely strike with <u>battle-darts</u> (*hildepilum*) the <u>loathsome foe</u> (*laðgewinnum*) from whom I have long fled.

I have called this creature a **strǣt-wyrhta**, a made-up Old English compound meaning 'street-maker'. The name points to this *dēor*'s first line of defence when it is attacked by predators: it will **wyrcan** (make) a **strǣt** (street or path).

Riddle 15 starts off with a list of physical characteristics, far more than we usually get in Old English animal descriptions. As we've seen in previous chapters, descriptions of animals usually focus on behaviours that are linked to an allegorical tale, not details about a *dēor*'s physical appearance. One need not describe an eagle if everyone knows what it looks like, and in that case it is the eagle's unique behaviours that are worth mentioning. But if you're trying to guess an animal from a riddle, physical traits are an important clue.

The *dēor* in *Riddle 15* has a white neck and is *fealu* on its neck and sides. **Fealu** might be translated as 'tawny' – basically yellow, but variously tinted with shades of red, brown or grey, pale in colour as opposed to vivid. Hair stands up on the creature's back and cheeks. The verb **hlīfian** means 'to tower' or 'to stand out prominently' and often refers to human creations (like mead-halls, sails and fortresses) or landscape features (like cliffs, hills, trees), but in this riddle it describes neither of these two categories and is instead applied to the creature's two ears, towering over its eyes. The *dēor* moves quickly on foot and bears a **beadu-wǣpen** (battle-weapon). What the *beadu-wǣpen* is exactly remains unclear – but it is fair to assume that it is not a typical 'battle-weapon' like a sword, spear or arrow (even if medieval illustrations might take liberties on this point – if you recall, the teeth tyrant of the illustration in Chapter 18 was grasping a spear in one of its forefeet). The riddle refers to this 'weapon' again when the creature steps through the grass, this time with multiple weapons, **ordas** (pointed weapons). Later, the creature defends itself fiercely with its **hilde-pīlas** (battle-darts). Claws then? Or teeth?

Despite being well armed and swift-moving, this *dēor*'s approach to danger differs significantly from the teeth tyrant's. If an enemy approaches, the creature is **forht-mōd** (timid in spirit), and it flees, carrying its children to safety. The *dēor* sounds like a digger, since it builds a *strǣt* (street) straight through a hill using its *fēþe-munda*. The literal translation of **fēþe-mund** is 'walking-hand' or 'hand for walking', a charming hapax for an animal's paw. *Fēþe-mund* emphasises the animal's skill and dexterity when it makes a **þyrel** (hole) through the earth. 'Thirl' is a fairly rare word for 'hole' in modern English, but you are more likely to be familiar with another related word: 'nostril'. Modern English 'nostril' comes from Old English **nos-þyrel**, literally 'nose-hole'.

Digging a *þyrel*, the *strǣt-wyrhta* makes a **dīgol** (secret) way out of its home to safety. The word *dīgol* inspired a character name in Tolkien's *The Lord of the Rings*. The hobbit Déagol discovers the cursed One Ring in a riverbed and refuses to give it to his friend and cousin Sméagol for his birthday. Enraged, Sméagol strangles Déagol and hides his body, a secret (*dīgol*) murder that will forever haunt him, even after he becomes the wicked creature Gollum. The name Sméagol, incidentally, comes from Old English **smēagan**, a verb meaning 'consider', 'ponder', 'examine', 'search' or 'seek an opportunity', things that this character often does to the detriment of himself and others.

The *strǣt* of the *strǣt-wyrhta* is called a **gegn-pæþ**, a 'hostile path' or 'opposing road', a place for a **gūþ-gemōt** (battle-meeting). Both *gegn-pæþ* and *gūþ-gemōt* are extremely rare words. *Gegn-pæþ* is a hapax composed of the components **gēan** (against, on the opposite side) + **pæþ** (path, track). The *gēan* prefix becomes the 'gain' of modern English 'gainsay', meaning 'to deny' or 'to speak against (something)'. But what is a 'gain-path'? Perhaps it refers to the force that the *strǣt-wyrhta* has to apply against the soil as it pushes its way along a difficult path, using its *fēþe-munda* to make its way forward.

Gegn-pæþ could alternatively be a reference to the fact that two opponents, the *strǣt-wyrhta* and its predator, will meet face to face (*gēan* each other) on the *pæþ* to fight it out. This idea works well with the word *gūþ-gemōt*, a meeting for battle or combat. *Gūþ-gemōt* appears only one other time in extant Old English literature, in a poetic retelling of Genesis. When he leads an army to rescue his kinsman Lot, Abraham makes a speech to his generals before the fight. The poem says: 'He had a great need for them to advance on two sides into the grim <u>battle-meeting</u> (*guðgemot*) with their guests, the difficult fight.' The poet describes Abraham's enemies as his **gystas**, his 'guests' or 'visitors', which alliterates nicely with *gūþ-gemōt*. The *strǣt-wyrhta*'s opponent is also called a *gyst*. The word not only alliterates with *gūþ-gemōt* and *gegn-pæþ*, it emphasises the fact that the enemy has breached an area where it doesn't belong. Such a hostile *gyst* must be dealt with accordingly.

The *strǣt-wyrhta*'s visitor is the worst kind of *gyst*, so bad it needs to be said three ways: a **nīþ-sceaða** (malignant foe), **lāð-gewinna** (hated opponent) and **wæl-hwelp** (slaughter-whelp). All three of these words are hapaxes, appearing nowhere else in Old English. The literal translation of *nīþ-sceaða* is 'hatred harmer' or 'hostility robber', while *lāð-gewinna* means 'hated adversary' or 'loathed foe'. Old English *hwelp* (Chapter 8) usually refers to a young dog, but can also be the cub of a lion or bear. (Today 'whelp' sounds quite old-fashioned, having been superseded by 'puppy'.) *Bosworth-Toller* defines *wæl-hwelp* as 'a dog that slays' or 'a dog for hunting', but given that a *hwelp* could be a cub of some sort, this animal isn't necessarily a dog. We can't really identify the creature chasing the *strǣt-wyrhta*; we only know that it is extremely hateful and hostile, possibly an animal's young offspring. It is also **wæl-grim** (slaughter-grim), cruel and bloodthirsty.

Unlike the baffling creatures of previous chapters, this *dēor* is a riddle, composed by someone who intended us to use clues to guess its identity. So what kind of *dēor* is the *strǣt-wyrhta*, an animal with a white belly and tall ears that uses its 'walking-hands' to make a path through a hill and its sharp weapons to fight off predators?

An expert burrower

To begin with, the riddle gives us several physical characteristics as clues. And so let's begin there, by asking: what animal would fit the description? The *hilde-pīlas* could be the sharp claws and teeth of a **brocc** (badger). *Brocc* derives from Celtic languages (compare it to Gaelic *broc* and Welsh *broch*) and means 'grey'. While today the defining image of the badger is of its black and white stripes, the hair of the European badger is silver-grey and could perhaps be described using the rather vague Old English colour term *fealu* (tawny). The badger's neck is white – like that of the riddle's *strǣt-wyrhta*. The *brocc* solution was first suggested by the Old English scholar Franz Dietrich as early as 1859, and since then it has been supported by many other readers.

Another strong argument in favour of the *brocc* is the *strǣt-wyrhta*'s skill at digging, for it can dig long tunnels quickly and easily. A badger has paws with five digits (like a human hand) and sharp claws, which it uses to dig extensive burrow systems called setts. Setts have many chambers connected by passageways and can extend over 100 metres and include as many as fifty entrances/exits. *Brocc* clans build these impressive 'streets' to keep themselves and their family safe. One can easily picture a badger bringing its young to a safer chamber, finding a *dīgol* (hidden) way through a hill.

But before we celebrate and lay down our riddle-solving hats, we must admit that the badger solution isn't as satisfying as it might at first seem. The main argument against it is not so much about the details included in the riddle, but those that are left out. *Riddle 15* makes no mention of what is arguably a *brocc*'s most distinctive feature, the black stripes on either side of its face that stretch across its eyes like a mask. Surely this is a more significant characteristic than ears that tower above its eyes. (For one thing, a badger's ears don't stick up that much, and certainly don't *tower* like cliffs.) Given the inclusion of several details concerning the *strǣt-wyrhta*'s colouring, it seems strange not to mention a black-masked face. Another argument against the *brocc* solution is that badgers are not known to be particularly quick-moving; they are short-legged, with what one field guide to Britain's mammals describes as a 'distinctive, unhurried trot'. The badger's waddle is a far cry from *Riddle 15*'s *strǣt-wyrhta*, who is 'swift on foot'.

Badgers digging a tunnel in the Harley Bestiary (England, *c*.1230–40)

The *brocc* also doesn't have a huge presence within extant Old English literature. The word mainly appears in glossaries, with a handful of examples in leechbooks. The medieval literature scholar Dieter Bitterli says the badger is 'virtually absent from the canonical works of classical and early medieval zoology', warranting only brief mentions in the writings of Pliny and Isidore. The first detailed description of the badger's characteristics is in the Flemish theologian Thomas of Cantimpré's encyclopaedia on nature written *c*.1240. In medieval bestiaries badgers are best known for digging holes together in the mountains, and the most common medieval illustration shows the badger's alleged digging method, one badger lying on its back with a stick in its mouth while its companions pile soil on to its belly. When the belly is piled high with earth, two of the badgers take either end of the stick in their teeth, dragging the 'pack-badger' away. You can see an example of this charming if totally unrealistic behaviour in the thirteenth-century Harley Bestiary. It's worth noting that in this illustration the distinctive black face stripes are also missing, so maybe in the Middle Ages they weren't considered essential for identifying the animal.

A tawny trickster

In 1927 the literature scholar Cyril Brett suggested a new solution that became popular: the *fox* (fox) or *fixen* (vixen). (*Fox* and *fixen*, incidentally, demonstrate how during the Old English period there is not yet a phonological difference between 'f' and 'v'.) A *fox* has reddish fur, often mingled with grey or yellow, a tawny combination that might be described as *fealu* in contrast to the white of its neck. Unlike badgers, foxes do have pointed ears that could be said to 'tower' over their eyes. They can run briskly when pursued so could arguably be 'swift on foot'.

Foxes, however, are not known to be great diggers. They might take up residence in the burrows of other animals, perhaps enlarging an abandoned rabbit warren or badger sett, but they are more likely to find homes above ground or near its surface, like in a rocky crevice or under a garden shed. And, perhaps most importantly, a *fox* certainly does not 'make streets' in the way that *Riddle 15* describes. Overall, I think it's fair to say that *fox* is a weaker solution than *brocc*.

But before we go burrowing for further possible answers to this riddle, let's take a moment to stay with the fox. The fox has long been associated with mischief, trickery and cunning. An Old English homily says the *fox* is the *geapest* of all animals, which is to say the most *geap* (crooked, crafty, deceitful). There's even a word in Old English, *foxunga*, that means 'foxlike wiles' or 'tricks'. The term is a hapax that appears in one of Ælfric's saints' lives. A man claims to want to follow Christ in his footsteps, but Christ sees that his desire comes from arrogance, not sincere faith. The man has *foxunga* dwelling inside him.

Although *foxunga* appears only once in Old English, it sticks around during the Middle English period, becoming the noun 'foxing'. The Middle English *Physiologus* gives an example of a 'foxing' or clever trick. The fox lies in a furrow or hole in the ground, scarcely breathing, playing dead, until some birds come along looking for carrion. As soon as the birds start to peck at the fox it repays their 'billing' (pecking) with 'illing' (evil doing). This method of deception is the most common subject for fox illustrations in medieval bestiaries. Bodley 764 says: 'The fox is the symbol of the devil, who appears dead to all living things until he has them by the throat and punishes them.' Often the strange behaviours of bestiary animals are assumed to be complete fabrication, but in this case it is supported by observation. You can see a fox playing dead to capture a crow in the 1961 film of a Russian naturalist at the Moscow Pavlov Institute.

A fox playing dead in a bestiary (England, early twelfth century)

A protective parent

But enough with foxes, let's get back to the real trickster of this chapter: the riddle itself. In 1944 the literature scholar Jean I. Young suggested yet another solution, an alternative to Dietrich's *brocc* and Brett's *fox*: the **wesle** (weasel). The *stræt-wyrhta*'s *hilde-pīlas* could be the *wesle*'s sharp claws or powerful canines. (The force of a weasel's bite is stronger relative to its size than that of a lion, tiger or bear!) Isidore says that the weasel 'practises deceit in the houses where it nurses its pups' by moving and changing its dwelling, which could correspond with the *stræt-wyrhta*'s carrying its children to a safer place.

In general, though, the *wesle* solution has not received much support. For starters, the colouring is all wrong. While they do have white on their undersides from the neck down along the belly, Britain's weasels are primarily chestnut-brown, too dark to be described as *fealu*. Weasels can scamper fairly quickly, but their small, rounded ears really can't be said to 'tower'. Like the *fox*, the *wesle* is not much of a burrower, sometimes taking over abandoned rodent dens but not doing the digging itself. Young thought the unidentified foe of the *stræt-wyrhta* could be a snake, and medieval sources like Isidore do say that the weasel preys upon snakes. One medieval manuscript illustration even depicts a tiny weasel ferociously attacking a much larger basilisk. It's true that the *stræt-wyrhta* does eventually turn back to fight its foe, but it seems unlikely for a weasel to flee in the first place if it regularly hunts snakes and fights basilisks.

A prickly hand-walker

If not a *brocc*, *fox* or *wesle*, what could the *stræt-wyrhta* be? A stronger contender than all these animals is the **igil** (hedgehog), which was first suggested by Brett as a less likely (in his opinion) alternative to his *fox* solution. (The word *igil*, incidentally, has a soft 'g' – IH-yill, not IH-gill – and you'll sometimes see it spelled with the 'g' dropped: *iil*.) The *igil*'s colouring isn't perfect – usually pale brown with a darker band at the tips of its quills and a grey or brown face and underparts. But what it lacks in colouring it makes up for in weapons: the *igil* is well armed, with more convincing *hilde-pīlas* than the *brocc*, *fox* or *wesle* put together, for its body is covered with approximately 6,000 sharp quills.

Like foxes and weasels, hedgehogs sometimes take up residence in uninhabited burrows dug by other creatures; they don't generally dig burrows themselves. Still, they are capable of digging when necessary – perhaps when in need of an escape route from a *nīþ-sceaða* (malignant foe). The Old English scholar Megan Cavell observes that they have 'powerful and clawed front limbs', which could very well be the *fēþe-munda* (walking-hands) to which *Riddle 15* refers. A hedgehog has five distinct digits on its forefeet, making it resemble a human hand and giving the riddler a good reason to use a term like *fēþe-munda* instead of *fēt* (feet).

The hedgehog works well as a solution, and it is also an animal that appears in medieval bestiaries as well as earlier texts that could have influenced the Old English riddler. Isidore describes the hedgehog as an animal with quills that stiffen when it's threatened, which transforms it into a tight, shielded ball – 'with these quills it is protected on all sides against attack'. Pliny, however, offers a more charming reason for the hedgehog's armour: when hedgehogs gather food for winter, they roll around on the ground so the fallen fruits stick to their quills. I'm sorry to tell you that this behaviour is not real – but it is such a beguiling idea that it became a popular subject of illustration in medieval bestiaries. After spearing as much fruit as possible, the hedgehog picks up one last piece in its mouth and carries it all back to its den.

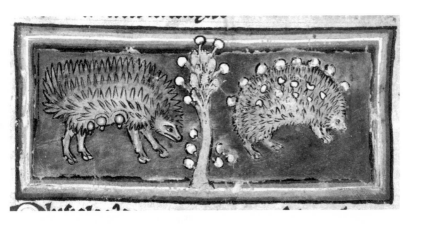

Hedgehogs collecting fruit in a bestiary (England, *c.*1200–1210)

If the hedgehog is the solution to *Riddle 15*, its quills make useful weapons for self-defence; but Christian allegory did not illuminate them in the most favourable light. In the Old English translation of Gregory the Great's *Pastoral Care*, for instance, the hedgehog's ability to roll itself into a secure, prickly ball represents aspects of the sinful soul:

> The <u>hedgehog</u> (*iil*) signifies <u>duplicity</u> (*twiefealdnesse*) of the <u>impure</u> (*unclænan*) mind, which is always cunningly making excuses, like the <u>hedgehog</u> (*iil*), whose <u>feet</u> (*fet*) and <u>head</u> (*heafod*) and whole <u>body</u> (*bodig*) can be seen before he is caught. But as soon as he is caught, he curls up into a <u>ball</u> (*cliewene*) and draws in his <u>feet</u> (*fet*) as much as he can and hides his <u>head</u> (*heafod*), so that when you have him in your hands, you cannot know what comes first, the <u>feet</u> (*fet*) or the <u>head</u> (*heafod*), although when you touched him before you could see both the <u>feet</u> (*fet*) and the <u>head</u> (*heafod*).

The **un-clǣne** (unclean or impure) mind cannot admit to its own faults, always creating cunning excuses, so it's impossible to tell *fet* from *hēafod* (head). The *igil* represents **twifealdness** (doubleness or duplicity) because it brings about **twēo** (doubt). You might feel doubt about whether a sinner can really be responsible for their sins, or whether you can distinguish the various parts of a hedgehog's **bodig** (body). How can you be sure when everything is curled up tightly into a **clȳwen** (ball)?

Clȳwen's etymology must be untangled like thread. Old English *clȳwen* means 'ball' or 'sphere', sometimes 'a ball of thread or yarn' more specifically. Over time the word became limited to the more specific 'ball of thread' definition. In the Greek legend of Theseus, the hero finds his way out of the Labyrinth of Crete by following Ariadne's 'clew' of thread that he unwinds on his way in. Because of this story, by the eighteenth century 'clew' had taken on a new definition having nothing to do with thread: 'indication to follow', 'slight direction' or 'key'. Nowadays, when we come across a 'clue' it is usually something that points the way or indicates a solution, like a piece of evidence to use in solving a crime, or even a sentence or phrase in a crossword puzzle that hints at the word or words to be inserted.

But during the Middle Ages, 'clues' were not associated with crimes or crosswords but with the *un-clǣne* mind. When a sinner's *un-clǣne* mind searches for excuses, their thoughts are wound up tightly like a *clȳwen* (ball of thread). If the sinner's logic is sufficiently wound up in a ball, it's harder to perceive the fault that needs correction, making it easier for a sinner to continue believing in their own innocence.

A 'greater hedgehog'

None of this negative symbolism is hinted at in *Riddle 15*, which is focused on the *dēor*'s appearance, protective nature and bravery. While the hedgehog lacks the street-maker's towering ears and correct colouring, it can dig when necessary with its walking-hands and defend itself with its sharp quills. But decades before Brett's *igil* explanation, the philologist John A. Walz suggested another, very similar one: the prickly porcupine. Dating from 1896, the porcupine solution has been around nearly as long as that of the badger, but it never achieved the same scholarly popularity. Like the hedgehog, the small ears of a porcupine don't exactly 'tower' above its eyes, and the animal doesn't usually move very fast.

But there are also some strong arguments in the porcupine's favour (similar to those for the hedgehog). It has hand-like feet (with four digits rather than five) and sharp, defensive quills (capable of killing an aggressive dog or *wæl-hwelp*). It can pick up its pace to a gallop when need be. Although porcupines take refuge in rocks and holes dug by other animals, they can also dig holes for themselves, living in deep burrows with multiple exits, where baby porcupines are secreted away for safekeeping. Although no porcupines lived in early medieval England, a term still exists for them in Old English: **māra igil**, or 'greater hedgehog', which is used as a gloss for *hystrix* (Latin for 'porcupine'). A traveller might see one while on pilgrimage to Rome.

Could the *dēor* of *Riddle 15* be one of these spiky, fierce, clever, burrow-dwelling creatures, the hedgehog or the porcupine? Cavell questions the need to choose between the two, since it's a distinction that probably did not exist in the Middle Ages. If a porcupine is a *māra igil* (greater *igil*), and a hedgehog is a **læssa igil** (smaller *igil*), then maybe the riddle's solution could simply be *igil*.

So what is the *strǣt-wyrhta*? Perhaps you've made up your own mind, or are vacillating between one solution and another. Are you swayed by the weaponry and *fēþe-munda* of the *igil*, or more convinced by the digging skills of the *brocc*? While the riddle doesn't mention the badger's most distinctive feature – its black mask – that characteristic is also missing from medieval bestiary illustrations. Really, it comes down to two questions: which clues are the most important, and which characteristics would the riddler have thought 'typical' of these animals? Maybe the *strǣt-wyrhta* is something else entirely, a solution yet to be proposed by modern scholars. Whether the creature is a prickly *igil* or burrowing *brocc*, wily *wesle* or *fealu* fox, this baffling *dēor* leaves us guessing.

Street-maker's Wordhord

beadu-wǣpen, noun (BEH-ah-duh-WAP-en / ˈbɛa-dʌ-ˌwæː-pɛn): Battle-weapon.

bodig, noun (BODD-ih / ˈbɔ-dɪj): Body.

brocc, noun (BROCK / ˈbrɔk): Badger.

clȳwen, noun (KLUE-wen / ˈklyː-wɛn): Ball, clew; (specifically) ball of thread or yarn.

dīgol, adjective (DEE-goll / ˈdiː-gɔl): Secret, hidden.

fealu, adjective (FEH-ah-luh / ˈfɛa-lʌ): Colour term of uncertain/ varied meaning: basically yellow but variously tinted with shades of red, brown or grey, often pale, always unsaturated (not vivid).

fēþe-mund, noun (FAY-thuh-MUND / ˈfeː-θə-ˌmʌnd): Animal paw ('foot-hand' or 'hand for walking') (plural: *fēþe-munda*).

fixen, noun (FICK-sen / ˈfɪk-sɛn): Vixen (female fox).

forht-mōd, adjective (FOR'HT-MOAD / ˈfɔrxt-ˌmoːd): Timid in spirit, afraid.

fox, noun (FAWKS / ˈfɔks): Fox.

foxunga, plural noun (FAWK-sung-ga / ˈfɔk-sʌŋ-ga): Foxlike wiles, tricks.

gēan, preposition (YAY-ahn / ˈjeːan): Against, on the opposite side.

geap, adjective (YEH-op / ˈjɛap): Crooked; deceitful, crafty, cunning.

gegn-pæþ, noun (YAIN-PATH / ˈjɛjn-ˌpæθ): Hostile path, opposing road.

gūþ-gemōt, noun (GOOTH-yeh-MOAT / ˈguːθ-jɛ-ˌmoːt): Battle-meeting, combat.

gyst, noun (YUEST / ˈjyst): Guest, visitor, stranger (plural: *gystas*).

hilde-pīl, noun (HILL-duh-PEEL / ˈhɪl-də-ˌpiːl): Battle-dart (plural: *hilde-pīlas*).

hlīfian, verb (H'LEE-vi-ahn / ˈhliː-vɪ-an): To stand high, tower, stand out prominently.

igil, noun (IH-yill / ˈɪ-jɪl): Hedgehog.

lāð-gewinna, noun (LAWTH-yeh-WIN-na / ˈlaːθ-jɛ-ˌwɪn-na): Hated opponent, enemy.

læssa igil, noun (LASS-ah IH-yill / ˈlæs-sa ˈɪ-jɪl): Hedgehog (smaller *igil*).

māra igil, noun (MA-ra IH-yill / ˈmaː-ra ˈɪ-jɪl): Porcupine (greater *igil*).

nīþ-sceaða, noun (NEETH-SHEH-ah-tha / ˈniːθ-ˌʃɛa-θa): Malignant foe.

nos-þyrel, noun (NOSS-THUE-rell / ˈnɔs-ˌθy-rɛl): Nostril (nose-hole).

ord, noun (ORD / ˈɔrd): Point, pointed weapon (plural: *ordas*).

pæþ, noun (PATH / ˈpæθ): Path, track.

rǣd, noun (RAD / ˈræːd): Counsel, advice; prudence, intelligence.

rǣdels, noun (RAD-ells / ˈræː-dɛls): Counsel, consideration; debate; conjecture, imagination, interpretation; enigma, riddle.

smēagan, verb (SMAY-ah-gahn / ˈsmeːa-gan): To consider, ponder, examine, search, seek an opportunity.

strǣt, noun (STRAT / ˈstræːt): Street, path.

strǣt-wyrhta, noun (STRAT-WUER-h'ta / ˈstræːt-ˌwyrx-ta): Street-maker (a compound invented by the author).

twēo, noun (TWAY-oh / ˈtweːɔ): Doubt, uncertainty.

twifealdness, noun (TWIH-veh-ald-ness / ˈtwɪ-vɛald-nɛs): Doubleness; duplicity, deceitfulness.

þyrel, noun (THUE-rell / ˈθy-rɛl): Hole.

un-clæne, adjective (UN-KLAN-uh / ˈʌn-ˌklæː-nə): Unclean, impure.

wæl-grim, adjective (WAEL-GRIM / ˈwæl-ˌɡrɪm): Slaughter-grim, cruel, destructive, bloodthirsty.

wæl-hwelp, noun (WAEL-H'WELP / ˈwæl-ˌhwɛlp): Slaughter-whelp, dog that slays, hunting dog.

wesle, noun (WEZ-luh / ˈwɛz-lə): Weasel.

wyrcan, verb (WUER-kahn / ˈwyr-kan): To make, work, labour.

20

Moving Spirit
(*ferende gæst*)

ET'S FLIP BACK a few pages of the Exeter Book, from *Riddle 15*'s
mysterious *strǣt-wyrhta*, through riddles whose suggested solutions range from 'wine cup' to 'barnacle goose', via chickens, a cuckoo,
a nightingale. (The barnacle goose, incidentally, is a strange creature
which is either a goose-shaped barnacle attached to driftwood until it
grows feathers and a beak and swims away, or a bird that grows hang-
ing from a tree until it is mature enough to drop down into the water
below.) Eventually we come to *Riddle 7*, which offers another baffling
animal description without an obvious solution:

> My <u>garment</u> (*hrægl*) <u>is silent</u> (*swigað*) when I <u>walk</u> (*trede*) upon the
> earth, keep to my dwelling or <u>agitate</u> (*drefe*) the waters.
>
> Sometimes I'm raised up by my <u>ornaments</u> (*hyrste*), a high breeze
> lifting me above human homes. The clouds' strength carries me far
> and wide over humankind.
>
> My <u>adornments</u> (*frætwe*) <u>rustle</u> (*swogað*) loudly, <u>make music</u>
> (*swinsiað*), <u>sing</u> (*singað*) brightly, when I touch neither water nor
> earth, a <u>moving spirit</u> (*ferende gæst*).

Without a name to hold on to (indeed, that's the whole point), I call this creature by the poetic final descriptor that the riddle offers: a *fērende gǣst* or moving spirit. (This is the same *gǣst* we saw describing the whale in Chapter 12.)

A moving spirit

Let's begin our investigations by looking at the facts that are on offer. *Riddle 7* provides even fewer clues about the creature's physical appearance and behaviour than *Riddle 15* in the previous chapter. We don't know the *dēor*'s colour, or even how exactly this moving spirit moves. It can **tredan** (tread) upon the earth and **drēfan** (agitate or disturb) the waters, but sometimes it touches neither water nor earth. It possesses a **hrægl** (garment), **hyrste** (ornaments) and *frætwe* (adornments), and it is these trappings, combined with a high breeze, that carry the creature up into the sky. The garment can **swīgan** (be silent) when the creature is on land or water, but in the air that changes. Suddenly, the *fērende gǣst*'s adornments can **swōgan** (rustle), **swinsian** (make music) and **singan** (sing).

The riddle never actually uses the words *feþer* or *feþra* ('feather' or 'wings'), but despite these omissions it's fairly clear that the *dēor* is a bird. It must be able to walk, swim and fly, and though this could equally refer to an insect, there is another clue that points us to a more feathery creature – the use of the words *hrægl* and *hyrste*. These words appear in other riddles to describe birds' plumage, like the chickens of *Riddle 13* (whose *hrægl* – possibly new down – is renewed) and the barnacle goose of *Riddle 10* (whose white *hyrste* – plumage – is caught by the wind, which lifts it into the air over the **seolh-bæþ** – seal-bath, a kenning for the sea).

One favourite solution

So the *ferende gæst* is very likely a bird, but what kind? Although we can never be certain about which animal the scribe was picturing, there is far more of a consensus for *Riddle 7*'s solution than *Riddle 15*'s. The universally favoured solution was first suggested in 1859 by Franz Dietrich, the same scholar who proposed *Riddle 15*'s badger solution. First, let's consider the repeated use of sw- words in the riddle: *swīgan, swōgan* and *swinsian*. Could this be a clue? Dietrich cites a letter written in Greek by St Gregory of Nazianzus, a fourth-century philosopher and theologian. In his letter, Gregory recounts a fable about swallows and swans whose wings produce a musical sound. This fable goes back at least as early as ancient Greece, since references to the sound of swan wings appear in the *Homeric Hymns* and a play by Aristophanes. Could the moving spirit be a **swan** (swan), whose name remains exactly the same in modern English?

In more recent years it's been suggested that the word *gæst* – assumed by most scholars to mean 'spirit' with a long 'æ' (as in 'mad') – could actually be **gæst** with a short 'æ' (as in 'that'), a word that means 'guest' or 'stranger'. (We saw an alternate spelling of *gæst* in the last chapter – a *gyst* that invades the *strǣt-wyrhta*'s burrows.) Although the words *gæst* and *gǣst* look quite similar – as do their modern forms 'guest' and 'ghost' – they are, as far as we know, unrelated etymologically. The name 'moving stranger' or 'travelling guest' (as opposed to 'moving spirit') could be appropriate for a swan, since some species do migrate within Britain, becoming 'guests' in different locations throughout the year. The ambiguity of this word could even have led the riddler to select it. The guesser is left wondering if the poem refers to the movement of a living spirit or that of a guest. (People don't 'guess', by the way, until Middle English; the Old English equivalent of 'to guess' is **rǣdan**, which is related to *rǣdels* and 'riddles'.)

If you are familiar with your swan species, then you might get even more particular with your solution: scholars in the know have suggested that *Riddle 7* must refer specifically to the mute swan, a species that lived in England year-round during the early medieval period. *Swanas*, or mute swans, aren't actually mute; they snort, hiss, growl, peep and even make a sound like a 'hoarse, muffled trumpet'. When mute swans fly, their wings make 'a rhythmic humming or whistling sound' that may be a form of communication.

A mute swan in the Harley Bestiary (England, *c.*1230–40)

The musicality of the swan crops up elsewhere too. The Old English *Phoenix* (Chapter 10) is largely based on a Latin poem by Lactantius, but the two poems differ, specifically in their descriptions of the phoenix's song. Lactantius says the phoenix's song is more beautiful than that of a 'dying swan', a reference to the legend of the swan song, but the Old English poet changes this to a comparison with the music of a swan's wings:

> The revelry of trumpets and horns, the sound of the harp, the voice of any hero on earth, the organ, the strain of a melody, the <u>wings of a swan</u> (*swanes feðre*) – none of those joys that the Lord created for humans' pleasure in this sorrowful world can match it.

If the sound of a *swan*'s wings sits alongside some of the most beautiful music on earth and is second only to the music of an immortal super-bird's song, then it is truly marvellous.

References to the swan's singing wings or feathers do not appear in later medieval bestiaries, though they still emphasise the animal's musical qualities, focusing instead on its beautiful voice. Supposedly, the swan sings the most sweetly right before its death, and this is why 'swan song' has become an idiom for a person's final performance or act. The swan's lovely voice is attributed to its neck, which, as one Old English text explains, is **lang-sweored** (long-necked) and curved like the windpipe of a musical instrument. Isidore claims that the Latin *cygnus* (whooper swan) comes from *canere* (singing) because the creature 'pours out a sweetness of song with its modulated voice'.

There is at least one Old English reference to a swan's song. In the poem *The Seafarer*, a lonely traveller describes his experience out on the ocean:

> I heard nothing but the roaring sea, the ice-cold waves. Sometimes I had for my amusement the <u>song</u> (*song*) of a <u>swan</u> (*ylfete*), the cry

of a <u>gannet</u> (*ganetes*) and the sound of a <u>curlew</u> (*huilpan*) instead of the laughter of men, or the singing of a <u>gull</u> (*mæw*) in place of mead-drinking.

Ilfette (or *ylfete* as it is spelled here) may refer to another species of swan, the whooper swan, although we can't be certain that people distinguished the two in early medieval England. Technically, this passage could still refer to the **sang** (song) of the swan's feathers, but alongside the bird calls of the **ganot** (gannet), the **hwilpa** (curlew) and the **mǣw** (gull), it makes more sense for it to be vocal. According to Cornell University's website *All About Birds*, the gannet makes 'a raucous, throaty, vibrato *arrrrr*', the curlew 'a low whistled *prreee*' and the gull 'a rich repertoire' including a *mew* call. (Perhaps that *mew*-ing is why the bird is called a *mǣw*.) If the *ilfette* is specifically a whooper swan, its *sang* is a low-pitched bugling.

In the Old English *Seafarer* poem, the sailor does not seem to take much pleasure in the *ilfette*'s song, so we can assume that either he's not very appreciative, or that whooper swans aren't as musically adept as their mute cousins. Or perhaps there's another reason. Aside from their singing, swans are not presented in a positive light in later medieval bestiaries. The swan's melodies are mournful, like a sinner regretfully remembering their evil deeds upon their deathbed. Because its white feathers hide black flesh, the swan often represents deception. After these white feathers are plucked the bird's black flesh is roasted, which Bodley 764 compares to the death of a rich man who is 'stripped of worldly pomp and goes down into the flames of hell'. While alive, the rich man holds his head up high, thinking too much of his worldly possessions, as a swan holds its head aloft on its long neck as it swims across the water. Despite these unsavoury associations, medieval sailors considered a swan to be a sign of good fortune because it does not dip down beneath the waves, always staying afloat. For this reason,

Bartholomaeus Anglicus calls the swan 'the most merriest bird in divinations'. Someone needed to tell the disconsolate sailor in *The Seafarer*.

Swans a-swimming

In Old English, too, swans are always afloat, travelling well upon the water. A swan-road today might be more associated with an ornamental pond or calm river, but the word **swan-rād** (swan-road) appears in Old English verse as a kenning for the ocean. One's fortune can vary when crossing the *swan-rād*. Some journeys are easy. When Beowulf crosses the *swan-rād*, sailing from his homeland to assist King Hrothgar with his monster dilemma, he has an easy journey on his excellent **ȳþ-lida** (wave-traverser or ship – remember *ȳþ-mearh*, 'sea-horse' or 'wave-horse', another 'ship' word from Chapter 12?). The language scholar Allan Metcalf says that in this particular context the kenning highlights the speed of Beowulf's ship, which floats swiftly and smoothly like a *swan*. Other ocean kennings that wouldn't emphasise speedy travel as much are **segl-rād** (sail-road) and *seolh-bæþ* (seal-bath). Similarly, when Elene, the mother of Emperor Constantine, sails back home to the land of the Greeks with good news, the **sīþ** (journey) on the *swan-rād* is **ge-sund** (favourable) for the **sige-cwēn** (victory-queen).

Crossing the *swan-rād* is not always smooth and *ge-sund*. In the Old English poem *Andreas*, St Andrew is afraid of sailing to Mermedonia to rescue St Matthew from the cannibals. He implores God to send someone else:

My Lord, Creator of the heavens, Ruler of glory – how may I travel faraway across the deep path so quickly, as you command with words? Your angel can easily accomplish that; from heaven, he knows the extent of the ocean, the salty sea-streams and <u>swan-road</u> (*swanrade*),

the <u>tumult</u> (*gewinn*) of the surf and the <u>water-terrors</u> (*wæterbrogan*),
the ways across vast lands ... The <u>battle-roads</u> (*herestræta*) across cold
water are unknown to me.

For Andrew, the *swan-rād* is a place of unnamed but threatening
wæter-brōgan (terrors of the deep). The way across the water is not
just a *swan-rād* but a **here-strǣt** (battle-road), where he must face the
ge-win (tumult or hostility) of cold waves. Perhaps the *sīþ* is swift, but
it's also dangerous. Why not send an angel instead?

Meanwhile, in the Old English poem *Juliana*, an evil governor exe-
cutes St Juliana before departing on a sea voyage. For a long time, the
governor is 'tossed about on the sea-flood, the <u>swan-road</u> (*swonrade*)'.
In the second half of the same line, **swylt** (death) seizes him and his
crew. All are drowned, and they must seek their place in hell without
hope. Alliteration on sw- makes it hard not to connect the words *swan-
rād* and *swylt*, which makes the former seem far less pleasant than its
name might suggest. Gone are any swift, smooth-sailing associations:
this 'swan' is not one of good fortune.

The *swan* is notable for the way in which it glides across the water,
whether that motion is fated or favourable, tame or tumultuous. In
Riddle 7, the *fērende* (moving) nature of the *gǣst* (spirit) is of central
importance, its travel on the *swan-rād* as well as in the sky. But only in
the sky will this *gǣst's* motion 'sing', its adornments making music as
they move in the wind.

Moving Spirit's Wordhord

drēfan, verb (DRAY-vahn / ˈdreː-van): To disturb, agitate, disquiet,
vex, trouble.

fērende, adjective (FAY-ren-duh / ˈfeː-rɛn-də): Moving, mobile.

ganot, noun (GAH-not / ˈga-nɔt): Sea-bird, probably a gannet.

gæst, noun (GAST / ˈgæst): Guest, visitor, stranger.

gǣst, noun (GAST / ˈgæːst): Spirit.

ge-sund, adjective (yeh-ZUND / jɛ-ˈzʌnd): Favourable, prosperous, safe, sound.

ge-win, noun (yeh-WIN / jɛ-ˈwɪn): Tumult, hostility, strife.

here-strǣt, noun (HEH-ruh-STRAT / ˈhɛ-rə-ˌstræːt): Battle-street, military road.

hrægl, noun (H'RAE-yull / ˈhræ-jəl): Garment, article of clothing.

hwilpa, noun (H'WILL-pa / ˈhwɪl-pa): Bird, probably a curlew.

hyrst, noun (HUERST / ˈhyrst): Ornament, adornment, decoration (plural: *hyrste*).

ilfette, noun (ILL-vet-tuh / ˈɪl-vɛt-tə): Swan (perhaps a whooper swan).

lang-sweored, adjective (LAHNG-SWEH-o-red / ˈlaŋ-ˌswɛɔ-rɛd): Long-necked.

mǣw, noun (MAE-ew / ˈmæːu): Gull.

rǣdan, verb (RAD-ahn / ˈræː-dan): To have an idea, suppose; to make out the meaning of a riddle; to learn by perusal; to read; to counsel, give advice; to resolve after deliberation.

sang, noun (SAHNG / ˈsaŋ): Song.

segl-rād, noun (SAIL-RAWD / ˈsɛjl-ˌraːd): Sail-road, a kenning for the sea.

seolh-bæþ, noun (SEH-ol'h-BATH / ˈsɛɔlx-ˌbæθ): Seal-bath, a kenning for the sea.

sige-cwēn, noun (SIH-yuh-KWAIN / ˈsɪ-jə-ˌkweːn): Victory-queen, victorious queen.

singan, verb (SING-gahn / ˈsɪŋ-gan): To sing.

sīþ, noun (SEETH / ˈsiːθ): Journey, voyage.

swan, noun (SWAHN / ˈswan): Swan (perhaps a mute swan) (plural: *swanas*).

swan-rād, noun (SWAHN-RAWD / ˈswan-ˌraːd): Swan-road, a kenning for the sea.

swīgan, verb (SWEE-gahn / ˈswiː-gan): To be silent.

swinsian, verb (SWIN-zi-ahn / ˈswɪn-zɪ-an): To make a pleasing sound, make music.

swōgan, verb (SWO-gahn / ˈswoː-gan): To make a sound, move with noise.

swylt, noun (SWUELT / ˈswylt): Death, destruction.

tredan, verb (TRED-ahn / ˈtrɛ-dan): To tread upon, step upon, walk upon.

wæter-brōga, noun (WAT-er-BRO-ga / ˈwæ-tɛr-ˌbroː-ga): Water-terror, terror of the deep (plural: *wæter-brōgan*).

ȳþ-lida, noun (UETH-LI-da / ˈyː-θ-ˌlɪ-da): Ship (wave-traverser).

Epilogue
Human or Beast?

IN THIS BOOK I have grouped the *dēor* of early medieval England into five categories – ordinary, extraordinary, good, bad and baffling – but you may have noticed that some creatures defy categorisation. You may find yourself puzzled by a commonplace animal like a *fox* or astonished by the extraordinary behaviour of a seemingly ordinary *ǣmette*. The much-maligned *wulf*, typically a symbol of evil, might end up coming to the aid of a saint.

And while 'animal' might seem like a clear enough category itself, distinct at the very least from human beings, the boundary in Old English between *mann* (human) and *dēor* is not always so straightforward. And so we end this *deorhord* by asking: what exactly makes us human in the eyes of Old English writers? And how are we different from – or similar to – the creatures that fill these pages and the natural world?

Human-to-animal transformation

Throughout history, there are stories of humans losing their human-ity and being transformed into animals. In fairy tales like *The Frog Prince* or *Beauty and the Beast*, a human character is cursed to live in an animal's form. Sometimes the enchantment is meant to teach a moral lesson – to avoid pride, selfishness or greed. It's only after the victim has learned their lesson that they are able to regain their human form. At other times the curse is a result of an angry deity or supernatural being: for instance, the goddess Artemis of Greek mythology turns the hunter Actaeon into a stag, to be pursued and killed by his own hunt-ing dogs. (Depending on the version of the story, this is either because Actaeon sees Artemis while she is bathing or because he claims to have superior hunting skills.)

In the case of King Nebuchadnezzar in the Old Testament, the human is transformed into an animal both as a moral lesson and as a punishment from God. God punishes the king for his excessive pride, which Ælfric explains in one of his homilies. A terrifying voice from heaven speaks to the king, saying:

> You, Nebuchadnezzar, shall be parted from your kingdom. You shall be cast out from the <u>humans</u> (*mannum*), and your dwelling shall be with <u>wild animals</u> (*wildeorum*). You shall eat grass as an <u>ox</u> (*oxa*) for seven years, until you know that God on high rules the kingdoms of men and gives kingdoms to whomever he wishes.

The homily tells how Nebuchadnezzar runs into the woods to dwell among the *wild-dēor* (wild animals), leaving behind the world of *menn* (humans). Just as the frightening voice foretold, he lives off grass like an *oxa* or *nȳten* (ox/beast) for seven years. Although his **feax** (hair) merely grows long like a woman's, his **næglas** (nails) become sharp like the **clawa** (talons) of an *earn* (eagle). Nebuchadnezzar becomes more *dēor* than *mann* because of his diet and the society he keeps, his body changing accordingly. After the seven-year period, he learns his lesson and his human mind comes back to him, allowing his return to civilisation. Only then is he able to become a *mann* again and leave his *dēor*-like existence behind.

Nebuchadnezzar's story is one of transformation – he is a *mann*, then a *dēor*, then a *mann* again. The transformation is not one he controls; it is a punishment for not living in accordance with God's wishes. It seems that humanity is something *deserved*, and it is God who decides who is worthy of being elevated above an animal's state. Nebuchadnezzar must live in a state lower than that of a human to learn that his status is far below God's. It is clear that *mann* transcends *dēor* in God's hierarchy.

Human-animal hybrids

But what about beings who live in a constant state of duality, neither fully *mann* nor *dēor*? In the Old English *Wonders of the East* we encountered a variety of creatures, some of which – while extraordinary – are clearly in the *dēor* category, like the self-immolating hens of Chapter 5, or the gold-hoarding ants of Chapter 6, or even the *griffus* of Chapter 5, a strange hybrid of real animals. But the text also describes other beings that are *menn* for the most part, with a few strange, animal-like qualities thrown in.

In *Wonders of the East*, for instance, there are *wīf* (women) who have the **tuscas** (tusks) of an *eofor* (wild boar). Thirteen feet tall, these women have pure-white bodies and *feax* so long it reaches their heels. The *tuscas* aren't their only *dēor*-like quality, for they also have the **tægl** (tail) of an *oxa*, the *fēt* (feet) of an *olfend* (camel), and the *tēþ* (teeth) of either an *eosol* (donkey) or an *eofor* – the two extant manuscripts disagree.

Tusked woman in the Tiberius manuscript's *Wonders of the East* (England, mid eleventh century)

The illustration in the eleventh-century Tiberius manuscript (which goes with *eoferes teð*, or boar's teeth) does a fairly good job of depicting all aspects of the text's description, with one rather small *tusc* visible that does resemble a boar's tusk more than a donkey's tooth.

The text explains that Alexander the Great killed these tusked women because of their **un-clǣnness**, a word that can refer to either physical or moral 'uncleanliness' or 'impurity'. This abhorrence for 'uncleanliness' probably had little to do with how frequently the women bathed. They were anomalies, with unfeminine (even inhuman) bodies, and they appear to have lived in a community without men – at least, no tusked men are mentioned. Indeed, if there *were* tusked men, would Alexander have also considered them *ǣwisc* (foul) of body and **un-weorþ** (of no value)? Would he have been disgusted by their *un-clǣnness*? It probably was no coincidence that the writer or scribe chose an adjective like *un-clǣne* (impure) for these *wīf* rather than something like 'fearsome' or 'frightening'. Since we are told nothing about the tusked women's behaviour or habits, we have to assume that they were judged as 'unworthy' to live solely because of their *un-clǣnness*, which is itself depicted through their *dēor*-like physical features. Although the *wīf* had qualities both human and animal, it seems that Alexander (or the scribe) saw them as more *dēor*, beneath *menn* in the social or moral hierarchy.

Not every animal-human hybrid is treated with this level of scorn and disgust. *Wonders of the East* tells of a land called Ciconia located in Gallia (probably Gaul, a region encompassing modern-day France, Belgium and Luxembourg, as well as parts of Switzerland, western Germany and northern Italy). The text says that the beings of this land are thought to be humans – *beoð menn gewenede* – but these *menn* are unlike any you will have encountered. Twenty feet tall, the *menn* of Ciconia have a mouth the size of a fan (a rather puzzling unit of measurement, but clearly very large) and a *hēafod* (head) with a lion's **manu** (mane). Unlike the tusked women, the text makes no judgements on their purity, cleanliness or right to live.

Perhaps the strangest feature of the *menn* of Ciconia is their reaction to being followed: they flee far away, sweating **blōd** (blood) as they go. **Swǣtan** (to sweat) blood is another characteristic borrowed from the animal world. In ancient Egypt, it was believed that hippos deliberately injured themselves in times of crisis, making themselves bleed. This, unlike some of the other medieval interpretations recounted in this book, was based on a real phenomenon that can still be observed today. For centuries people puzzled over the hippo's blood-like sweat, a red substance thicker than human perspiration. It wasn't until the year 2000 that a group of Japanese chemists began to gather hippo 'sweat' samples, a process that the science writer Sam Kean describes as 'tiptoeing into the hippo pen at the local zoo to dab the beasts with paper towels'. They published the results of their study in 2004, having learned that the liquid is clear right after it's emitted from the skin but turns red a few minutes later. The substance is not blood or even sweat, although like sweat it can help regulate the hippo's body temperature. This red mucus works as a natural sunscreen and may also have antiseptic properties. Whether the medieval scribe who wrote about people who sweat *blōd* had a hippo in mind will, of course, remain a mystery.

Despite their monstrous appearance – twenty feet tall, lion-maned, giant-mouthed – these beings of Ciconia are thought to be *menn*, not *dēor*. Their bodies exude *blōd* in an unusual way, yet there is no mention of their *un-clǣnness*. (Would it be the same if they were all *wīf*, or would the uncontrolled shedding of *blōd* then be considered *un-clǣne*, perhaps associated with the 'impurity' of menstrual blood?) There is something about the tusked women's hybridity that is more disconcerting than the Ciconians' own mixed-up physiognomy. One's gender, it seems, can put human-ness further out of reach.

Hound or human?

Wonders of the East, as in most of its descriptions, offers limited information about the blood-sweating Ciconians and the tusked women, but some of its creatures appear in other Old English texts. This gives us a lot more to go on when determining a writer's opinion on a being's human- or animal-ness. Not all texts treat hybridity in the same way. A hybrid might be more *dēor* in one text, more *mann* in another. *Healfhundingas*, for instance, appear not only in *Wonders of the East* but also in *Alexander's Letter to Aristotle* and in saints' lives, and the extent of the creature's humanity varies between these sources.

A **healfhunding** (half-dog) is a person who is half-dog and half-human. Called a *cynocephalus* (dog-headed) in Latin, the *healfhunding* is essentially human aside from its dog-head – whether that counts as **healf** (half) a *hund* is up for debate.

In *Wonders of the East* the *healfhundingas* are described as having other animal qualities: in addition to a *hēafod* of a *hund* (dog), they have the *manu* of a *hors* (horse) and the *tuscas* of an *eofor*. Their monstrosity is further emphasised by their *oroþ* (breath), which is like a fire's flame. (Whether that means they breathe fire or simply have very hot exhalations is unclear.) These *healfhundingas* don't sound very human, yet they live near cities filled with earthly wealth in 'Egypt' (which during antiquity was thought to lie next to 'India'). In other words, they are not that far removed from civilisation. In one of the surviving copies of *Wonders of the East*, the Nowell Codex, there is an illustration of a *healfhunding* which, though very animal-like, appears to wear human clothes. Does modesty (wearing clothes) and proximity to 'civilised' society lend these otherwise beast-like creatures an air of humanity?

Alexander the Great encounters *healfhundingas* during his campaign in *Indea*. He doesn't have much to say about them in his *Letter to Aristotle*, only that the beings emerge from a forest for the express

Healfhunding in the Nowell Codex's *Wonders of the East* (England, *c.*1000)

purpose of wounding his troops. (How exactly he knew their intentions is not explained – presumably, by their actions, or maybe he just assumes everyone is out to get him.) He doesn't comment on their physical characteristics at all, so apparently he believes Aristotle (or rather, the Old English scribe thought their audience) sufficiently well informed to know what a *healfhunding* is. Alexander, in his typical belligerent approach, commands his warriors to shoot arrows at the *healfhundingas* until they retreat into the **wudu-bearwas** (groves of trees). While the *healfhundingas* of *Wonders of the East* lived near cities, the *Letter to Aristotle*'s *healfhundingas* come from the forest. The fact that they dwell in the *wudu-bearwas*, home to wolves, wild boars and teeth tyrants, makes them seem less human than their counterparts in other tales. Forests are outside the bounds of human civilisation; the historian John Block Friedmann points out that monstrous beings ordinarily reside 'in mountains, caves, deserts, rivers, or woods ... barren or savage landscapes'. Does the location of the *healfhundingas*' home suggest more of a similarity to *wild-dēor* (wild animals) than to *menn?* It seems that these Indian hybrids are further from human-ness than the properly dressed, suburban Egyptian ones.

Holy hybrid

While some of the *healfhundingas* have had human qualities thus far – wearing clothes or living near cities – they have been much more *dēor*-like overall. We don't get any sense that they are capable of rational thought or speech. When King Nebuchadnezzar was made to live as a *dēor*, he lost his ability to think and speak like a *mann*. Are such capabilities a prerequisite for humanity in Old English texts? Are *healfhundingas* ultimately more *hund* than *mann*? The image of the more *dēor*-like *healfhunding* is greatly altered in hagiography, a popular medieval genre consisting of stories about the saints.

So far we've met a number of saints who had special relationships with animals – St Daria with her protective lioness, St Edmund with his head-guarding wolf, St Giles with his foster-mother deer. We have seen how saints can be associated with certain animals – St John the Evangelist with an eagle and St Luke with a calf. But we have yet to encounter a saintly animal-human hybrid.

The first time I came across St Christopher was in a taxi; the driver had placed an image of him on a small card attached to his rear-view mirror. It was a picture of him carrying the child Christ across a river. This is the most common depiction of St Christopher that's around today (and his name literally means 'bearer of Christ'), making him an ideal patron saint to those who travel a lot or work in transportation (drivers, sailors, etc.). But this particular story about St Christopher does not appear even once in early medieval England. The legend of St Christopher as ferryman most likely originates in twelfth-century Germany. Instead, Old English hagiography dwells on the saint's most unusual physical characteristic – his dog-head.

One Old English text tells how Christopher came from the land of the *healfhundingas* to the city of Samos during King Dagnus' reign in the third century CE. The text describes him as **healf-hundisc** (half-canine). Half-dog, the newly arrived Christopher knows nothing about God, nor can he invoke God's name, lacking the ability to speak. Although unable to speak, Christopher is capable of rational thought, and after learning about God he decides to receive **fulluht** (baptism) and become Christian.

The text known as the Old English *Martyrology* contains a far more detailed account of the story, which is also set in third-century Samos but features an Emperor Decius instead of a King Dagnus. One day Christopher arrives in Samos from a place 'where humans have the heads of dogs' and 'where people eat one another'. Unlike the Old English text mentioned above, which focuses on the fact that the saint is *healf-hundisc*, half-canine, the *Martyrology* emphasises his human half – these *healfhundingas* are described as 'humans' and as 'people', but in the same moment their own actions seem to undo their humanity. They are cannibals – they commit acts that are among the most taboo in Christian culture. This puts them further beyond the bounds of civilisation than living in a forest ever could, their eating habits being more bestial than Nebuchadnezzar's vegetarian diet of *oxa*-like grass-eating. Christopher himself conforms to common descriptions of the *healfhundingas* – he is not marked out as special. As well as the *hēafod* of a *hund* he has teeth as sharp as the *tuscas* of an *eofor*. His hair is wild, and his eyes shine as brightly as the **morgen-steorra** (morning star). Although a *morgen-steorra* sounds rather lovely, it is in fact another name for Lucifer or the Devil, and so his brightly shining eyes mark Christopher and his kind as demonic.

But Christopher stands out from his cannibalistic brethren in one crucial element, and it is this that draws him closer to humanity in a way which might teach us what truly distinguished man from beast in the medieval period. The *Martyrology* explains that Christopher is **ge-lēafful** (faithful) to God in his heart, and perhaps it is this faith that has led him to the city, out of the forest and away from his kin (the text itself provides no reason). Given that, like other *healfhundingas*, he lacks the ability to speak like a *mann*, Christopher prays to God to be granted human **ge-sprec** (the power of speech, yeh-SPRETCH). Christopher's prayers are answered: a man dressed in white appears at his side and breathes into his mouth, an act reminiscent of the way God breathes life into Adam, the very first *mann*. Afterwards, Christopher has a gift that seems just as precious: he can **sprecan** (speak, SPREH-kahn) like a *mann*. (Notice how the 'c' in the noun and verb match the modern English pronunciations of 'speech' and 'speak?) But why is speech so important to Christopher? We've already seen that despite their dog-heads and cannibalistic ways, the *healfhundingas* are still seen as at least *half* human. Given that he's left behind his old ways and drawn himself into civilisation, why wouldn't Christopher pray to complete the outward transformation and render himself fully, visibly human? Christopher's prayer for speech instead of a human head highlights a core element of medieval humanity: it is speech, after all, that is needed to praise God, not a new face.

Understandably, Emperor Decius is keen to see the *healfhunding* for himself, and he orders 200 warriors to go and fetch him. Christopher is so intimidating that no warrior dares approach him, but he genially complies anyway. When Decius sees Christopher, he is so shocked at the sight of the dog-headed man that he falls off his throne. After pulling himself together, Decius proceeds to offer Christopher gold and silver if only he gives up his faith in Christ. When Christopher refuses, Decius tortures him, and when torture has no effect he commands the poor *healfhunding* to be led to his **be-hēafdung** (beheading). Thus, in the same moment that Christopher is martyred and brought closest to God, he finally loses the last vestige of his inhuman-ness, his dog-head.

The power of speech

Each of these Old English texts reveals a curiosity about distinguishing *mann* from *dēor*, whether it is through what they wear or where they live, what they eat or whether they can speak. Throughout there is evidence of a desire to distinguish the rational from the irrational; it is this classification, after all, that reveals who is and who isn't capable of attaining salvation in the medieval Christian Church.

During the mid ninth century (the middle of the Old English period), two monks of the Frankish Empire were exchanging letters in Latin on this very subject, specifically on the humanity of the *cynocephali*, the dog men who counted St Christopher among their ranks. Rimbert, a monk and missionary known as 'the apostle of the North', wrote a letter to Ratramnus of Corbie in northern France, a respected thinker and commentator on various theological controversies. Rimbert wanted to know more about the *cynocephali* for a practical reason: at this time they were believed to dwell in the northernmost regions of the world, and Rimbert was heading to Scandinavia on a mission.

Although both classical sources and later medieval texts often locate the world's strangest creatures in India or Ethiopia, this is not the case during the seventh to eleventh centuries, when the monstrous could be found in the North, places like northern Germany, Scandinavia and the Baltic. Even writers who spent a lot of time in northern Europe placed their monsters there, which the historian Ian Wood says is 'a contradiction to the notion that the monstrous races were always far away'. Instead, monsters roamed 'just over the horizon'. This may be because the North was an area just opening up for these writers, an area accessible but not fully understood and thus ripe for tales of extraordinary beings. With such creatures so close to hand, the question was not whether they existed but whether they were human; 'if they were,' Wood explains, 'they were to be the object of mission; if they were not, they were to be killed'.

It seems that Rimbert and Ratramnus corresponded both before and after Rimbert's mission, but only one letter survives: that of Ratramnus, which conveniently summarises important points from their previous exchanges. From Ratramnus' letter, we can infer what questions Rimbert asked and what he observed during his mission, as well as Ratramnus' conclusion on the matter. Rimbert wanted to know what he should do if he encountered a *cynocephalus*. Were the *cynocephali* human (people he could convert to Christianity) or animal?

It's clear from Ratramnus' letter that Rimbert did in fact meet the *cynocephali* on his mission, and his field report provided solid first-hand evidence for their humanity. The *cynocephali* lived in communities, thus abiding by social contracts and laws, demonstrating a sense of morality. They practised agriculture, proving they were rational creatures. They wore clothing, which showed they were modest. Finally, they themselves were keepers of domesticated animals, and animals are not in the habit of domesticating other animals.

While Ratramnus was partly swayed by Rimbert's eyewitness account, he relied mostly upon his own research at the monastery library to come to his conclusion. In particular, he was convinced by the answer he found in a Latin translation of the *Life of St Christopher*. For Ratramnus, rationality was the most essential quality for defining a human, and this, he believed, was demonstrated with the power of speech. God hears Christopher's (presumably silent) prayers and grants him the power to speak early on in the narrative of his martyrdom. Thus God recognised Christopher, a *cynocephalus*, as a human being, and what's good enough for God was good enough for Ratramnus. His conclusion is quite clear: *cynocephali* are not animals but humans with rational minds.

This conclusion would have seemed perfectly rational to speakers of Old English, a language in which **reord-berend** (speech-bearer) is another word for 'human'. Speech is not just a way for people to communicate with one another, it is a way to praise God, to repent and pray for salvation. In the case of St Christopher, his prayer is answered and God grants the *cynocephalus* human *ge-sprec*, the power of speech, because he is *ge-lēafful*, faithful to him in his heart. Christianity is a religion of the book and was spread through speech. The Gospel of John begins: 'In the beginning was the Word' (*On frymðe wæs word*, in Old English), but this *word* doesn't simply represent language; it ultimately derives from Greek *logos*, thought or reason. And so we can see the links that tied humanity so closely to language, and thus to God and to reason.

However, we might also feel uncomfortable with this version of humanity. While rooting it so fundamentally in the power of speech might uplift an animal, it may also denigrate a human. To say that any single ability determines one's humanity is, of course, to immediately exclude a whole range of people from this category. This would have been as problematic in the past as it is today: speech, like sight, hearing, walking or any other function, is an ability that comes and goes, whether through birth, age, accident or illness. It can also be narrowly judged by those who consider 'speech' and a specific language so entwined as to exclude other languages. St Christopher might be deemed worthy of God's gifts, but his dual status as *healfhunding* and saint is unusual: others whose humanity was put into such question might not have been so lucky.

Throughout the Middle Ages, for instance, Christian writers were known to associate the *cynocephali* with the Saracens, anyone who professed the religion of Islam. Knowing this, we might see descriptions of the dog-headed men in a new light. Rather than observing or admiring the humanity of the *cynocephalus*, the writers may have been intent on undermining the intelligence and dignity of a race of real people. When we stop marvelling at the human hybrids, we can start to ask what the speaker might really have been trying to communicate. Are the tusked women called *æwisc* (indecent) because of their tusks or because they appear to live in a society without men? Are the tusks themselves merely a way for the writer to manifest their disgust? If tusked women and *cynocephali* were real peoples, then the animal terminology is a way of dehumanising them, a device to inspire repulsion. This is a tool seen across cultures and eras, weaponised in colonialism and racism and war – and it can be rare to hear from those whose humanity has been stripped in such a way. There are no records of what the *cynocephali* thought, or how the tusked women might have described themselves.

Stories are passed down through speech – both written and oral – and the ones that have survived form our connection to those bearers of Old English from so long ago. Through them, we might find another reason why speech was seen as so important: we feel their authors' humanity, communicated in voice and words, and we get a glimpse of what it meant to be human at the time.

Writers, translators and readers of Old English would have understood this particular power of language: in these texts, a creature's ability to speak for itself affects how well humans can identify with it. Creatures who are unable to speak, like the antagonist Grendel in *Beowulf*, are described as monstrous and seen as more *dēor* than *mann*. His speechlessness communicates his monstrosity – it becomes more difficult to identify with Grendel when we can't hear his side of the story.

And this brings us back to the largest community of those who can't speak: the creatures that share the earth with us, and who have populated this book. In texts like the Old English Exeter Book riddles *dēor* are often given the ability to speak for themselves, and even in other texts their behaviour and actions 'speak' through the textual interpretations of the writers. Normally, animals' 'speech' is inaccessible to us because they communicate without 'words' – these writers bring them closer by making them speak our language. But what do they communicate? Not the reality of their own everyday lives, certainly – they articulate human concerns of good and evil, honour and endurance, treachery and fear. We are encouraged to identify with them not through an understanding of their real nature, but through how close to our own they might be.

Giving a voice to an *igil* (hedgehog) or a *swan* is not humanising them so much as giving us humans a way to understand another way of being ourselves. From Old English poetry and prose of the early medieval period to the *Physiologus* texts from antiquity and the bestiary lore of the later Middle Ages, people have used animals to illuminate the human experience. It's the reason why a medieval poet imagines a spider that's just being a spider as cruel and cowardly, and it's why a fox merely going about its business in the urban wilderness might be praised as a 'polite neighbour'.

Speech-bearer, human, animal – these distinctions are less important, it seems, as we end *The Deorhord*. In Old English stories, we find a desire to better understand humans themselves through animals. The fact that this understanding comes through animals is less important than what the stories' words communicate. A *gange-wæfre*'s (spider's) industrious web-weaving reminds us that all we do on earth is transient and fleeting compared to the eternity of the afterlife. The *hwæl* (whale) warns us that if something looks too good to be true, it probably is. The fact that both *lēo* (lioness) and *hind* look after the saints shows us how the fierce and the meek can each serve God in their own ways. And the *stræt-wyrhta* (street-maker) – whatever it might be – demonstrates a parent's bravery and devotion to their children when facing danger.

So what does it mean to be a human being in Old English? Ask the animals of *The Deorhord*. These *dēor* show humanity at its best and its worst, through deception, greed and hatred, but also through empathy, self-sacrifice and love. At the end of the day, in Old English *dēor* and *menn* are not so far away from each other: they are both *sceaft* (creation), sharing a single planet, and perhaps this is the ultimate lesson they can teach us.

The Epilogue's Wordhord

ǣwisc, adjective (AE-wish / ˈæːˌwɪʃ): Foul, shameless, indecent.

be-hēafdung, noun (beh-HAY-ahv-dung / bɛˈheːavˌdʌŋ): Beheading.

blōd, noun (BLOAD / ˈbloːd): Blood.

clawu, noun (KLA-wuh / ˈklaˌwʌ): Claw, talon (plural: *clawa*).

feax, noun (FEH-ahks / ˈfɛaks): Hair.

fulluht, noun (FULL-uh't / ˈfʌl-lʌxt): Baptism.

ge-lēafful, adjective (yeh-LAY-ahf-full / jɛˈleːafˌfʌl): Full of belief, faithful.

ge-sprec, noun (yeh-SPRETCH / jɛˈsprɛtʃ): The power of speech.

healf, adjective (HEH-alf / ˈhɛalf): Half.

healfhunding, noun (HEH-alf-HUN-ding / ˈhɛalf-ˌhʌn-dɪŋ): *Cynocephalus*, one of a fabled race of half-canine men or men with dogs' heads (plural: *healfhundingas*).

healf-hundisc, adjective (HEH-alf-HUN-dish / ˈhɛalf-ˌhʌn-dɪʃ): Half-canine.

manu, noun (MA-nuh / ˈma-nʌ): Mane.

morgen-steorra, noun (MOR-gen-STEH-or-ra / ˈmɔr-gɛn-ˌstɛɔr-ra): Morning star (epithet for Satan or the Devil).

nægl, noun (NA-yull / ˈnæ-jəl): Nail (plural: *næglas*).

reord-berend, noun (REH-ord-BEH-rend / ˈrɛɔrd-ˌbɛ-rɛnd): Speech-bearer, human.

sprecan, verb (SPREH-kahn / ˈsprɛ-kan): To speak.

swǣtan, verb (SWAE-tahn / ˈswæː-tan): To sweat.

tægl, noun (TA-yull / ˈtæ-jəl): Tail.

tusc, noun (TUSK / ˈtʌsk): Tusk (plural: *tuscas*).

un-clǣnness, noun (UN-KLAN-ness / ˈʌn-ˌklæːn-nɛs): Impurity, foulness (in a physical sense); impurity, obscenity (in a moral sense).

un-weorþ, adjective (UN-WEH-orth / ˈʌn-ˌwɛɔrθ): Of no value; of no dignity; unworthy.

wudu-bearu, noun (WUH-duh-BEH-ah-ruh / ˈwʌ-dʌ-ˌbɛa-rʌ): Grove of trees (plural: *wudu-bearwas*).

Þanc-word (thank-words)

This book began many years ago as an idea I had as a postgraduate. I had learned about medieval bestiaries, which so perfectly combined two interests of mine – medieval storytelling and animals. I was fascinated by the stories people told in these texts about animals, and also by the curious animal illustrations with their varying levels of realism. I thought, how fun would it be for a modern-day artist, unfamiliar with medieval tales, to illustrate these animals according to the descriptions given in Old and Middle English? I was fortunate enough to find a brilliant illustrator to collaborate with me in this endeavour: James Merry. The result was a blog called *Deorhord: A Medieval and Modern Bestiary*. While the scope of this book ended up being quite different from the original blog, I am indebted to James for his extraordinary illustrations, which inspired me to think about these bizarre animal descriptions in new ways. You can see my Old English and Middle English translations along with James Merry's artwork at medievalandmodernbestiary.com. Thanks are also due to Ryan Lintott for working out how to do medieval-style interlinear 'glosses' on WordPress.

Thanks to my PhD supervisor, Clare Lees, who always encouraged me to find my place in a field that tends to undervalue non-academic work. I feel especially fortunate to have had a supervisor who actively promoted and supported both the creativity and individuality of all her students. Thanks also to Craig Davis, the professor who inspired my *lufu* of Old English in the first place.

I am grateful for the support of my agent Charlie Campbell and everyone at Profile who helped make *The Deorhord* a reality. Thanks especially to Louisa Dunnigan, my *snotor* and talented editor, whose ideas, recommendations and critiques have improved this book in so many ways. I am also grateful to Linden Lawson for her *earn*-eyed edits, and to Joanna Lisowiec for creating a truly *wlitig* collection of animal illustrations.

Thanks to the patient readers of the rough draft of this manuscript, who generously provided encouragement and advice: Teresa Crist, Ryan Lintott and Kathryn Maude.

I am grateful to the Toronto *Dictionary of Old English*, especially Stephen Pelle, for sponsoring my access to library resources at the University of Toronto. I could not have researched this book without that support.

Thanks to all the academics on social media who have answered my random queries and provided access to sources. I am also grateful to Katherine Hindley for her assistance in reading some medieval French manuscripts.

Thanks to the members of my writers' group whose encouragement, passion for writing and friendship continue to inspire me.

I am grateful for the generosity of all the gold-givers on Patreon, who have supported my work over the years.

Thanks to my wonderful parents, who encourage and support me in all I do and who nurtured a little girl's love of both words and animals.

I am incredibly grateful for the love and support of my husband Ryan, who encouraged me to focus on writing this book while he took care of everything else throughout my pregnancy. Thanks also to Crash and Knives for providing their *dēor's* perspective, walking in front of the screen purring and batting at notes. And I like to think that Kai was involved in the editorial process, giving little kicks as I read through the good parts (but it'll be a few years before I can confirm this).

Sources

General

Bosworth-Toller Anglo-Saxon Dictionary: bosworthtoller.com
Douay-Rheims and Latin Vulgate Bible: drbo.org/drl/index.htm
The Medieval Bestiary: bestiary.ca
Middle English Compendium: quod.lib.umich.edu/m/middle-english-dictionary
Oxford English Dictionary: oed.com
Thesaurus of Old English: oldenglishthesaurus.arts.gla.ac.uk
Toronto *Dictionary of Old English: A to I*: doe.utoronto.ca

Prologue

URBAN WILDLIFE

A. Anthony, 'Urban foxes: Are they "fantastic" or a growing menace?',
Guardian (15 October 2022), theguardian.com/environment/2022/
oct/15/urban-foxes-are-they-fantastic-or-a-growing-menace; A.
Dempsey, 'Toronto built a better green bin and – oops – maybe a
smarter raccoon', *Toronto Star* (30 August 2018), thestar.com/news/
gta/2018/08/30/toronto-built-a-better-green-bin-and-oops-maybe-
a-smarter-raccoon.html; H. Williamson, 'Inside the secret world of
London's urban foxes', *Metro* (8 September 2018), metro.co.uk/2018/09/08/
inside-the-secret-world-of-londons-urban-foxes-7923273.

THE *PHYSIOLOGUS* AND BESTIARIES

M. J. Curley, *Physiologus: A Medieval Book of Nature Lore* (2009); I. Dines,
'Bestiaries, Latin', in *The Encyclopedia of Medieval Literature in Britain*,
ed. S. Echard and R. Rouse (2017), pp. 1–5; B. Dykema, 'Preaching the
Book of Creation: Memory and moralization in medieval bestiaries',
Peregrinations 3.2 (2011), 96–121; E. Harlitz-Kern, 'To see the antisemitism

of medieval bestiaries, look for the owl', *Aeon* (24 March 2020), aeon.co/
ideas/to-see-the-antisemitism-of-medieval-bestiaries-look-for-the-owl;
S. C. M. Lindquist and A. S. Mittman, *Medieval Monsters: Terrors, Aliens,
Wonders* (2018); F. McCulloch, *Medieval Latin and French Bestiaries* (1962);
E. Runde, 'Books of beasts in the British Library: The medieval bestiary
and its context', *Catalogue of Illuminated Manuscripts* (British Library),
bl.uk/catalogues/illuminatedmanuscripts/TourBestiaryGen.asp; D. H.
Strickland, 'The bad side of the medieval bestiary', *Getty Iris* (21 May 2019),
blogs.getty.edu/iris/the-bad-side-of-the-medieval-bestiary.

ISIDORE'S *ETYMOLOGIES*
S. A. Barney et al., trans. and ed., *The Etymologies of Isidore of Seville* (2006).

LANGUAGE HISTORY
C. Breay and J. Story, *Anglo-Saxon Kingdoms: Art, Word, War* (2018); D.
Crystal, *The Cambridge Encyclopedia of the English Language* (1995).

1 Eagle

BIRD TERMINOLOGY
C. H. Whitman, 'The birds of Old English literature', *Journal of English and
Germanic Philology* 2.2 (1898), 149–98.

EVANGELISTS AND THEIR ANIMALS
A. H. Collins, *Symbolism of Animals and Birds Represented in English Church
Architecture* (1913); S. C. M. Lindquist and A. S. Mittman, *Medieval Monsters:
Terrors, Aliens, Wonders* (2018); C. Thomas, 'How the four evangelists
became gospel writers and acquired their symbols', *Early Irish Manuscripts*
(Trinity College Dublin) (6 April 2016), tcd.ie/library/early-irish-mss/how-
the-four-evangelists-became-gospel-writers-and-acquired-their-symbols/.

BEASTS OF BATTLE
H. Estes, 'Feasting with Holofernes: Digesting Judith in Anglo-Saxon
England', *Exemplaria* 15 (2003), 325–50.

2 Spider

SPIDER BITE REMEDIES
T. Porck, 'Creepy crawlies in early medieval England: Anglo-Saxon medicine and minibeasts', *ThijsPorck.com* (11 March 2018), thijsporck. com/2018/03/11/creepy-crawlies.

SPIDERS IN THE PSALMS
M. Cavell, 'Arachnophobia and Early English Literature', *New Medieval Literatures* 18 (2018), 1–43; E. R. Harvey, 'The swallow's nest and the spider's web', in *Studies in English Language and Literature: 'Doubt wisely': Papers in Honour of E. G. Stanley*, ed. M. J. Toswell and E. M. Tyler (1996), pp. 327–41; K. Michalski and S. Michalski, *Spider* (2010).

3 Field Creature

FARMING AND ANIMAL HUSBANDRY
D. Banham and R. Faith, *Anglo-Saxon Farms and Farming* (2014); R. Gameson, 'The material fabric of early British books', in *The Cambridge History of the Book in Britain: Volume 1, c.400–1100*, ed. R. Gameson (2011), pp. 13–93; M. Gardiner, 'Late Saxon Settlements', in *The Oxford Handbook of Anglo-Saxon Archaeology*, ed. H. Hamerow et al. (2011), pp. 198–220; W. G. Hoskins, *The Making of the English Landscape* (1955); C. Lee, 'Earth's Treasures: Food and Drink', in *The Material Culture of Daily Living in the Anglo-Saxon World*, ed. M. C. Hyer and G. R. Owen-Crocker (2011), pp. 142–56; S. Payne, 'Animal Husbandry', in *The Blackwell Encyclopaedia of Anglo-Saxon England*, ed. M. Lapidge et al. (1999), pp. 38–9; D. Yalden, *The History of British Mammals* (1999).

4 Dove

COLOUR SYMBOLISM
F. McCulloch, *Mediaeval Latin and French Bestiaries* (1962); A. Payne, *Medieval Beasts* (1990); H. Pulliam, 'Color', *Studies in Iconography* 33 (2012), 3–14.

DOVE SYMBOLISM

H. Collins, *Symbolism of Animals and Birds Represented in English Church Architecture* (1913).

HUMOURS

E. Sears, *The Ages of Man: Medieval Interpretations of the Life Cycle* (1986).

GRAMMATICAL GENDER

A. Curzan, *Gender Shifts in the History of English* (2003).

5 Animals Unheard Of

ALEXANDER THE GREAT

A. E. Knock, 'Wonders of the East: A synoptic edition of the Letter of Pharasmanes and the Old English and Old Picard translations' (unpublished doctoral thesis, Birkbeck, University of London, 1981); R. Stoneman, *Legends of Alexander the Great* (2011).

SCOTTISH WITCHCRAFT CHARGES

Ancient Criminal Trials in Scotland (1488–1624), compiled by R. Pitcairn (1833); M. Wasser, 'Scotland's First Witch-Hunt: The Eastern Witch-Hunt of 1568–1569', in *Scottish Witches and Witch-Hunters*, ed. J. Goodare (2013), pp. 17–33.

VALKYRIES

L. M. Hollander, 'The Lay of Harold (Haraldskvathi or Hrajnsmól)', in *Old Norse Poems: The Most Important Non-Skaldic Verse Not Included in the Poetic Edda* (1936).

GRIFFINS

A. Apps, trans., *Gaius Iulius Solinus and his Polyhistor* (2011); C. H. Whitman, 'The birds of Old English literature', *Journal of English and Germanic Philology* 2.2 (1898), 149–98.

VASA MORTIS

T. Major, 'Philistine Doomsday and the *Vasa Mortis* of *Solomon and Saturn II*', *Neophilologus* 100 (2016), 143–60.

6 Ant

ST MALCHUS
C. Gray, Jerome, *'Vita malchi': Introduction, Translation, and Commentary* (2015).

MONASTICISM
C. H. Lawrence, *Medieval Monasticism: Forms of Religious Life in Western Europe in the Middle Ages* (2001).

MEDIEVAL PLACE NAMES
J. B. Friedmann, *The Monstrous Races in Medieval Art and Thought* (1981); P. Gravestock, 'Did Imaginary Animals Exist?', in *The Mark of the Beast: The Bestiary in Art, Life and Literature*, ed. D. H. Strickland (2013), pp. 119–39; R. Stoneman, *Legends of Alexander the Great* (2011).

GOLD-DIGGING ANTS
R. Barber, *Bestiary: MS Bodley 764* (1992); M. Cesario, 'Ant-lore in Anglo-Saxon England', *Anglo-Saxon England* 40 (2012), 273–91; W. George and W. B. Yapp, *The Naming of the Beasts: Natural History in the Medieval Bestiary* (1991); J. Rizvi and G. M. Kakpori, 'Review: Lost kingdoms of the gold-digging ants', *India International Centre Quarterly* 15.2 (1988), 131–47.

7 Elephant

ELEPHANT FACTS
World Wildlife Fund, wwf.org.uk.

HENRY III'S ELEPHANT
S. Lewis, *The Art of Matthew Paris in the 'Chronica Majora'* (1987).

ALEXANDER'S LETTER TO ARISTOTLE
R. D. Fulk, *The 'Beowulf' Manuscript: Complete Texts and 'The Fight at Finnsburg'* (2010); R. Stoneman, *Legends of Alexander the Great* (2011).

ELEPHANT LORE
R. Barber, *Bestiary: MS Bodley 764* (1992); G. C. Druce, 'The elephant in

medieval legend and art', *Journal of the Royal Archaeological Institute* 76
(1919), 1–73; N. Nicholas and G. Baloglou, *An Entertaining Tale of Quadrupeds:
Translation and Commentary* (2003); H. Rackham, trans. and ed., *Pliny:
Natural History* (1967); R. Steele, *Mediaeval Lore from Bartholomew Anglicus*
(1905); H. Wirtjes, *The Middle English 'Physiologus'* (1991).

8 Lion

LIONS AND SAINTS

A. H. Collins, *Symbolism of Animals and Birds Represented in English Church
Architecture* (1913); S. C. M. Lindquist and A. S. Mittman, *Medieval Monsters:
Terrors, Aliens, Wonders* (2018); K. Walker-Meikle, *Medieval Pets* (2012).

LION LORE

R. Barber, *Bestiary: MS Bodley 764* (1992); M. Haist, 'The Lion, Bloodline,
and Kingship', in *The Mark of the Beast: The Medieval Bestiary in Art, Life, and
Literature*, ed. D. H. Strickland (2013), pp. 3–21; G. C. Macaulay, *The History of
Herodotus* (1890); H. Rackham, trans. and ed., *Pliny: Natural History* (1967); R.
Steele, *Mediaeval Lore from Bartholomew Anglicus* (1905).

9 Deer

DEER IN BRITAIN

D. Couzens et al., *Britain's Mammals Updated Edition: Field Guide to Mammals
of Great Britain and Ireland* (2021); D. Yalden, *The History of British Mammals*
(1999).

MILKING DEER

D. Nosowitz, 'Deer milk is apparently a real thing (in New Zealand)',
Modern Farmer (27 June 2018), modernfarmer.com/2018/06/deer-milk-is-
apparently-a-real-thing-in-new-zealand; J. E. Salisbury, *The Beast Within:
Animals in the Middle Ages* (2011).

CHRIST'S LEAPS

D. Hurst, *Gregory the Great: Forty Gospel Homilies* (1990).

DOMNE EAFE AND HER HIND

S. Hollis, 'The Minster-in-Thanet foundation story', *Anglo-Saxon England* 27 (1998), 41–64; J. Davies, 'The landscapes of Thanet and the legend of St Mildrith: Human and nonhuman voices, agencies and histories', *English Studies* 96.5 (2015), 487–506; E. Parker, 'St Mildred and the foundation of Minster-in-Thanet', *A Clerk of Oxford* (22 July 2012), aclerkofoxford. blogspot.com/2012/07/st-mildred-of-thanet.html.

10 Phoenix

PHOENIX LORE

J. S. Hill, 'The phoenix', *Religion and Literature* 16.2 (1984), 61–6; V. Jones, 'The Phoenix and the Resurrection', in *The Mark of the Beast: The Medieval Bestiary in Art, Life, and Literature*, ed. D. H. Strickland (2013), pp. 99–115.

OLD ENGLISH *PHOENIX* POEM

N. F. Blake, *The Phoenix* (1990); D. G. Calder, 'The vision of paradise: A symbolic reading of the Old English phoenix', *Anglo-Saxon England* 1 (1972), 167–81; H. Maring, 'Birds of creation in Old English poetry', *Journal of English and Germanic Philology* 120.4 (2021), 429–64.

SPICES AND FRAGRANCES

J. H. Wheatcroft, 'Classical Ideology in the Medieval Bestiary', in *The Mark of the Beast: The Medieval Bestiary in Art, Life, and Literature*, ed. D. H. Strickland (2013), pp. 141–59.

NATURE

J. Neville, *Representations of the Natural World in Old English Poetry* (1999).

BENNU BIRD

P. G. P. Meyboom, *The Nile Mosaic of Palestrina: Early Evidence of Egyptian Religion in Italy* (1994); R. H. Wilkinson, *The Complete Gods and Goddesses of Ancient Egypt* (2003).

HEORU-DREORIG

K. P. Wentersdorf, 'On the meaning of O.E. *dreorig* in *Brunanburh* 54', *Neuphilologische Mitteilungen* 74.2 (1973), 232–7; K. P. Wentersdorf, 'On the meaning of O.E. *heorodreorig* in *The Phoenix* and other poems', *Studia Neophilologica* 45.1 (1973), 32–46.

OLD ENGLISH *PHYSIOLOGUS* FRAGMENT

M. D. C. Drout, '"The Partridge" is a phoenix: Revising the Exeter Book *Physiologus*', *Neophilologus* 91 (2007), 487–503; M. C. Hoek, 'Anglo-Saxon innovation and the use of the senses in the Old English *Physiologus* Poems', *Studia Neophilologica* 69 (1997), 1–10; A. Rossi-Reder, 'Beasts and baptism: A new perspective on the Old English *Physiologus*', *Neophilologus* 83 (1999), 461–77.

11 Panther

NAME ETYMOLOGY

S. A. Barney et al., trans. and ed., *The Etymologies of Isidore of Seville* (2006); A. H. Collins, *Symbolism of Animals and Birds Represented in English Church Architecture* (1913).

PANTHER LORE

R. Barber, *Bestiary: MS Bodley 764* (1992); F. N. M. Diekstra, 'The *Physiologus*, the bestiaries and medieval animal lore', *Neophilologus* 69.1 (1985), 142–55; M. C. Hoek, 'Anglo-Saxon innovation and the use of the senses in the Old English *Physiologus* poems', *Studia Neophilologica* 69 (1997), 1–10.

12 Whale

OLD ENGLISH *WHALE* POEM

M. C. Hoek, 'Anglo-Saxon innovation and the use of the senses in the Old English *Physiologus* poems', *Studia Neophilologica* 69 (1997), 1–10; J. Neville, *Representations of the Natural World in Old English Poetry* (1999).

HEOLOÞ-HELM

M. Fox, 'Feðerhama and hæleðhelm: The equipment of devils', *Florilegium* 26 (2009), 131–57.

JASCONIUS

C. Van Duzer, 'Floating islands seen at sea: Myth and reality', *Anuario do Centro de Estudos de História do Atlântico* 1 (2009), 110–20.

LEVIATHAN

C. C. Coulter, 'The "Great Fish" in ancient and medieval story', *Transactions and Proceedings of the American Philological Association* 57 (1926), 32–50.

13 Snake

ORANGE ETYMOLOGY

D. S. Kastan, *On Color* (2018).

SNAKE LORE

R. Barber, *Bestiary: MS Bodley 764* (1992); F. N. M. Diekstra, 'The *Physiologus*, the bestiaries and medieval animal lore', *Neophilologus* 69.1 (1985), 142–55; J. Neville, *Representations of the Natural World in Old English Poetry* (1999); H. Rackham, trans. and ed., *Pliny: Natural History* (1967); J. H. Wheatcroft, 'Classical Ideology in the Medieval Bestiary', in *The Mark of the Beast: The Medieval Bestiary in Art, Life, and Literature*, ed. D. H. Strickland (2013), pp. 141–59.

CERASTES

K. F. Kitchell Jr, *Animals in the Ancient World from A to Z* (2014); A. E. Knock, 'Wonders of the East: a synoptic edition of the Letter of Pharasmanes and the Old English and Old Picard translations' (unpublished doctoral thesis, Birkbeck College, University of London, 1981).

14 Dragon

CHRONICLES

M. Swanton, trans. and ed., *The Anglo-Saxon Chronicles* (1996).

ST MARGARET

T.-A. Cooper, 'Why Is Margaret's the Only *Life* in London, BL, Cotton MS Tiberius A.iii?', in *Writing Women Saints in Anglo-Saxon England*, ed. P. E. Szarmach (2013), pp. 55–81; S. C. M. Lindquist and A. S. Mittman, *Medieval Monsters: Terrors, Aliens, Wonders* (2018).

DIOCLETIAN PERSECUTION

M. Gaddis, *There Is No Crime for Those Who Have Christ: Religious Violence in the Christian Roman Empire* (2005).

DRAGONS (AND OTHER FIRE-BREATHERS)

R. Barber, *Bestiary: MS Bodley 764* (1992); A. K. Brown, 'The fire-drake in *Beowulf*', *Neophilologus* 64.3 (1980), 439–60; Y. Byghan, *Sacred and Mythological Animals: A Worldwide Taxonomy* (2020); M. E. Goldsmith, *The Mode and Meaning of 'Beowulf'* (1970); A. Payne, *Medieval Beasts* (1990); C. Van Duzer, *Sea Monsters on Medieval and Renaissance Maps* (2014).

15 Wolf

PREDATORY ANIMALS IN EARLY MEDIEVAL ENGLAND

J. Neville, *Representations of the Natural World in Old English Poetry* (1999).

WOLF EXTERMINATION

D. Couzens et al., *Britain's Mammals Updated Edition: Field Guide to Mammals of Great Britain and Ireland* (2021); D. Yalden, *The History of British Mammals* (1999).

WOLF'S ASSOCIATION WITH THE DEVIL

J. Neville, *Representations of the Natural World in Old English Poetry* (1999).

'WOLF'S HEAD' AND OUTLAWRY

B. O'Brien, trans. and ed., *Digital Edition of 'Leges Edwardi Confessoris'*, earlyenglishlaws.ac.uk/law/ecf1; F. Tupper Jr, *The Riddles of the Exeter Book* (1910).

PERSONAL NAMES

F. Colman, *The Grammar of Names in Anglo-Saxon England: The Linguistics and Culture of the Old English Onomasticon* (2014).

16 Water-monster

NICOR

J. Neville, *Representations of the Natural World in Old English Poetry* (1999); M. S. Serjeantson, 'The vocabulary of folklore in Old and Middle English', *Folklore* 47.1 (1936), 42–73.

MIDDLE ENGLISH TEXTS

E. Mason, trans. and ed., *Arthurian Chronicles: Wace and Layamon* (1962); H. Weber, *Metrical Romances of the Thirteenth, Fourteenth, and Fifteenth Centuries*, vol. I (1810).

NIX

Editors of the Encyclopaedia Britannica, 'Nix', *Britannica* (2022), britannica.com/topic/nix-German-mythology.

KNUCKER

'Dragons & serpents in Sussex', *Sussex Archaeology & Folklore*, sussexarch. org.uk/saaf/dragon.html.

NUCKELAVEE

W. T. Dennison, 'Orkney folklore. Sea myths', *Scottish Antiquary* 5.19 (1891), 130–33.

DEPTFORD CREEK NECKER

'Drowned lair: The Deptford Creek Necker', *Portals of London* (13 January 2019), portalsoflondon.com/2019/01/13/drowned-lair-the-deptford-creek-necker.

17 Moon-head

ALEXANDER'S LETTER TO ARISTOTLE
R. D. Fulk, *The 'Beowulf' Manuscript: Complete Texts and 'The Fight at Finnsburg'* (2010); V. Di Marco and L. Perelman, *The Middle English Letter of Alexander to Aristotle* (1978); E. Pettit, *The Waning Sword: Conversion Imagery and Celestial Myth in 'Beowulf'* (2020).

CROCODILE LORE
R. Barber, *Bestiary: MS Bodley 764* (1992); S. A. Barney et al., trans. and ed., *The Etymologies of Isidore of Seville* (2006); O. L. Kuhns, *Bestiaries and Lapidaries*, vol. IV (1896); F. McCulloch, *Mediaeval Latin and French Bestiaries* (1962); A. Payne, *Medieval Beasts* (1990); H. Rackham, trans. and ed., *Pliny: Natural History* (1967).

18 Teeth Tyrant

DENTES TYRANNUM AND ODONTOTYRANNOS
R. D. Fulk, *The 'Beowulf' Manuscript: Complete Texts and 'The Fight at Finnsburg'* (2010); E. M. Moacdieh, 'Odontotyrannus', *A Book of Creatures* (10 October 2016), abookofcreatures.com/2016/10/10/odontotyrannus; R. Stoneman, *Legends of Alexander the Great* (2011).

INDUS WORM
J. W. McCrindle, trans. and ed., *Ancient India as described by Ktêsias the Knidian* (1882).

RHINOS
C. Fountain, 'Three-horned rhinos', *International Zoo News* 27.4 (1980), 17; J. Gibson, 'Three horned rhino in Namibia', *Rhino Resource Center* (2015), rhinoresourcecenter.com/images/Three-horned-rhino-in-Namibia_ i1459169465.php; H. G. Liddell and R. Scott, *A Greek–English Lexicon, revised and augmented edition* (1940).

FOURTEENTH-CENTURY ILLUSTRATION
Bibliothèque nationale de France, Français 24364, f. 54v.

19 Street-maker

RIDDLE 15 SOLUTIONS

D. Bitterli, 'Exeter Book Riddle 15: Some points for the porcupine', *Anglia* 120.4 (2002), 461–87; M. Cavell, 'The *Igil* and Exeter Book *Riddle 15*', *Notes and Queries* 64.2 (2017), 206–10.

BRITISH MAMMALS

D. Couzens et al., *Britain's Mammals Updated Edition: Field Guide to Mammals of Great Britain and Ireland* (2021).

FOX, WEASEL AND HEDGEHOG LORE

R. Barber, *Bestiary: MS Bodley 764* (1992); S. A. Barney et al., trans. and ed., *The Etymologies of Isidore of Seville* (2006); F. N. M. Diekstra, 'The *Physiologus*, the bestiaries and medieval animal lore', *Neophilologus* 69.1 (1985), 142–55; R. B. Parker, '*Volpone* and *Reynard the Fox*', *Renaissance Drama* 7 (1976), 3–42.

20 Moving Spirit

RIDDLE 7 SOLUTION

D. Bitterli, *Say What I am Called: The Old English Riddles of the Exeter Book and the Anglo-Latin Riddle Tradition* (2009).

BIRD CALLS

Cornell University, *The Cornell Lab: All About Birds*, allaboutbirds.org/guide.

SWAN LORE

R. Barber, *Bestiary: MS Bodley 764* (1992); S. A. Barney et al., trans. and ed., *The Etymologies of Isidore of Seville* (2006); A. Payne, *Medieval Beasts* (1990); R. Steele, trans. and ed., *Mediaeval Lore from Bartholomew Anglicus* (1905).

SWANS IN OLD ENGLISH

P. Kitson, 'Swans and geese in Old English riddles', *Anglo-Saxon Studies in Archaeology and History* 7 (1994), 79–84; A. Metcalf, 'Ten natural animals in Beowulf', *Neuphilologische Mitteilungen* 64.4 (1963), 378–89.

Epilogue

HIPPO 'SWEAT'

S. Kean, 'Sweating blood', *Science History Institute* (29 July 2018), sciencehistory.org/distillations/sweating-blood; Y. Saikawa et al., 'The red sweat of the hippopotamus', *Nature* 429 (27 May 2004), 363.

ST CHRISTOPHER

S. M. Kim, '"In his heart he believed in God, but he could not speak like a man": Martyrdom, Monstrosity, Speech and the Dog-Headed Saint Christopher', in *Writers, Editors and Exemplars in Medieval English Texts*, ed. S. M. Rowley (2020), pp. 235–50; S. C. Thomson, 'Grotesque, fascinating, transformative: The power of a strange face in the story of Saint Christopher', *Essays in Medieval Studies* 34 (2018), 83–98.

THE MONSTROUS IN THE MIDDLE AGES

J. B. Friedmann, *The Monstrous Races in Medieval Art and Thought* (1981); I. Wood, '"The ends of the earth?": The Bible, Bibles, and the Other in Early Medieval Europe', in *The Calling of the Nations: Exegesis, Ethnography and Empire in a Biblical-Historic Present*, ed. M. Vessey et al. (2011), pp. 200–216; I. Wood, 'Where the Wild Things Are', in *Visions of Community in the Post-Roman World: The West, Byzantium and the Islamic World, 300–1100*, ed. W. Pohl et al. (2012), pp. 531–42.

RATRAMNUS AND RIMBERT ON *CYNOCEPHALI*

S. G. Bruce, 'Hagiography as Monstrous Ethnography: A Note on Ratramnus of Corbie's Letter Concerning the Conversion of the Cynocephali', in *Insignis sophiae arcator: Medieval Latin Studies in Honour of Michael Herren on his 65th Birthday*, ed. G. R. Wieland et al. (2006), pp. 45–56.

GREEK *LOGOS*

H. G. Liddell and R. Scott, *An Intermediate Greek Lexicon* (1889).

Old English Words

Below is a list of all the Old English words in this book with their definitions and pronunciations.

a-bysgian, verb (ah-BUEZ-yi-ahn / a-'byz-jɪ-an): To busy, engage, involve, preoccupy. *See page 89*

a-cǣglod, adjective (ah-KAG-lodd / a-'kæː-glɔd): Pegged, studded with pegs; serrated (definition uncertain). *See page 233*

āglǣca, noun (AH-GLACK-ah / 'aː-ˌglæː-ka): Hostile fighter, fierce combatant, great opponent. *See page 168*

ancor, noun (AN-kor / 'an-kɔr): Recluse, hermit, anchorite. *See page 127*

and-wrāþ, adjective (AND-WRAWTH / 'and-ˌwraːθ): Hostile, antagonistic (towards something). *See page 158*

ān-haga, noun (AHN-HA-ga / 'aːn-ˌha-ga): Solitary being. *See page 139*

ān-stapa, noun (AHN-STAH-pa / 'aːn-ˌsta-pa): Lone wanderer (one-stepper). *See page 158*

ār-lēas, adjective (AR-LAY-ahs / 'aːr-ˌleːas): Impious, wicked; dishonourable, shameful. *See page 125*

aspide, noun (AH-spih-duh / 'a-spɪ-də): Asp. *See page 113*

attor, noun (AHT-tor / 'at-tɔr): Venom, poison. *See page 183*

attor-coppa, noun (AHT-tor-KOP-pa / 'at-tɔr-ˌkɔp-pa): Spider (plural: *attor-coppan*). *See page 33*

attor-cræft, noun (AHT-tor-KRAFT / 'at-tɔr-ˌkræft): Art of using poison or poisonous potions, witchcraft, sorcery. *See page 70*

a-weallan, verb (ah-WEH-al-lahn / a-'wɛal-lan): To well up; to abound in numbers, swarm; to be hot, burn, well up with heat. *See page 227*

a-wurpan, verb (ah-WURP-ahn / a-'wʌr-pan): To cast away. *See page 180*

a-wyrgda, noun (ah-WUERG-da / a-'wyrg-da): The cursed, the Devil. *See page 208*

æcer-mann, noun (ACK-er-MAHN / 'æ-kɛr-ˌman): Farmer. *See page 43*

æferþe, noun (AE-ver-thuh / 'æ-vɛr-θə): Unidentified medicinal herb. *See page 34*

ǣmette, noun (AM-et-tuh / 'æː-mɛt-tə): Ant (plural: *ǣmettan*). *See page 82*

ǣmett-hyll, noun (AM-et-HUELL / 'æː-mɛt-ˌhyl): Anthill. *See page 84*

ǣmtig, adjective (AM-tih / 'æːm-tij): Empty, devoid of; bearing or having nothing; not engaged in any activity, at leisure; unmarried. *See page 85*

ǣnlīc, adjective (ANN-leech / 'æːn-liːtʃ): Unique, peerless, incomparable. *See page 140*

æsc-þrote, noun (ASH-THROT-uh / 'æʃ-ˌθrɔ-tə): Verbena, vervain. *See page 35*

ǣwisc, adjective (AE-wish / 'æː-wiʃ): Foul, shameless, indecent. *See page 281*

bān-fæt, noun (BAHN-VAT / 'baːn-ˌvæt): Bone-vessel, the body. *See page 149*

bār, noun (BAR / 'baːr): Boar. *See page 183*

basilisca, noun (BA-zih-liss-ka / 'ba-zɪ-lis-ka): Basilisk. *See page 113*

bēacen, noun (BAY-ah-kun / 'beːa-kən): Sign, portent (plural: *bēacen*). *See page 190*

beadu-wǣpen, noun (BEH-ah-duh-WAP-en / 'bɛa-dʌ-ˌwæː-pɛn): Battle-weapon. *See page 252*

bēag, noun (BAY-ahg / 'beːag): Circular ornament; necklace; crown, circlet (plural: *bēagas*). *See page 142*

beard, noun (BEH-ard / 'bɛard): Beard. *See page 193*

be-gyllan, verb (beh-YUEL-lahn / bɛ-'jyl-lan): To cry out against or in answer to. *See page 27*

be-hēafdung, noun (beh-HAY-ahv-dung / bɛ-'heːav-dʌŋ): Beheading. *See page 287*

beorht, adjective (BEH-orh't / 'bɛɔrxt): Bright, clear, lucid. *See page 29*

bera, noun (BEH-ra / 'bɛ-ra): Bear (plural: *beran*). *See page 95*

bern, noun (BERN / 'bɛrn): Barn. *See page 43*

be-swīcan, verb (beh-ZWEE-kahn / bɛ-'zwiː-kan): To deceive, seduce, evade, betray. *See page 100*

bile-wit, adjective (BILL-uh-wit / 'bɪ-lə-wɪt): Meek, peaceable, gentle, merciful, pure, innocent, virtuous. *See page 62*

blæc, adjective (BLACK / 'blæːk): Black, or of dark hue. *See page 158*

blǣd, noun (BLADD / 'blæːd): Blowing, breath, breathing. *See page 195*

blīþe, adjective (BLEE-thuh / 'bliː-θə): Happy, joyful; gentle, kind, gracious. *See page 29*

blōd, noun (BLOAD / 'bloːd): Blood. *See page 282*

bodig, noun (BODD-ih / 'bɔ-dɪj): Body. *See page 262*

brægen, noun (BRAE-yen / 'bræ-jɛn): Brain. *See page 183*

brēost, noun (BRAY-ost / 'breːɔst): Breast, chest. *See page 234*

bridd, noun (BRID / 'brɪd): Young bird, chick. *See page 19*

brim-hlæst, noun (BRIM-H'LAST / 'brɪm-ˌhlæst): Fish (sea-cargo). *See page 10*

brocc, noun (BROCK / 'brɔk): Badger. *See page 254*

buc, noun (BUCK / 'bʌk): Buck, male deer, perhaps the roe deer specifically (plural: *bucas*). *See page 120*

burn, noun (BURN / 'bʌrn): Stream, brook, river. *See page 144*

cat, noun (KAHT / 'kat): Cat (plural: *catas*). *See page 10*

cǣg, noun (KAG / 'kæːg): Key. *See page 233*

cealf, noun (CHEH-alf / 'tʃɛalf): Calf (plural: *cealfru*). *See page 47*

cēol, noun (CHAY-oll / 'tʃeːɔl): Ship, sea-going vessel. *See page 170*

cicen, noun (CHIH-chen / 'tʃɪ-tʃɛn): Chicken (plural: *cicenu*). *See page 44*

clawu, noun (KLA-wuh / 'kla-wʌ): Claw, talon (plural: *clawa*). *See page 279*

clǣne, adjective (KLAN-uh / 'klæː-nə): Pure, purified, cleansed. *See page 145*

clipian, verb (KLIH-pi-ahn / 'klɪ-pɪ-an): To call, cry out. *See page 110*

clȳwen, noun (KLUE-wen / 'klyː-wɛn): Ball, clew; (specifically) ball of thread or yarn. *See page 262*

cop, noun (KOP / 'kɔp): Top, summit. *See page 33*

copp, noun (KOP / 'kɔp): Cup, vessel. *See page 33*

corn-hūs, noun (KORN-hoos / 'kɔrn-huːs): Granary. *See page 44*

crist, noun (KRIST / 'krɪst): Jesus Christ. *See page 59*

cū, noun (KOO / 'kuː): Cow. *See page 44*

culfre, noun (KULL-vruh / 'kʌl-vrə): Dove (plural: *culfran*). *See page 54*

cū-meoluc, noun (KOO-MEH-o-luk / 'kuː-ˌmɛɔ-lʌk): Cow's milk. *See page 46*

cwic-sūsl, noun (KWITCH-SOO-zull / ˈkwɪtʃ-ˌsuː-zəl): Living torment, eternal punishment; hell. *See page 173*

cyre, noun (KUE-ruh / ˈky-rə): Choice, free will. *See page 72*

dā, noun (DAH / ˈdaː): Doe, perhaps the roe deer specifically (plural: *dān*). *See page 120*

dēaþ, noun (DAY-ath / ˈdeːaθ): Death. *See page 23*

dēaþ-sele, noun (DAY-ath-SEH-luh / ˈdeːaθ-ˌsɛ-lə): Hall of death. *See page 171*

dēaw, noun (DAY-aw / ˈdeːaw): Dew. *See page 143*

dēofol, noun (DAY-oh-voll / ˈdeːɔ-vɔl): Devil, demon; Satan, the Devil. *See page 173*

dēofol-gyld, noun (DAY-oh-voll-YUELD / ˈdeːɔ-vɔl-ˌjyld): Idol, statue of a pagan god. *See page 125*

dēor, noun (DAY-or / ˈdeːɔr): Animal (plural: *dēor*). *See page 10*

dīgol, adjective (DEE-goll / ˈdiː-gɔl): Secret, hidden. *See page 253*

domne, noun (DOM-nuh / ˈdɔm-nə): Lord or lady, referring to a person of high status. *See page 130*

draca, noun (DRAH-ka / ˈdra-ka): Dragon (plural: *dracan*). *See page 113*

drēfan, verb (DRAY-vahn / ˈdreː-van): To disturb, agitate, disquiet, vex, trouble. *See page 268*

drēor, noun (DRAY-or / ˈdreːɔr): Blood. *See page 147*

drēorig, adjective (DRAY-oh-rih / ˈdreːɔ-rɪj): Suffering from or causing anguish, grief, horror or misery. *See page 147*

dumb, adjective (DUMB / ˈdʌmb): Mute, unable to speak. *See page 131*

dūn, noun (DOON / ˈduːn): Mountain, hill. *See page 76*

dūn-scræf, noun (DOON-SHRAFF / ˈduːn-ˌʃræf): Mountain gorge, mountain cave (plural: *dūn-scræfu*). *See page 160*

dūru, noun (DOO-ruh / ˈduː-rʌ): Door. *See page 137*

dyrstig, adjective (DUER-stih / ˈdyr-stɪj): Daring, bold, rash. *See page 88*

ēa, noun (AY-ah / ˈeːa): River. *See page 89*

ēad, noun (AY-ahd / ˈeːad): Happiness, well-being. *See page 23*

ēage, noun (AY-ah-yuh / ˈeːa-jə): Eye (plural: *ēagan*, pronounced AY-ah-gahn). *See page 184*

ēa-land, noun (AY-ah-LOND / ˈeːa-ˌland): Island. *See page 170*

eardung, noun (EH-ar-dung / ˈɛar-dʌŋ): Habitation, dwelling. *See page 224*

earm, adjective (EH-arm / ˈɛarm): Wretched, miserable. *See page 222*

earmincg, noun (EH-ar-minj / ˈɛar-mɪndʒ): Miserable being, unhappy or unfortunate wretch. *See page 116*

earn, noun (EH-arn / ˈɛarn): Eagle (plural: *earnas*). *See page 17*

ēaster, noun (AY-ah-ster / ˈeːa-stɛr): Easter. *See page 153*

ecg, noun (EDGE / ˈɛdʒ): Sword. *See page 61*

ege, noun (EH-yuh / ˈɛ-jə): Fear, terror, dread; awe, respectful fear, reverence. *See page 57*

egeslic, adjective (EH-yez-litch / ˈɛ-jɛz-lɪtʃ): Terrible, dreadful, frightening, terrifying. *See page 188*

ēhtan, noun (AY-h'tahn / ˈeːx-tan): To pursue or chase. *See page 23*

ellen, noun (EL-len / ˈɛl-lɛn): Courage, strength. *See page 161*

ellen-rōf, adjective (EL-len-ROAF / ˈɛl-lɛn-ˌroːf): Brave, strong. *See page 161*

elpend, noun (EL-pend / ˈɛl-pɛnd): Elephant (plural: *elpendas*). *See page 98*

elpend-bān, noun (EL-pend-BAHN / ˈɛl-pɛnd-ˌbaːn): Ivory (elephant-bone). *See page 102*

Engla þēod, noun (ENG-gla-THAY-od / ˈɛŋ-gla-ˌθeːɔd): Country or nation of the English. *See page 96*

englisc, noun (ENG-glish / ˈɛŋ-glɪʃ): English, the English language. *See page 7*

eofor, noun (EH-ov-or / ˈɛɔ-vɔr): Wild boar (plural: *eoforas*). *See page 241*

eorþ-tilia, noun (EH-orth-TIH-li-ah / ˈɛɔrθ-ˌtɪ-lɪ-a): Farmer, tiller of the earth. *See page 43*

eosol, noun (EH-oh-zoll / ˈɛɔ-zɔl): Donkey, ass. *See page 74*

ēowo-meoluc, noun (AY-o-wo-MEH-o-luk / ˈeːɔ-wɔ-ˌmɛɔ-lʌk): Ewe's milk. *See page 46*

etan, noun (EH-tahn / ˈɛ-tan): To eat. *See page 23*

fæder, noun (FADD-er / ˈfæ-dɛr): Father (a human father or God the Father). *See page 59*

fæsten, noun (FAST-en / ˈfæs-tɛn): Fastness; place by its nature fortified against incursion. *See page 232*

fæþm, noun (FATH-um / ˈfæ-θəm): Bosom, embrace; grasp, clutch, possession; fathom (a unit of measurement). *See page 201*

fealu, adjective (FEH-ah-luh / ˈfɛa-lʌ): Colour term of uncertain/varied meaning: basically yellow but variously tinted with shades of red, brown or grey, often pale, always unsaturated (not vivid). *See page 252*

fear, noun (FEH-ar / ˈfɛar): Bull, ox. *See page 183*

feax, noun (FEH-ahks / ˈfɛaks): Hair. *See page 278*

feld, noun (FELD / ˈfɛld): Field, pasture (plural: *feldas*). *See page 47*

fell, noun (FELL / ˈfɛl): Skin, hide. *See page 180*

feng, noun (FENG / ˈfɛŋ): Grip, grasp, clasp; the act of seizing. *See page 223*

fēnix, noun (FAY-niks / ˈfeː-nɪks): Phoenix. *See page 136*

fenn, noun (FEN / ˈfɛn): Fen, marsh. *See page 232*

feoh, noun (FEH-oh / ˈfɛɔx): Cattle, livestock; property, wealth, money; value, price, fee; name of the F-rune ᚠ. *See page 42*

feoh-hord, noun (FEH-oh-HORD / ˈfɛɔx-ˌhɔrd): Hoard of money or wealth. *See page 46*

feoh-spilling, noun (FEH-oh-SPIL-ling / ˈfɛɔx-ˌspɪl-lɪŋ): Wasting of money. *See page 46*

feoh-strang, adjective (FEH-oh-STRONG / ˈfɛɔx-ˌstraŋ): Rich (money-strong). *See page 46*

fēond, noun (FAY-ond / ˈfeːɔnd): Fiend, devil; enemy. *See page 173*

feorm, noun (FEH-orm / ˈfɛɔrm): Food, provisions; entertainment, feast; benefit, profit. *See page 43*

feormere, noun (FEH-or-meh-ruh / ˈfɛɔr-mɛ-rə): One who supplies with food, purveyor. *See page 43*

feormian, verb (FEH-or-mi-ahn / ˈfɛɔr-mɪ-an): To foster or maintain; to entertain or welcome a guest; to harbour a fugitive or criminal; to maintain someone with basic necessities; to supply food as an obligation or rent; to provide a feast for someone. *See page 43*

fērende, adjective (FAY-ren-duh / ˈfeː-rɛn-də): Moving, mobile. *See page 268*

fēþe-mund, noun (FAY-thuh-MUND / ˈfeː-θə-ˌmʌnd): Animal paw ('foot-hand' or 'hand for walking') (plural: *fēþe-munda*). *See page 252*

feþer, noun (FEH-ther / ˈfɛ-θɛr): Feather; (in plural) wings (plural: *feþra*). *See page 20* *fisc*, noun (FISH / 'fıʃ): Fish; any animal that lives exclusively in the water (plural: *fiscas*). *See page 168*

fisca cynn, noun (FISK-ah KUEN / 'fı-ska 'kyn): Fish-kind. *See page 168*

fiþer-fōte, adjective (FITH-er-FOAT-uh / 'fı-θɛr-ˌfoː-tə): Four-footed. *See page 77*

fixen, noun (FICK-sen / 'fık-sɛn): Vixen (female fox). *See page 257*

flǣsc, noun (FLASH / 'flæː-ʃ): Flesh. *See page 211*

flēogende, verb (FLAY-oh-yen-duh / 'fleː-ɔ-jɛn-də): Flying. *See page 89*

flocc, noun (FLOCK / 'flɔk): Assembly of people; herd or flock of animals. *See page 123*

foddor, noun (FOD-dor / 'fɔd-dɔr): Food. *See page 160*

fola, noun (FOLL-ah / 'fɔ-la): Young animal (mainly equine but also the young of camels and elephants) (plural: *folan*). *See page 89*

folc-gedrēfnes, noun (FOLK-yeh-DRAVE-ness / 'fɔlk-jɛ-ˌdreː-v-nɛs): Disturbance of the people, confusion of mankind (people-trouble). *See page 39*

folc-sceaða, noun (FOLK-SHEH-ah-tha / 'fɔlk-ˌʃɛa-θa): Tyrant (people-harmer). *See page 242*

foran-hēafod, noun (FOR-on-HAY-ah-vod / 'fɔ-ran-ˌheː-a-vɔd): Forehead. *See page 243*

ford, noun (FORD / 'fɔrd): Ford; a shallow place, natural or artificial, across a stream, river or other water, by which a crossing can be made. *See page 47*

for-dǣdla, noun (for-DAD-la / fɔr-'dæː-d-la): Destroyer. *See page 223*

fore-bēacen, noun (FOR-uh-BAY-ah-kun / 'fɔ-rə-ˌbeː-a-kən): Foretoken, portent, sign (plural: *fore-bēacen*). *See page 190*

fore-stihtung, noun (FOR-uh-STI'H-tung / 'fɔ-rə-ˌstıx-tʌŋ): Predestination, preordination. *See page 124*

forht-mōd, adjective (FOR'HT-MOAD / 'fɔrxt-ˌmoː-d): Timid in spirit, afraid. *See page 252*

for-swelgan, verb (for-SWELL-gahn / fɔr-'swɛl-gan): To swallow (something/someone) entirely, devour (something/someone) utterly. *See page 191*

fōstor-cild, noun (FOH-stor-CHILLD / ˈfoː-stɔr-ˌtʃɪld): Foster-child. *See page 128*

fōstor-mōdor, noun (FOH-stor-MO-dor / ˈfoː-stɔr-ˌmoː-dɔr): Foster-mother. *See page 128*

fōt, noun (FOAT / ˈfoːt): Foot (plural: *fēt*, pronounced FATE). *See page 80*

fox, noun (FAWKS / ˈfɔks): Fox. *See page 257*

foxunga, plural noun (FAWK-sung-ga / ˈfɔk-sʌŋ-ga): Foxlike wiles, tricks. *See page 257*

frætwe, noun (FRAT-wuh / ˈfræt-wə): Adornments, ornaments, treasure; sometimes used figuratively to refer to 'fruits of the earth'. *See page 141*

frēond, noun (FRAY-ond / ˈfreːɔnd): Friend. *See page 158*

frocga, noun (FRAW-ja / ˈfrɔ-dʒa): Frog. *See page 39*

fugel, noun (FUH-yell / ˈfʌ-jɛl): Bird (plural: *fuglas*). *See page 19*

fugel-timber, noun (FUH-yell-TIM-ber / ˈfʌ-jɛl-ˌtɪm-bɛr): Bird material (which forms the fledgling), the young bird which develops. *See page 149*

fulluht, noun (FULL-uh't / ˈfʌl-lʌxt): Baptism. *See page 286*

fūlnes, noun (FOOL-ness / ˈfuː-lnɛs): Foulness, stench. *See page 194*

fȳr, noun (FUER / ˈfyːr): Fire. *See page 117*

fyrd-lēoþ, noun (FUERD-LAY-oth / ˈfyrd-ˌleːɔθ): Battle-song. *See page 211*

fȳrene, adjective (FUE-reh-nuh / ˈfyː-rɛ-nə): Fiery, flaming with fire, fire-producing. *See page 190*

fyrn, adjective (FUERN / ˈfyrn): Long ago, ancient. *See page 159*

fyrn-geflita, noun (FUERN-yeh-VLIT-ah / ˈfyrn-jɛ-ˌvlɪ-ta): Ancient enemy, long-standing foe. *See page 159*

gange-wæfre, noun (GONG-guh-WAV-ruh / ˈgaŋ-gə-ˌwæv-rə): Spider (walker-weaver). *See page 32*

ganot, noun (GAH-not / ˈga-nɔt): Sea-bird, probably a gannet. *See page 272*

gāt, noun (GAHT / ˈgaːt): Goat (plural: *gǣt*). *See page 45*

gāte meoluc, noun (GAH-tuh MEH-o-luck / ˈgaː-tə ˈmɛɔ-lʌk): Goat's milk. *See page 46*

gærs-hoppa, noun (GARZ-HOP-pa / ˈgærz-ˌhɔp-pa): Grasshopper. *See page 33*

gærs-stapa, noun (GARZ-STAH-pa / ˈgærz-ˌsta-pa): Locust (grass-stepper). *See page 33*

gæst, noun (GAST / 'gæst): Guest, visitor, stranger. *See page 269*

gǣst, noun (GAST / 'gæːst): Spirit. *See page 171*

gealla, noun (YEH-al-la / 'jɛal-la): Gall, bile, or any bitter substance; bitterness. *See page 60*

gēan, preposition (YAY-ahn / 'jeːan): Against, on the opposite side. *See page 253*

geap, adjective (YEH-op / 'jɛap): Crooked; deceitful, crafty, cunning. *See page 257*

gebūr, noun (yeh-BOOR / jɛ-'buːr): Farmer, a free but economically dependent peasant. *See page 42*

ge-cynd, noun (yeh-KUEND / jɛ-'kynd): Nature, kind, condition; gender. *See pages 60 and 142*

ge-fēa, noun (yeh-VAY-ah / jɛ-'veːa): Joy, gladness. *See page 24*

ge-fēra, noun (yeh-VAY-ra / jɛ-'veːra): Companion, comrade (plural: ge-fēran). *See page 210*

ge-flit, noun (yeh-VLIT / jɛ-'vlɪt): Contention, discord; dispute, quarrel or altercation; separation (resulting from conflict). *See page 159*

gefrǣge, adjective (yeh-FRAE-yuh / jɛ-'fræːjə): Known, celebrated, famous. *See page 69*

gegn-pæþ, noun (YAIN-PATH / 'jɛjn-ˌpæθ): Hostile path, opposing road. *See page 253*

ge-gyrwan, verb (yeh-YUER-wahn / jɛ-'jyr-wan): To prepare, make ready; to clothe, equip; to ornament, adorn. *See page 234*

ge-hæg, noun (yeh-HAIE / jɛ-'hæj): Enclosed piece of land. *See page 121*

gehroden, adjective (yeh-H'ROD-en / jɛ-'hrɔ-dɛn): Adorned. *See page 139*

ge-lēafful, adjective (yeh-LAY-ahf-full / jɛ-'leːaf-fʌl): Full of belief, faithful. *See page 287*

ge-myndig, adjective (yeh-MUEN-dih / jɛ-'myn-dɪj): Mindful, remembering. *See page 84*

genēat, noun (yeh-NAY-aht / jɛ-'neːat): Companion, associate, vassal. *See page 49*

ge-scēad, noun (yeh-SHAY-odd / jɛ-'ʃeːad): Reason, discretion. *See page 98*

ge-scēadwīs, adjective (yeh-SHAY-odd-wees / jɛ-'ʃeːad-wiːs): Reasonable, rational, intelligent. *See page 116*

ge-sēnian, verb (yeh-SAY-ni-ahn / jɛ-'seː-nɪ-an): To sign, mark with the sign of the cross, bless. *See page 127*

ge-sprec, noun (yeh-SPRETCH / jɛ-'sprɛtʃ): The power of speech. *See page 287*

ge-sund, adjective (yeh-ZUND / jɛ-'zʌnd): Favourable, prosperous, safe, sound. *See page 273*

ge-tēon, verb (yeh-TAY-on / jɛ-'teːɔn): To do, effect, cause; to determine a course of action. *See page 223*

ge-tēþed, adjective (yeh-TAY-thed / jɛ-'teː-θɛd): Toothed, provided with teeth. *See page 234*

ge-wǣpnod, adjective (yeh-WAP-nod / jɛ-'wæːp-nɔd): Armed, equipped with weapons. *See page 243*

ge-win, noun (yeh-WIN / jɛ-'wɪn): Tumult, hostility, strife. *See page 274*

gim, noun (YIM / 'jɪm): Gem, precious stone, jewel. *See page 141*

gīw, noun (YEE-ew / 'jiːw): Griffin. *See page 78*

glæs, noun (GLASS / 'glæs): Glass. *See page 141*

glida, noun (GLID-ah / 'glɪ-da): Kite, glede (a bird of prey). *See page 63*

godes gāst, noun (GOD-ess GAHST / 'gɔd-ɛs 'gaːst): God's Spirit (Holy Spirit). *See page 58*

gold, noun (GOLD / 'gɔld): Gold. *See page 86*

gold-fæt, noun (GOLD-VAT / 'gɔld-ˌvæt): Thin plate of gold. *See page 141*

gold-hord, noun (GOLD-HORD / 'gɔld-ˌhɔrd): Treasure, a hoard of valuables. *See page 87*

gōs, noun (GOHS / 'goːs): Goose (plural: *gēs*). *See page 50*

gram, adjective (GROM / 'gram): Angry, wrathful; hostile, fierce. *See page 100*

grāp, noun (GRAWP / 'graːp): Grasp, grip. *See page 223*

grǣdig, adjective (GRADD-ih / 'græː-dɪj): Greedy, covetous. *See page 25*

griffus, noun (GRIFF-fuss / 'grɪf-fʌs): Griffin. *See page 76*

grislīc, adjective (GRIZZ-leech / 'grɪz-liːtʃ): Grim, horrible; inspiring terror, horror or awe. *See page 226*

grund, noun (GRUND / 'grʌnd): Bottom, lowest part of anything; solid bottom or earth underlying something; abyss; ground. *See page 171*

grymettan, verb (GRUE-met-tahn / 'gry-mɛt-tan): To roar, bellow; to cry out, howl. *See page 110*

grymettung, noun (GRUE-met-tung / ˈgry-mɛt-tʌŋ): Roaring, bellowing; loud outcry, howling. *See page 110*

grytt, noun (GRUET / ˈgryt): Dust. *See page 39*

gūþ-fugel, noun (GOOTH-FUH-yell / ˈguːθ-ˌfʌ-jɛl): War-bird (an epithet for the eagle). *See page 25*

gūþ-gemōt, noun (GOOTH-yeh-MOAT / ˈguːθ-jɛ-ˌmoːt): Battle-meeting, combat. *See page 253*

gūþ-hafoc, noun (GOOTH-HA-vock / ˈguːθ-ˌha-vɔk): War-hawk (an epithet for the eagle). *See page 25*

gylden, adjective (YUEL-den / ˈjyl-dɛn): Golden. *See page 193*

gyllan, verb (YUEL-lahn / ˈjyl-lan): To make a loud cry, to screech; to bay, howl; to make a strident, grating or crashing noise. *See page 27*

gyst, noun (YUEST / ˈjyst): Guest, visitor, stranger (plural: *gystas*). *See page 253*

hālga gāst, noun (HALL-ga GAHST / ˈhaːl-ga ˈgaːst): Holy Spirit. *See page 58*

hamer, noun (HA-mer / ˈha-mɛr): Hammer (plural: *hameras*). *See page 238*

hasu-pāda, noun (HA-zuh-PAH-da / ˈha-zʌ-ˌpaː-da): Grey-cloaked one (an epithet for the eagle). *See page 18*

haswig-feþera, adjective (HA-zwih-FETH-er-ah / ˈhaz-wɪj-ˌfɛ-θɛ-ra): Having grey feathers; used as a substantive to mean 'the grey-feathered one'. *See page 144*

hǣlend, noun (HAL-end / ˈhæː-lɛnd): Saviour, Christ; healer. *See page 183*

hǣleþ, noun (HAL-eth / ˈhæ-lɛθ): Hero, (noble) man (plural: *hæleþas*). *See page 27*

hǣþ, noun (HATH / ˈhæːθ): Heath; open, uncultivated ground. *See page 210*

hǣþen, noun (HATH-en / ˈhæː-θɛn): Heathen, pagan, person who is not Christian (plural: *hæþenan*). *See page 116*

hǣþ-stapa, noun (HATH-STAH-pa / ˈhæːθ-ˌsta-pa): Heath-stepper, heath-wanderer. *See page 123*

hē, pronoun (hay / heː): He (or a pronoun that refers to a grammatically masculine noun). *See page 61*

hēa-dēor, noun (HAY-ah-DAY-or / ˈheːa-ˌdeːɔr): Stag, deer (lofty-animal). *See*

page 120

hēafod, noun (HAY-ah-vod / 'heːa-vɔd): Head (plural: *hēafdu*). *See page 182*

healf, adjective (HEH-alf / 'hɛalf): Half. *See page 283*

healfhunding, noun (HEH-alf-HUN-ding / 'hɛalf-ˌhʌn-dɪŋ): *Cynocephalus*, one of a fabled race of half-canine men or men with dogs' heads (plural: *healfhundingas*). *See page 283*

healf-hundisc, adjective (HEH-alf-HUN-dish / 'hɛalf-ˌhʌn-dɪʃ): Half-canine. *See page 286*

hēap, noun (HAY-op / 'heːap): Group, company, multitude, crowd. *See page 84*

heaþu-grimm, adjective (HEH-ah-thuh-GRIM / 'hɛa-θʌ-ˌgrɪm): Battle-grim, fierce (as the fray of battle). *See page 222*

hege, noun (HEH-yuh / 'hɛ-jə): Hedge, fence; boundary wall (plural: *hegeas*). *See page 121*

hell, noun (HELL / 'hɛl): Hell. *See page 171*

helle-fȳr, noun (HELL-uh-VUER / 'hɛl-lə-ˌvyːr): Hell-fire. *See page 199*

helle-mūþ, noun (HELL-uh-MOOTH / 'hɛl-lə-ˌmuːθ): Hell-mouth, the entrance to hell. *See page 200*

henn, noun (HEN / 'hɛn): Hen. *See page 67*

hēo, pronoun (hay-oh / heːɔ): She (or a pronoun that refers to a grammatically feminine noun). *See page 61*

heofon, noun (HEH-oh-von / 'hɛɔ-vɔn): Heaven. *See page 137*

heofon-hrōf, noun (HEH-oh-von-H'ROAF / 'hɛɔ-vɔn-ˌhroːf): Roof or vault of heaven. *See page 145*

heofon-rīce, noun (HEH-oh-von-REE-chuh / 'hɛɔ-vɔn-ˌriː-tʃə): Kingdom of heaven. *See page 137*

heoloþ-cynn (HEH-oh-loth-KUEN / 'hɛɔ-lɔθ-ˌkyn): Concealment-kind, the inhabitants of hell, possibly 'race living in concealment or darkness'. *See page 174*

heoloþ-helm, noun (HEH-oh-loth-HELM / 'hɛɔ-lɔθ-ˌhɛlm): Helmet of concealment or deception. *See page 173*

heorot, noun (HEH-o-rot / 'hɛɔ-rɔt): Male deer, hart, stag (occasionally also used of the female), perhaps the red deer specifically (plural: *heorotas*).

See page 120

heorþ-genēat, noun (HEH-orth-yeh-NAY-aht / ˈhɛɔrθ-jɛ-ˌneːat): Hearth-companion. *See page 49*

heoru, noun (HEH-or-uh / ˈhɛɔ-rʌ): Sword. *See page 147*

heoru-drēor, noun (HEH-or-uh-DRAY-or / ˈhɛɔ-rʌ-ˌdreːɔr): Blood, gore (caused by a battle). *See page 147*

heoru-drēorig, adjective (HEH-or-uh-DRAY-oh-rih / ˈhɛɔ-rʌ-ˌdreːɔ-rɪj): Blood-stained, drenched in blood; very sad, disconsolate; used as a substantive to mean 'the disconsolate one'. *See page 147*

heoru-swealwe, noun (HEH-oh-ruh-SWEH-all-wuh / ˈhɛɔ-rʌ-ˌswɛal-wə): Falcon, hawk. *See page 45*

here-feoh, noun (HEH-reh-FEH-oh / ˈhɛ-rɛ-ˌfɛɔx): Booty, spoils of war. *See page 46*

here-hūþ, noun (HEH-ruh-HOOTH / ˈhɛ-rə-ˌhuːθ): Spoils of war, booty, loot, plunder. *See page 168*

here-strǣt, noun (HEH-ruh-STRAT / ˈhɛ-rə-ˌstræːt): Battle-street, military road. *See page 274*

hergung, noun (HER-gung / ˈhɛr-gʌŋ): Plundering, pillaging, looting, ravaging. *See page 190*

hilde-lēoþ, noun (HILL-duh-LAY-oth / ˈhɪl-də-ˌleːɔθ): Battle-song. *See page 27*

hilde-pīl, noun (HILL-duh-PEEL / ˈhɪl-də-ˌpiːl): Battle-dart (plural: *hilde-pīlas*). *See page 252*

hilde-swāt, noun (HILL-duh-SWAHT / ˈhɪl-də-ˌswaːt): Hostile vapour (battle-sweat). *See page 197*

hind, noun (HIND / ˈhɪnd): Hind, female deer, perhaps the red deer specifically (plural: *hinde*). *See page 120*

hin-sīþ, noun (HIN-SEETH / ˈhɪn-ˌsiːθ): Departure (journey hence), death. *See page 210*

hīw, noun (HEE-ew / ˈhiːw): Form, figure, appearance, likeness. *See page 58*

hlǣw, noun (H'LAEW / ˈhlæːw): Barrow, burial mound; low rounded hill. *See page 196*

hlēapende, verb (H'LAY-ah-pen-duh / ˈhleːa-pɛn-də): Leaping, jumping, running. *See page 131*

hlīfian, verb (H'LEE-vi-ahn / 'hliː-vɪ-an): To stand high, tower, stand out prominently. *See page 252*

hlȳp, noun (H'LUEP / 'hlyːp): Leap, jump (plural: *hlȳpas*). *See page 132*

hold, noun (HOLD / 'hɔld): Corpse, carcass. *See page 23*

hord, noun (HORD / 'hɔrd): Hoard. *See page 10*

hord-weard, noun (HORD-WEH-ard / 'hɔrd-ˌwɛard): Hoard-guardian, guardian of treasure. *See page 197*

hord-wynn, noun (HORD-WUEN / 'hɔrd-ˌwyn): Delightful treasure (hoard-joy). *See page 197*

horn, noun (HORN / 'hɔrn): Horn, antler (plural: *hornas*). *See page 123*

hornede, adjective (HORN-eh-duh / 'hɔr-nɛ-də): Horned. *See page 186*

hors, noun (HORS / 'hɔrs): Horse (plural: *hors*). *See page 44*

hræfn, noun (H'RAV-un / 'hræ-vən): Raven. *See page 25*

hrægl, noun (H'RAE-yull / 'hræ-jəl): Garment, article of clothing. *See page 268*

hremn, noun (H'REH-mun / 'hrɛ-mən): Raven. *See page 55*

hrēol, noun (H'RAY-ol / 'hreːɔl): Reel, spool. *See page 234*

hring, noun (H'RING / 'hrɪŋ): Ring, circlet. *See page 142*

hrycg, noun (H'RUEDG / 'hrydʒ): Back, spine. *See page 233*

hrycg-hǣr, noun (H'RUEDG-HAER / 'hrydʒ-ˌhæːr): Hair on the back of an animal. *See page 211*

hrȳþer, noun (H'RUE-ther / 'hryː-θɛr): Ox, cow. *See page 47*

hund, noun (HUND / 'hʌnd): Dog, hound (plural: *hund*). *See page 44*

hungor, noun (HUNG-gor / 'hʌŋ-gɔr): Hunger; famine. *See page 190*

hungrig, adjective (HUNG-grih / 'hʌŋ-grɪj): Hungry, famished. *See page 214*

hunig, noun (HUN-ih / 'hʌ-nɪj): Honey. *See page 143*

hunta, noun (HUN-tah / 'hʌn-ta): Hunter; possibly a venomous spider or a hunting spider. *See pages 33 and 121*

hūs, noun (HOOS / 'huːs): House. *See page 95*

hūsel, noun (HOO-zull / 'huː-zəl): The Eucharist (especially the bread or wafer). *See page 59*

hwæl, noun (H'WAL / 'hwæl): Whale (also referring to any of various large marine mammals). *See page 167*

hwæt, adjective (H'WAT / 'hwæt): Quick, swift; vigorous, active; bold, brave.

See page 168

hwelp, noun (H'WELP / 'hwɛlp): Cub of a lion or bear; (in other contexts) young dog. *See page 112*

hwilpa, noun (H'WILL-pa / 'hwɪl-pa): Bird, probably a curlew. *See page 272*

hwistlung, noun (H'WIST-lung / 'hwɪst-lʌŋ): Hissing, whistling. *See page 187*

hwīt, adjective (H'WEET / 'hwiːt): White. *See page 18*

hȳra, noun (HUE-rah / 'hyː-ra): Hireling, one who works for pay, a hired servant. *See page 206*

hyrde, noun (HUER-duh / 'hyr-də): Shepherd, herdsman; keeper, guardian. *See page 206*

hyrd-rǣden, noun (HUERD-RADD-en / 'hyrd-ˌræː-dɛn): Guardianship, care, keeping. *See page 214*

hyrst, noun (HUERST / 'hyrst): Ornament, adornment, decoration (plural: *hyrste*). *See page 268*

hȳð, noun (HUETH / 'hyːθ): Landing place for boats, low shore, port. *See page 47*

igil, noun (IH-yill / 'ɪ-jɪl): Hedgehog. *See page 259*

ilfette, noun (ILL-vet-tuh / 'ɪl-vɛt-tə): Swan (perhaps a whooper swan). *See page 272*

Indea, noun (IN-deh-ah / 'ɪn-dɛa): 'India', an imprecise term for a broad geographical region in southern Asia. *See page 88*

innoþ, noun (IN-noth / 'ɪn-nɔθ): The inner part of the body, innards (stomach, womb, bowels, etc.). *See page 194*

irfe, noun (IR-vuh / 'ɪr-və): Inherited property, property that passes to an heir. *See page 47*

irþ, noun (IRTH / 'ɪrθ): Ploughing, tilling; ploughed land. *See page 43*

irþling, noun (IRTH-ling / 'ɪrθ-lɪŋ): Ploughman, farmer. *See page 43*

īsen, noun (EE-zen / 'iː-zɛn): Iron. *See page 193*

lāc, noun (LAHK / 'laːk): Battle, struggle; a gift, present, grace, favour; a message (offering of words); medicine. *See page 70*

lamb, noun (LAHMB / 'lamb): Lamb. *See page 57*

lang-sweored, adjective (LAHNG-SWEH-o-red / 'laŋ-ˌswɛɔ-rɛd): Long-necked. *See page 271*

lāð, adjective (LAWTH / 'laːθ): Hostile, malign, bearing hate toward another. *See page 100*

lāð, noun (LAWTH / 'laːθ): What is hateful or harmful, harm, evil, injury, hurt, trouble, grief, pain, enmity. *See page 223*

lāð-getēona, noun (LAWTH-yeh-TAY-on-ah / 'laːθ-jɛ-ˌteːɔ-na): Evil-doer (plural: *lāð-getēonan*). *See page 223*

lāð-gewinna, noun (LAWTH-yeh-WIN-na / 'laːθ-jɛ-ˌwɪn-na): Hated opponent, enemy. *See page 254*

lǣce, noun (LATCH-uh / 'læː-tʃə): Doctor, physician. *See page 70*

lǣce-bōc, noun (LATCH-uh-BOAK / 'læː-tʃə-ˌboːk): Leechbook, book of medical remedies (plural: *lǣce-bēc*, pronounced LATCH-uh-BAYCH). *See page 33*

lǣce-wyrt, noun (LATCH-uh-WUERT / 'læː-tʃə-ˌwyrt): Ribwort plantain, a medicinal herb. *See page 34*

lǣne, adjective (LAN-uh / 'læː-nə): Loaned, not permanent, transitory, temporary. *See page 169*

lǣssa igil, noun (LASS-ah IH-yill / 'læs-sa 'ɪ-jɪl): Hedgehog (smaller *igil*). *See page 263*

lēo, noun (LAY-oh / 'leːɔ): Lion (plural: *lēon*). *See page 20*

lēod-hata, noun (LAY-od-HA-ta / 'leːɔd-ˌha-ta): Tyrant (people-hater). *See page 242*

lēoþ, noun (LAY-oth / 'leːɔθ): Song, poem, ode. *See page 27*

lēoþ-cræft, noun (LAY-oth-KRAFT / 'leːɔθ-ˌkræft): The art of poetry. *See page 27*

līc-hama, noun (LEECH-HA-ma / 'liːtʃ-ˌha-ma): Body. *See page 72*

līg, noun (LEE / 'liːj): Flame. *See page 245*

līþe, adjective (LEE-thuh / 'liː-θə): Soft, gentle, mild, serene. *See page 29*

lobbe, noun (LOB-buh / 'lɔb-bə): Spider. *See page 39*

locc, noun (LOCK / 'lɔk): Hair, lock of hair (plural: *loccas*). *See page 193*

lox, noun (LOCKS / 'lɔks): Lynx. *See page 205*

lufu, noun (LUH-vuh / 'lʌ-vʌ): Love. *See page 57*

lyb, noun (LUEB / 'lyb): Medicine, drug. *See page 70*

lybbestre, noun (LUEB-bes-truh / 'lyb-bɛs-trə): Witch, sorcerer. *See page 70*

lyb-lāc, noun (LUEB-lahk / 'lyb-la:k): Sorcery, witchcraft. *See page 70*

lyft-floga, noun (LUEFT-FLO-ga / 'lyft-ˌflɔ-ga): Flier in the air. *See page 197*

lyft-sceaþa, noun (LUEFT-SHEH-ah-tha / 'lyft-ˌʃɛa-θa): Robber of the air (an epithet for the raven). *See page 25*

lystan, verb (LUE-stahn / 'ly-stan): To desire, to lust for (something/someone). *See page 168*

lytel, adjective (LUE-tell / 'ly-tɛl): Little. *See page 63*

mān, adjective (MAHN / 'ma:n): Wicked, false. *See page 223*

mān-fordǣdla, noun (MAHN-vor-DAD-la / 'ma:n-vɔr-ˌdæ:d-la): Wicked destroyer (plural: *mān-fordǣdlan*). *See page 223*

mann, noun (MAHN / 'man): Man, human being (plural: *menn*). *See page 20*

manu, noun (MA-nuh / 'ma-nʌ): Mane. *See page 281*

māra igil, noun (MA-ra IH-yill / 'ma:-ra 'ɪ-jɪl): Porcupine (greater *igil*). *See page 263*

mæden, noun (MADD-en / 'mæ:-dɛn): Virgin, maiden. *See page 116*

mægen, noun (MAE-yen / 'mæ-jɛn): Power, might. *See page 113*

mær-līc, adjective (MAER-leech / 'mæ:r-li:tʃ): Great, magnificent, glorious, splendid, illustrious. *See page 20*

mǣw, noun (MAE-ew / 'mæ:u): Gull. *See page 272*

mearh, noun (MEH-ar'h / 'mɛarx): Horse; marrow. *See pages 171 and 211*

mēce, noun (MAY-chuh / 'me:-tʃə): Sword. *See page 61*

mele-dēaw, noun (MELL-uh-DAY-aw / 'mɛ-lə-ˌde:aw): Honey-dew, nectar. *See page 143*

meolc, noun (MEH-olk / 'mɛɔlk): Milk. *See page 46*

mere-dēor, noun (MEH-ruh-DAY-or / 'mɛ-rə-ˌde:ɔr): Sea animal (plural: *mere-dēor*). *See page 223*

mere-fisc, noun (MEH-ruh-FISH / 'mɛ-rə-ˌfiʃ): Sea-fish. *See page 222*

mere-weard, noun (MEH-ruh-WEH-ard / 'mɛ-rə-ˌwɛard): Sea-guardian, one who keeps guard in the sea. *See page 168*

micel, adjective (MIH-chell / 'mɪ-tʃɛl): Great in size, in quantity, or in a metaphorical sense. *See page 242*

middan-geard, noun (MID-dahn-YEH-ard / 'mɪd-dan-ˌjɛard): Middle-dwelling (between heaven and hell), the earth, world. *See page 144*

miht, noun (MI'HT / 'mɪxt): Power, might. *See page 116*

mildheortness, noun (MILD-HEH-ort-ness / 'mɪld-ˌhɛɔrt-nɛs): Mercy, compassion. *See page 124*

missenlīc, adjective (MISS-sen-leech / 'mis-sɛn-li:tʃ): Different, diverse, various. *See page 186*

mist-glōm, noun (MIST-GLOAM / 'mɪst-ˌglo:m): Mist-gloom, darkness caused by mist. *See page 174*

mōd, noun (MOAD / 'mo:d): Inner person, soul, mind, heart, spirit. *See page 28*

mōna, noun (MO-na / 'mo:-na): Moon. *See page 233*

mōnaþ-gecynd, noun (MO-nath-yeh-KUEND / 'mo:-naθ-jɛ-ˌkynd): Period, menstruation. *See page 46*

mōr-berige, noun (MOR-BEH-ri-yuh / 'mo:r-ˌbɛ-rɪ-jə): Mulberry (plural: *mōr-berian*). *See page 98*

morgen-steorra, noun (MOR-gen-STEH-or-ra / 'mɔr-gɛn-ˌstɛɔr-ra): Morning star (epithet for Satan or the Devil). *See page 286*

munt, noun (MUNT / 'mʌnt): Mountain, hill (plural: *muntas*). *See page 95*

mūs, noun (MOOS / 'mu:s): Mouse (plural: *mȳs*). *See page 50*

mūþ, noun (MOOTH / 'mu:θ): Mouth (plural: *mūþas*). *See page 162*

nǣdre, noun (NADD-ruh / 'næ:-drə): Snake, serpent, adder, viper (plural: *nǣdran*). *See page 180*

nægl, noun (NA-yull / 'næ-jəl): Nail (plural: *næglas*). *See page 278*

ne, adverb (neh / nɛ): Not. *See page 35*

nēat, noun (NAY-aht / 'ne:at): Ox or cow; beast, animal. *See page 47*

neorxnawang, noun (NEH-ork-snah-WAHNG / 'nɛɔrk-sna-ˌwaŋ): Paradise. *See page 137*

nēotan, verb (NAY-o-tahn / 'ne:ɔ-tan): To enjoy, have the benefit of, make use of. *See page 49*

nett, noun (NET / 'nɛt): Web, net. *See page 37*

nicor, noun (NICK-or / 'nɪ-kɔr): Water-monster (plural: *nicoras*). *See page 219*

nicor-hūs, noun (NICK-or-HOOS / 'nɪ-kɔr-ˌhu:s): Home of a *nicor* (plural: *nicor-hūs*). *See page 223*

nīten, noun (NEE-ten / 'ni:-tɛn): Animal; cattle. *See page 95*

nīten-cynn, noun (NEE-ten-KUEN / 'ni:-tɛn-ˌkyn): Kind of animal. *See page 95*

nīþ, noun (NEETH / 'niːθ): Hatred, enmity, rancor, spite, malice. *See page 23*

nīþ-draca, noun (NEETH-DRAH-ka / 'niːθ-ˌdra-ka): Hate-dragon, a hostile or malicious dragon. *See page 197*

nīþ-sceaða, noun (NEETH-SHEH-ah-tha / 'niːθ-ˌʃɛa-θa): Malignant foe. *See page 254*

nos-þyrel, noun (NOSS-THUE-rell / 'nɔs-ˌθy-rɛl): Nostril (nose-hole). *See page 252*

nosu, noun (NO-zuh / 'nɔ-zʌ): Nose. *See page 193*

nytan, verb (NUE-tahn / 'ny-tan): To not know. *See page 35*

nyten, adjective (NUE-ten / 'ny-tɛn): Ignorant. *See page 124*

nȳten, noun (NUE-ten / 'nyː-tɛn): Animal, beast (plural: *nȳtenu*). *See page 20*

ōfer, noun (OH-ver / 'oː-vɛr): Edge, border, margin; land that borders water, a bank or shore. *See page 170*

olfend, noun (OL-vend / 'ɔl-vɛnd): Camel (plural: *olfendas*). *See page 88*

olfend-mere, noun (OL-vend-MEH-ruh / 'ɔl-vɛnd-ˌmɛ-rə): Female camel (plural: *olfend-meran*). *See page 89*

on-grislīc, adjective (ON-GRIZZ-leech / 'ɔn-ˌgrɪz-liːtʃ): Horrible, dreadful. *See page 225*

ord, noun (ORD / 'ɔrd): Point, pointed weapon (plural: *ordas*). *See page 252*

or-mǣte, adjective (OR-MAT-uh / 'ɔr-ˌmæː-tə): Immense. *See page 95*

oroþ, noun (OR-oth / 'ɔ-rɔθ): Breath, breathing. *See page 188*

or-þanc, noun (OR-thonk / 'ɔr-θɔnk): Skilful contrivance or work, artifice. *See page 141*

oxa, noun (AWK-sa / 'ɔk-sa): Ox (plural: *oxan*). *See page 44*

Oxna-ford, noun (AWK-sna-vord / 'ɔk-sna-vɔrd): Oxford. *See page 47*

panþer, noun (PAHN-ther / 'pan-θɛr): Panther. *See page 156*

pard, noun (PARD / 'pard): Leopard or panther (plural: *pardas*). *See page 95*

pæþ, noun (PATH / 'pæθ): Path, track. *See page 253*

pipor, noun (PIP-or / 'pɪ-pɔr): Pepper. *See page 185*

rā, noun (RAH / 'raː): Roe deer (plural: *rān*). *See page 120*

rǣd, noun (RAD / 'ræːd): Counsel, advice; prudence, intelligence. *See page 250*

rǣdan, verb (RAD-ahn / 'ræː-dan): To have an idea, suppose; to make out the meaning of a riddle; to learn by perusal; to read; to counsel, give advice; to resolve after deliberation. *See page 269*

rǣdels, noun (RAD-ells / ˈræː-dɛls): Counsel, consideration; debate; conjecture, imagination, interpretation; enigma, riddle. *See page 250*

rǣden, noun (RAD-en / ˈræː-dɛn): Condition. *See page 214*

rǣsan, verb (RAZ-ahn / ˈræː-zan): To rush, move violently or impetuously. *See page 246*

rēad, adjective (RAY-ahd / ˈreːad): Red. *See page 69*

rēafian, verb (RAY-ah-vi-ahn / ˈreːa-vɪ-an): To plunder, rifle, spoil, waste, rob. *See page 208*

rēafigende, adjective (RAY-ah-vi-yen-duh / ˈreːa-vɪ-jɛn-də): Ravening, rapacious. *See page 208*

renge, noun (RENG-guh / ˈrɛŋ-gə): Spider. *See page 39*

reord-berend, noun (REH-ord-BEH-rend / ˈrɛɔrd-ˌbɛ-rɛnd): Speech-bearer, human. *See page 290*

reordian, verb (REH-or-di-ahn / ˈrɛɔr-di-an): To speak, say. *See page 26*

rest, noun (REST / ˈrɛst): Bed, couch; a place of rest; (in other contexts) rest, repose, sleep. *See page 76*

rēðe, adjective (RAY-thuh / ˈreː-θə): Fierce, cruel, savage, wild. *See page 112*

rōf, adjective (ROAF / ˈroːf): Valiant, strong, brave. *See page 161*

rȳung, noun (RUE-ung / ˈryː-ʌŋ): Grunting, groaning, roaring. *See page 101*

saluwig-pād, adjective (SA-luh-wi-PAWD / ˈsa-lʌ-wɪj-ˌpaːd): Dark-cloaked, having dark plumage. *See page 18*

sang, noun (SAHNG / ˈsaŋ): Song. *See page 272*

sǣ-draca, noun (SAE-DRAH-ka / ˈsæː-ˌdra-ka): Sea-dragon (plural: *sǣ-dracan*). *See page 223*

sǣ-fisca cynn, noun (SAE-FISK-ah KUEN / ˈsæː-ˌfɪ-ska ˈkyn): Sea-fish-kind, any creature that lives in the sea. *See page 168*

sǣ-mearh, noun (SAE-MEH-ar'h / ˈsæː-ˌmɛarx): Ship (sea-horse). *See page 171*

sceaft, noun (SHEH-oft / ˈʃɛaft): Creation. *See page 9*

scēap, noun (SHAY-op / ˈʃeːap): Sheep (plural: *scēap*). *See page 44*

scip, noun (SHIP / ˈʃɪp): Ship. *See page 170*

scop, noun (SHOP / ˈʃɔp): Poet. *See page 27*

scræf, noun (SHRAFF / 'ʃræf): Cave, hollow place in the earth; miserable dwelling, den. *See page 160*

searu-gim, noun (SEH-ah-ruh-YIM / 'sɛa-rʌ-ˌjɪm): Curious gem, precious stone (plural: *searu-gimmas*). *See page 193*

secgan, verb (SEDG-ahn / 'sɛdʒ-an): To say words, tell. *See page 26*

segl-rād, noun (SAIL-RAWD / 'sɛjl-ˌraːd): Sail-road, a kenning for the sea. *See page 273*

seolh-bæþ, noun (SEH-ol'h-BATH / 'sɛɔlx-ˌbæθ): Seal-bath, a kenning for the sea. *See page 268*

seonu-wealt, adjective (SEH-on-uh-WEH-alt / 'sɛɔ-nʌ-ˌwɛalt): Round, circular, spherical. *See page 233*

seonuwealtian, verb (SEH-on-uh-WEH-all-ti-ahn / 'sɛɔ-nʌ-ˌwɛal-tɪ-an): To reel, not stand firmly. *See page 233*

sige-cwēn, noun (SIH-yuh-KWAIN / 'sɪ-jə-ˌkweːn): Victory-queen, victorious queen. *See page 273*

sige-wang, noun (SIH-yuh-WAHNG / 'sɪ-jə-ˌwaŋ): Victory-plain, a plain where victory is won, a plain where evil is overcome. *See page 139*

sinc-fæt, noun (SINK-VAT / 'sɪnk-ˌvæt): Costly vessel, vessel of gold or of silver. *See page 196*

singan, verb (SING-gahn / 'sɪŋ-gan): To sing. *See page 268*

sīþ, noun (SEETH / 'siːθ): Journey, voyage. *See page 273*

slecg, noun (SLEDGE / 'slɛdʒ): Mallet, sledgehammer (plural: *slecga*). *See page 238*

slincan, verb (SLINK-ahn / 'slɪn-kan): To crawl; to slink away. *See page 188*

smēagan, verb (SMAY-ah-gahn / 'smeːa-gan): To consider, ponder, examine, search, seek an opportunity. *See page 253*

smeoru, noun (SMEH-or-uh / 'smɛɔ-rʌ): Fat, grease, suet, tallow. *See page 183*

smiþ, noun (SMITH / 'smɪθ): Smith, usually someone who works in metals or wood (plural: *smiþas*). *See page 141*

smoca, noun (SMOCK-ah / 'smɔ-ka): Smoke. *See page 193*

snaca, noun (SNAH-ka / 'sna-ka): Snake, reptile, perhaps even a scorpion (plural: *snacan*). *See page 181*

snōd, noun (SNOAD / 'snoːd): Headdress, snood. *See page 234*

snotor, adjective (SNOT-or / ˈsnɔ-tɔr): Prudent, wise. *See page 182*

sōfte, adverb (SOAF-tuh / ˈsoːf-tə): Softly, without disturbance; at ease, without trouble; gently; without discord; easily, without opposition. *See page 246*

solor, noun (SOLL-or / ˈsɔ-lɔr): Upper chamber; sunny room, solarium. *See page 146*

spearca, noun (SPEH-ar-ka / ˈspɛar-ka): Spark (plural: *spearcan*). *See page 201*

spere, noun (SPEH-ruh / ˈspɛ-rə): Spear, lance (plural: *speru*). *See page 238*

spor, noun (SPOR / ˈspɔr): Track, trace; mark left by anything. *See page 211*

sprecan, verb (SPREH-kahn / ˈsprɛ-kan): To speak. *See page 287*

spyrian, verb (SPUE-ri-ahn / ˈspy-rɪ-an): To track; to make a track; to inquire, investigate, search after, seek to attain. *See page 212*

stān, noun (STAHN / ˈstaːn): Stone, rock. *See page 170*

stēda, noun (STAY-da / ˈsteː-da): Stallion (mainly equine but also used for a male camel) (plural: *stēdan*). *See page 89*

stefn, noun (STEH-vun / ˈstɛ-vən): Voice. *See page 162*

stenc, noun (STENCH / ˈstɛntʃ): Smell, scent, odour (plural: *stencas*). *See page 137*

stirc, noun (STIRK / ˈstɪrk): Calf. *See page 20*

strǣl, noun (STRAL / ˈstræːl): Arrow, shaft, dart (plural: *strǣla*). *See page 246*

strǣt, noun (STRAT / ˈstræːt): Street, path. *See page 251*

strǣt-wyrhta, noun (STRAT-WUER-h'ta / ˈstræːt-ˌwyrx-ta): Street-maker (a compound invented by the author). *See page 251*

sum, adjective (sum / sʌm): Some, one of many, certain. *See page 151*

sund-hwæt, adjective (SUND-H'WAT / ˈsʌnd-ˌhwæt): Water-quick, active in swimming. *See page 168*

sundor-gecynd, noun (SUN-dor-yeh-KUEND / ˈsʌn-dɔr-jɛ-ˌkynd): Peculiar or unique nature. *See page 158*

swan, noun (SWAHN / ˈswan): Swan (perhaps a mute swan) (plural: *swanas*). *See page 269*

swan-rād, noun (SWAHN-RAWD / ˈswan-ˌraːd): Swan-road, a kenning for the sea. *See page 273*

swǣtan, verb (SWAE-tahn / ˈswæː-tan): To sweat. *See page 282*

swefen-reccere, noun (SWEH-ven-REH-cheh-ruh / 'swɛ-vɛn-,rɛ-tʃɛ-rə): Interpreter of dreams, soothsayer. *See page 23*

swēg-hlēoþor, noun (SWAY-H'LAY-oh-thor / 'sweːj-,hleːɔ-θɔr): Sound, voice. *See page 162*

swelce, adverb (SWELL-chuh / 'swɛl-tʃə): As, like. *See page 233*

sweord, noun (SWEH-ord / 'swɛɔrd): Sword. *See page 61*

swift, adjective (SWIFT / 'swɪft): Swift, moving or capable of moving quickly. *See page 242*

swīgan, verb (SWEE-gahn / 'swiː-gan): To be silent. *See page 268*

swīn, noun (SWEEN / 'swiːn): Pig, swine (plural: *swīn*). *See page 44*

swinsian, verb (SWIN-zi-ahn / 'swɪn-zɪ-an): To make a pleasing sound, make music. *See page 268*

swīðe, adverb (SWEE-thuh / 'swiː-θə): Very, much, exceedingly. *See page 241*

swōgan, verb (SWO-gahn / 'swoː-gan): To make a sound, move with noise. *See page 268*

swylt, noun (SWUELT / 'swylt): Death, destruction. *See page 274*

syllic, adjective (SUEL-litch / 'syl-lɪtʃ): Strange, wonderful. *See page 95*

tācn, noun (TAH-kun / 'taː-kən): Token, sign. *See page 144*

tam, adjective (TAHM / 'tam): Tame, the opposite of wild. *See page 214*

tama, noun (TAH-ma / 'ta-ma): Tameness. *See page 115*

tægl, noun (TA-yull / 'tæ-jəl): Tail. *See page 279*

tægl-hǣr, noun (TA-yull-HAER / 'tæ-jəl-,hæːr): Hair of an animal's tail. *See page 211*

tīdre, adjective (TEE-druh / 'tiː-drə): Fragile, weak, easily broken. *See page 37*

tiger, noun (TIH-gur / 'tɪ-gər): Tiger (plural: *tigras*). *See page 95*

tord, noun (TORD / 'tɔrd): Turd, dung. *See page 35*

tōþ, noun (TOATH / 'toː θ): Tooth, tusk (plural: *tēþ*, pronounced TAYTH). *See page 193*

tredan, verb (TRED-ahn / 'trɛ-dan): To tread upon, step upon, walk upon. *See page 268*

trum, adjective (TRUM / 'trʌm): Strong, firm, sound. *See page 123*

tunece, noun (TUN-eh-chuh / 'tʌ-nɛ-tʃə): Tunic, coat. *See page 157*

tunge, noun (TUNG-guh / 'tʌŋ-gə): Tongue. *See page 193*

tusc, noun (TUSK / 'tʌsk): Tusk (plural: *tuscas*). *See page 279*

twēo, noun (TWAY-oh / 'twe:ɔ): Doubt, uncertainty. *See page 262*

twifealdness, noun (TWIH-veh-ald-ness / 'twɪ-vɛald-nɛs): Doubleness; duplicity, deceitfulness. *See page 262*

þæcele, noun (THATCH-el-uh / 'θæ-tʃɛ-lə): Torch, light. *See page 188*

þel-fæsten, noun (THELL-FAST-en / 'θɛl-ˌfæs-tɛn): Plank-fortress (Noah's ark). *See page 55*

þēof, noun (THAY-off / 'θe:ɔf): Thief. *See page 196*

þēow, noun (THAY-oh / 'θe:ɔw): Servant, enslaved person. *See page 127*

þrimilce-mōnaþ, noun (THRI-mill-chuh-MO-nath / 'θrɪ-mɪl-tʃə-ˌmo:-naθ): May (three-milkings-month). *See page 45*

þrinness, noun (THRIN-ness / 'θrɪn-nɛs): Trinity, as in the Holy Trinity (Father, Son and Holy Spirit). *See page 59*

þrowend, noun (THRO-wend / 'θrɔ-wɛnd): Scorpion. *See page 181*

þrymm, noun (THRUEM / 'θrym): Power, might; glory, majesty, magnificence, greatness. *See page 161*

þyrel, noun (THUE-rell / 'θy-rɛl): Hole. *See page 252*

ūht-sceaþa, noun (OO'HT-SHEH-ah-tha / 'u:xt-ˌʃɛa-θa): One who robs in the time just before dawn. *See page 197*

un-āræfnedlīc, adjective (UN-ah-RAV-ned-leech / 'ʌn-a:-ˌræv-nɛd-li:tʃ): Intolerable, impossible to bear. *See page 186*

un-ārīmed, adjective (UN-ah-REE-med / 'ʌn-a:-ˌri:-mɛd): Unnumbered, countless. *See page 186*

un-clǣne, adjective (UN-KLAN-uh / 'ʌn-ˌklæ:-nə): Unclean, impure. *See page 261*

un-clǣnness, noun (UN-KLAN-ness / 'ʌn-ˌklæ:n-nɛs): Impurity, foulness (in a physical sense); impurity, obscenity (in a moral sense). *See page 281*

un-gefrǣgelīcan, adjective (UN-yeh-FRAE-yuh-lee-kahn / 'ʌn-jɛ-ˌfræ:-jə-li:-kan): Unheard of, unusual, extraordinary. *See page 69*

un-gelēaful, adjective (UN-yeh-LAY-ah-vull / 'ʌn-jɛ-ˌle:a-vʌl): Unbelieving, incredulous. *See page 116*

un-hearmgeorn, adjective (UN-HEH-arm-yeh-orn / 'ʌn-ˌhɛarm-jɛɔrn): Not eager for harm. *See page 60*

un-hīrlīc, adjective (UN-HEER-leech / ˈʌn-ˌhiːr-liːtʃ): Fierce, savage. *See page 226*

un-land, noun (UN-LOND / ˈʌn-ˌland): False land. *See page 170*

unriht-hǣmed, noun (UN-ri'ht-HAM-ed / ˈʌn-rɪxt-ˌhæː-mɛd): Unlawful cohabitation, illicit intercourse, adultery, fornication. *See page 128*

un-sceþþignes, noun (UN-SHETH-thi-ness / ˈʌn-ˌʃɛθ-θɪ-nɛs): Innocence, harmlessness. *See page 60*

un-sōfte, adverb (UN-SOAF-tuh / ˈʌn-ˌsoːf-tə): With difficulty, with trouble; (in other contexts) not at ease, in discomfort, not gently. *See page 246*

un-weorþ, adjective (UN-WEH-orth / ˈʌn-ˌwɛɔrθ): Of no value; of no dignity; unworthy. *See page 281*

wang, noun (WAHNG / ˈwaŋ): Field, plain. *See page 137*

wæfer-gange, noun (WAV-er-GONG-guh / ˈwæ-vɛr-ˌgaŋ-gə): Spider (weaver-walker). *See page 32*

wæl, noun (WAEL / ˈwæl): The slain, the dead; slaughter, carnage. *See page 72*

wæl-cēasiga, noun (WAEL-CHAY-ah-zi-ga / ˈwæl-ˌtʃeːa-zɪ-ga): Chooser of the slain (an epithet for the raven). *See page 25*

wæl-cyrige, noun (WAEL-KUE-ri-yuh / ˈwæl-ˌky-rɪ-jə): Valkyrie, chooser of the slain. *See page 72*

wæl-grim, adjective (WAEL-GRIM / ˈwæl-ˌgrɪm): Slaughter-grim, cruel, destructive, bloodthirsty. *See page 254*

wæl-hwelp, noun (WAEL-H'WELP / ˈwæl-ˌhwɛlp): Slaughter-whelp, dog that slays, hunting dog. *See page 254*

wæter-brōga, noun (WAT-er-BRO-ga / ˈwæ-tɛr-ˌbroː-ga): Water-terror, terror of the deep (plural: *wæter-brōgan*). *See page 274*

weald, noun (WEH-ald / ˈwɛald): High land covered with woods, forest. *See page 211*

wealte, noun (WEH-all-tuh / ˈwɛal-tə): Ring. *See page 233*

weder, noun (WEH-der / ˈwɛ-dɛr): Weather. *See page 138*

weorc, noun (WEH-ork / ˈwɛɔrk): Work, action, deed (plural: *weorc*). *See page 117*

weorold-þing, noun (WEH-oh-rold-THING / ˈwɛɔ-rɔld-ˌθɪŋ): Worldly thing, matter or affair (plural: *weorold-þing*). *See page 206*

weorþ-mynd, noun (WEH-orth-muend / ˈwɛɔrθ-mynd): Honour, glory, favour, fame. *See page 23*

wer, noun (WEHR / ˈwɛr): Man, male (plural: *weras*). *See page 142*

wer-gild, noun (WEHR-YILD / ˈwɛr-ˌjɪld): Man-price, recompense to which a victim's family is entitled in case of wrongful death, set according to the victim's status. *See page 131*

wērig, adjective (WAY-rih / ˈweː-rɪj): Weary. *See page 222*

wesle, noun (WEZ-luh / ˈwɛz-lə): Weasel. *See page 259*

wēsten, noun (WAY-sten / ˈweː-stɛn): Desert, wilderness. *See page 83*

wēsten-setla, noun (WAY-sten-SET-la / ˈweː-stɛn-ˌsɛt-la): Wilderness-dweller, hermit, anchorite. *See page 128*

weþer, noun (WEH-ther / ˈwɛ-θɛr): Ram. *See page 184*

wicce-cræft, noun (WITCH-uh-KRAFT / ˈwɪ-tʃə-ˌkræft): Witchcraft, sorcery. *See page 70*

wīf, noun (WEEF / ˈwiːf): Woman, female (plural: *wīf*). *See page 142*

wīf-mann, noun (WEEV-mahn / ˈwiːv-man): Woman. *See page 61*

wīg-hūs, noun (WEE-HOOS / ˈwiːj-ˌhuːs): Battle-house, war-house, a tower or fortification. *See page 98*

wild-dēor, noun (WILLD-DAY-or / ˈwɪld-ˌdeːɔr): Wild animal (plural: *wild-dēor*). *See page 121*

wilde, adjective (WILL-duh / ˈwɪl-də): Wild, not tamed. *See page 115*

wil-wang, noun (WILL-WAHNG / ˈwɪl-ˌwaŋ): Delightful plain, pleasant land. *See page 139*

wīsdōm, noun (WEEZ-doam / ˈwiːz-doːm): Wisdom, knowledge, learning, philosophy. *See page 28*

witan, verb (WIT-ahn / ˈwɪ-tan): To know, be aware. *See page 35*

wlitig, adjective (WʼLI-tih / ˈwlɪ-tɪj): Beautiful. *See page 124*

wōd, adjective (WOAD / ˈwoːd): Mad, raving, raging, furious. *See page 246*

word, noun (WORD / ˈwɔrd): Word. *See page 8*

wordhord, noun (WORD-HORD / ˈwɔrd-ˌhɔrd): Word-hoard, a store of words. *See page 10*

wrāþ, adjective (WRAWTH / ˈwraːθ): Angry, wrathful, incensed. *See page 158*

wrǣt, noun (WRAT / ˈwræːt): Work of art, a jewel or ornament. *See page 157*

wrǣt-līc, adjective (WRAT-leech / 'wræːt-liːtʃ): Wondrous, curious, excellent. *See page 141*

wudu-bearu, noun (WUH-duh-BEH-ah-ruh / 'wʌ-dʌ-ˌbɛa-rʌ): Grove of trees (plural: *wudu-bearwas*). *See page 284*

wulf, noun (WULF / 'wʌlf): Wolf (plural: *wulfas*). *See page 25*

wulf-heort, adjective (WULF-HEH-ort / 'wʌlf-ˌhɛɔrt): Wolf-hearted, cruel. *See page 209*

wundor-līc, adjective (WUN-dor-leech / 'wʌn-dɔr-liːtʃ): Wondrous, exciting admiration or surprise. *See page 151*

wyn-sum, adjective (WUEN-zum / 'wyn-zʌm): Pleasant, agreeable; joyous. *See page 137*

wyrcan, verb (WUER-kahn / 'wyr-kan): To make, work, labour. *See page 251*

wyrd, noun (WUERD / 'wyrd): Fate, fortune, chance; event, occurrence, circumstance; what happens (to a person), lot, condition. *See page 222*

wyrm, noun (WUERM / 'wyrm): Worm, insect, snake, dragon, reptile (plural: *wyrmas*). *See page 32*

ylp, noun (UELP / 'ylp): Elephant (plural: *ylpas*). *See page 94*

yrfe, noun (UER-vuh / 'yr-və): Cattle. *See page 47*

ȳþ-lida, noun (UETH-LI-da / 'yːθ-ˌlɪ-da): Ship (wave-traverser). *See page 273*

ȳþ-mearh, noun (UETH-MEH-ar'h / 'yːθ-ˌmɛarx): Ship (wave-steed) (plural: *ȳþ-mearas*). *See page 174*

Images

I am grateful to the British Library for making the images from their online Catalogue of Illuminated Manuscripts free to access, download and reuse. Catalogue information is made available under a Creative Commons CC0 1.0 Universal Public Domain Dedication.

page 21
St John the Evangelist and his eagle in the Lindisfarne Gospels (England, *c.*700). British Library, Cotton MS Nero D IV, f. 209v.

page 36
Spiders in the Old English *Herbarium* (England, eleventh century). British Library, Cotton MS Vitellius C III, f. 23v.

page 45
A shepherd tending sheep on a calendar page for May (England, eleventh century). British Library, Cotton MS Julius A VI, f. 5r.

page 48
St Luke and his calf in the Lindisfarne Gospels (England, *c.*700). British Library, Cotton MS Nero D IV, f. 137v.

page 56
A white dove returning to Noah with an olive branch in the Old English *Hexateuch* (England, late eleventh to early twelfth century). British Library, Cotton MS Claudius B IV, f. 15v.

page 71
Hens in the Tiberius manuscript's *Wonders of the East* (England, mid eleventh century). British Library, Cotton MS Tiberius B V/1, f. 79r.

page 73
Two-headed beast in the Nowell Codex's *Wonders of the East* (England, c.1000). British Library, Cotton MS Vitellius A XV, f. 99r.

page 75
Lertex in the Nowell Codex's *Wonders of the East* (England, c.1000). British Library, Cotton MS Vitellius A XV, f. 102r.

page 77
Griffin in the Tiberius manuscript's *Wonders of the East* (England, mid eleventh century). British Library, Cotton MS Tiberius B V/1, f. 86v.

page 87
Gold-digging ants in the Tiberius manuscript's *Wonders of the East* (England, mid eleventh century). British Library, Cotton MS Tiberius B V/1, f. 80v.

page 97
Matthew Paris's drawing of the elephant given to Henry III in the *Liber Additamentorum* (England, 1250–59). British Library, Cotton MS Nero D I, f. 169v.

page 99
Elephant and castle in the Rochester Bestiary (England, c.1230). British Library, Royal MS 12 F XIII, f. 11v.

page 111
St Mark and his lion in the Lindisfarne Gospels (England, c.700). British Library, Cotton MS Nero D IV, f. 93v.

page 114
Lions licking their cubs in a bestiary (England, c.1200–1210). British Library, Royal MS 12 C XIX, f. 6r.

page 126
A deer faces off with a snake in the Rutland Psalter (England, c.1260). British Library, Add MS 62925, f. 87r.

page 148
Bestiary sequence showing the phoenix collecting twigs for its pyre and
then burning up (England, *c*.1200–1210). British Library, Royal MS 12 C
XIX, f. 49v.

page 159
A panther is loved by all animals but the dragon in this bestiary illustration
(England, *c*.1200–1210). British Library, Royal MS 12 C XIX, f. 16r.

page 172
Sailors mistake a whale for an island in the Harley Bestiary (England,
c.1230–40). British Library, Harley MS 4751, f. 69r.

page 185
Two-headed snake in the Tiberius manuscript's *Wonders of the East*
(England, mid eleventh century). British Library, Cotton MS Tiberius B
V/1, f. 79v.

page 199
Dragon with a knotted tail in a bestiary (England, early twelfth century).
British Library, Stowe MS 1067, f. 5r.

page 200
A hell-mouth illustration from the Guthlac Roll (England, 1175–1215).
British Library, Harley Y 6, roundel 8.

page 208
A wolf faces three sheep in a bestiary (England, *c*.1170). British Library, Add
MS 11283, f. 9r.

page 220
An assortment of sea creatures (*pisces*, or 'fish' according to the label), some
more realistic than others, in the Harley Bestiary (England, *c*.1230–40).
British Library, Harley MS 4751, f. 68r.

page 248

Alexander fighting an *arine* (France, early fifteenth century). British Library, Royal MS 20 B XX, f. 51v.

page 256

Badgers digging a tunnel in the Harley Bestiary (England, *c.*1230–40). British Library, Harley MS 4751, f. 30r.

page 258

A fox playing dead in a bestiary (England, early twelfth century). British Library, Stowe MS 1067, f. 2r.

page 261

Hedgehogs collecting fruit in a bestiary (England, *c.*1200–1210). British Library, Royal MS 12 C XIX, f. 8v.

page 270

A mute swan in the Harley Bestiary (England, *c.*1230–40). British Library, Harley MS 4751, f. 41v.

page 280

Tusked woman in the Tiberius manuscript's *Wonders of the East* (England, mid eleventh century). British Library, Cotton MS Tiberius B V/1, f. 85r.

page 284

Healfhunding in the Nowell Codex's *Wonders of the East* (England, *c.*1000). British Library, Cotton MS Vitellius A XV, f. 100r.

A Note from the Author

If you enjoyed this book and would like more Old English words in your life, you can find the Old English Wordhord on Facebook, Instagram, Mastodon and Twitter, or download the app for a new word every day.

oldenglishwordhord.com